Allen Postma

BASEBALL

Felip
Filipe
Felipe

IMPROVING YOUR
HEALTH

*A Total Program for
Health and Physical Fitness*

IMPROVING YOUR

HEALTH

OLIVER E. BYRD, M.D.,
Executive Head, Department of Health Education, and Professor of Education, Stanford University, Stanford, California.

EDWINA JONES,
Supervisor, Physical Education, Cleveland Public Schools, Cleveland, Ohio.

PAUL E. LANDIS,
Assistant Commissioner, Ohio High School Athletic Association, Columbus, Ohio.

EDNA MORGAN,
Principal, Paul Revere School, Curriculum Center for Health and Physical Education, Cleveland, Ohio.

LAIDLAW BROTHERS • PUBLISHERS

River Forest, Illinois

Summit, N. J.   Palo Alto, Calif.   Dallas   Atlanta

Art Director — RAYMON NAYLOR

• The illustrations for this book were made by Raymon Naylor, Stanley Fleming, Mrs. Bea Leonard, Bob Bonfils, Vern Milem, and Paul Hazelrigg. The anatomical drawings are by Morton Blatt. The photographs on pages 10, 42, 57, and 96 were furnished by H. Armstrong Roberts. The photographs on pages 37, 50, 59, and 228 were furnished by United Press International. Ewing Galloway furnished the photograph on page 38, and Harold M. Lambert Studios furnished the photographs on pages 161, 220, 248, and 249. The photograph on page 107 is used through the courtesy of the American Dental Association.

The publications of such organizations as the American Medical Association, American Dental Association, National Safety Council, and the American Red Cross have been most helpful to the authors. The advice and assistance given by members of each are gratefully acknowledged. Grateful acknowledgment is also made to the staff members of the Hinsdale Health Museum of Hinsdale, Illinois, for making available the resources of the Museum.

TABLE OF CONTENTS

1. Body Chemistry and Mental Health

Your Glands and Your Mental Health

Why you feel as you do. Have you ever awakened in the morning feeling "on top of the world," happy and full of energy? Or, some other morning, perhaps you awakened feeling vaguely unhappy for no particular reason that you could think of. You had not lost sleep. You had eaten the same as usual, and you had exercised enough. There may have been many reasons why you felt as you did, not just one. One of the reasons could have been your body chemistry, or the chemicals in your body.

Do you know that there are powerful chemicals in your body that have an influence on the way you feel, think, and act? There is still much more to be discovered about the effects of these chemicals upon you; but we do know something about them.

We know that the chemicals that are *secreted* (sĕ·krēt′ ĕd), or given off, by some of your glands produce certain changes and effects on different parts of your body, including your brain. To some extent, then, these chemicals affect the way you feel and act.

6

There is a close relationship between the way you feel and act and the way you think. Probably you have all at some time or another experienced some of the feelings listed below. It would be interesting, perhaps, to discuss them with the other members of the class and try to decide, for each of the situations described, whether it was primarily the mind which affected the way the body felt, or the way the body was functioning that affected the mind.

▼

Have a
Discussion

▲

1. On days of big tests at school I sometimes have a headache or some other ailment.

2. When I have a bad cold, I can't seem to think as well as usual.

3. Just before I go on the stage to take my part in a play, I notice that sometimes my mouth gets dry or my hands perspire.

4. I may feel tired after school, but if someone asks me to go to a movie I don't feel tired any more.

7

What is good mental health? Good mental health is more than just not being mentally ill. It is a positive quality. There are many characteristics of a mentally healthy person. You can recognize one who is mentally healthy by some of the ways in which he adjusts to the people and things in his environment. For example, a mentally healthy person usually gets along well with other people. In order to have these good relationships with others, he has found it helpful to learn how to control his emotions. He has also learned how to direct his efforts to accomplish what he wants to do.

There are many other characteristics that could be listed. Among them are the ability to think clearly and realistically; the ability to face difficulties and problems rather than run away from them; and the ability to find solutions for problems. Most people can develop each of these abilities.

Think for Yourself

Why is the development of good mental health important to me now, and why will it be important to me in the future?

heredity   habit   environment   attitude

8

Factors affecting mental health. Your glands are only one of the things that have an effect on your mental health. You probably know that you have inherited some characteristics from your parents, your grandparents, and other ancestors. Your *environment* (ĕn · vī′ rŭn mĕnt) also has played a part in the building of your mental health and personality. It includes everything around you, as you may know. The books you read, the television programs you choose, the people you are with—all these have an effect on you.

Just as important as heredity and environment, however, are the habits and attitudes that you have developed as a result of the ways in which you have reacted to your environment. Some of these habits and attitudes will be discussed in another chapter of this book. It is well to know about all of these things that affect the development of your personality. In this chapter you will discover some of the effects that your glands have on you and the development of your mental health and personality.

The Work of the Glands

Kinds of glands. As you have learned, glands give off, or secrete,

I these affect your mental health and personality.

chemical substances. Glands are able to manufacture chemical substances from materials which they take from the blood. Some glands secrete chemical substances into *ducts*, or small tubes. The secretions of the sweat glands, for example, are carried by ducts to the surface of the skin, where they serve their purpose of helping to maintain the proper body temperature.

Some glands do not have ducts. They are called ductless, or *endocrine* (ĕn′ dȯ · krīn), *glands*. The secretions from these glands, called

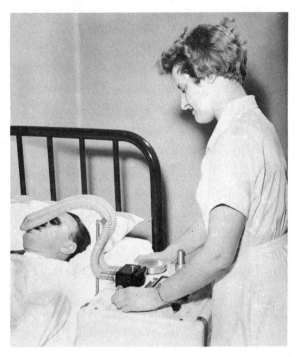

Metabolism tests indicate the oxygen used per minute for each pound of body weight.

act. For example, some people are always active; others just want to sit and do little. A function known as *basal metabolism* (bās′ ăl mĕ · tăb′ ȯ · lĭz′m) has something to do with these differences in people. Your basal metabolism is the rate at which your body makes energy and heat from the oxygen and the food substances in your blood.

Secretions from one of the endocrine glands, the *thyroid* (thī′ roid), regulate your metabolism. This gland also has other effects on the body and the mind. You will learn more about the work of the thyroid gland later in the chapter.

Secretions from glands which are a part of the endocrine system affect your growth, your muscle

hormones (hôr′ mōnz), enter directly into the blood stream, through which they may travel to various parts of the body. This ability of the hormones to travel to various parts of the body has led some to call them "chemical messengers." The endocrine glands, which you will read about in this chapter, are the ones which secrete the powerful chemicals that affect your body in various ways.

What the hormones do. You know that there are many differences in people and the way they

A newsboy deals with many people.

control, your appetite or lack of it, and other things as well.

Changes in body chemistry. The amount of hormones produced by the various glands of the body is not always the same each day in the year. This is one reason why you can feel different on different days. Changes of this kind, within the range of changes that most people show from time to time, are normal and natural.

As you have learned, other things also affect the way you feel; and your glands usually work amazingly well, maintaining a delicate balance of chemicals within your body. Therefore, you should be careful not to blame your endocrine glands for all your personality difficulties.

On the other hand, it is well to realize that you have to learn to adjust to the natural and normal bodily changes caused by these glands. You should know, for example, that because of the chemicals secreted by these glands it may be harder for you, on some days, to remain calm, cheerful, and well-balanced.

Try This

List some occupations in which a well-balanced personality is essential to doing a good job. List especially occupations which require that you meet with other people, or occupations in which you would have an influence on many other people.

The Endocrine Glands

The glands of internal secretion. The pituitary, the pineal, the thyroid, the parathyroids, the thymus, the adrenals, the pancreas, and the reproductive are the glands in the endocrine system.

You have read something about the thyroid gland, and you will read more about it and other endocrine glands in the pages that follow. There are two glands about

which we know very little—the pineal and the thymus. However, we know a great deal about the other glands of the endocrine system and their functions.

The thyroid gland. This gland is located in the neck near the windpipe. It has two lobes, or parts, one on each side of the windpipe. There is a narrow band of tissue that passes in front of the wind-

SOME OF YOUR IMPORTANT GLANDS

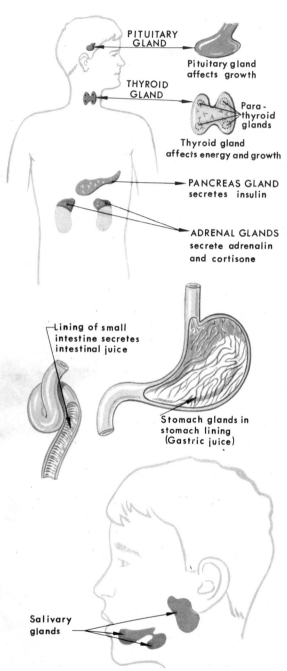

PITUITARY GLAND

Pituitary gland affects growth

THYROID GLAND

Para-thyroid glands

Thyroid gland affects energy and growth

PANCREAS GLAND secretes insulin

ADRENAL GLANDS secrete adrenalin and cortisone

Lining of small intestine secretes intestinal juice

Stomach glands in stomach lining (Gastric juice)

Salivary glands

pipe connecting the two parts. The hormone made by the thyroid gland, called *thyroxin* (thī rŏk′ sĭn), is very important to your physical and mental development and your personality.

As you have learned, thyroxin controls the basal metabolism, or the rate at which your body uses oxygen and food substances to make heat and energy. The amount of thyroxin secreted, then, has an influence on how you act— whether you tend to act slowly or quickly, as you know. Your rate of growth is also affected by secretions from your thyroid gland.

The brain, too, has to have the right amount of thyroxin in order to function properly. Too much or too little of this chemical can change your personality. If too little thyroxin is secreted, a person becomes sluggish in his thinking. He is not as alert as the average person. A lack of this essential hormone shows up very early in life. For example, a very young baby would show signs of a lack of this hormone. His mental and physical development would be retarded.

Too much thyroxin in the body is harmful, also. It can make a person highly nervous and over-active. He may also be restless and *apprehensive*, or worried. To be apprehensive means to expect the worst and to be fearful and worried about things that are not really important.

A person whose thyroid gland is secreting too much thyroxin may not be able to sleep well at night. He burns up energy very fast; and, though he has an unusually big appetite, he remains thin because he uses up so much energy.

Iodine is an important part of thyroxin. In order to function properly, the thyroid gland must have an adequate supply of iodine. Most likely you are getting enough iodine from the water you drink and the food you eat.

The parathyroid glands. The *parathyroid* (păr′ à thī′ roid) *glands* are located on the thyroid gland in the neck. Usually there are four of these glands. They are quite small, but they are very important to your well-being.

The connection between these glands and your development is quite obvious when you know about the functions of the parathyroid glands. A lack of the proper amount of the hormone secreted by the parathyroid glands causes a deficiency, or lack, of calcium in the blood stream. This, in turn, affects the nerves and muscles. The muscles go into spasm, or an unnatural contraction of the muscles. If this condition continues, a person develops a disease called tetany.

You can see that if one were not getting enough of the hormone secreted by the parathyroid glands and his muscles went into spasm much of the time, he would not be able to live a normal life and do the things that other people can do. For example, a boy probably could not take part in athletics.

Too much of the hormone secreted by the parathyroid glands also has bad effects. Too much of this chemical results in a decrease in the calcium deposits which are found in the bone. The bones become generally thinner. There is a great deal of muscle weakness, lack of appetite, and even pain. A person having this difficulty tires easily and tends to be irritable.

You can see that your mental health and your personality could be greatly affected by this body chemical. It is fortunate that most of us have the right amount of it.

The diabetic must be careful about his diet.

The pancreas gland. This gland, is located behind the stomach. One of the hormones it produces is *insulin* (ĭn′ sŭ · lĭn). It also secretes *enzymes* (ĕn′ zīmz), or digestive juices, to help digest your food; but it is the insulin with which we are concerned here. Insulin is necessary for the control of the amount of sugar in the blood.

If too little insulin is secreted, *diabetes mellitus* (dī′ ȧ · bē′ tĕz mĕl ė′ tŭs) may develop. A person with diabetes cannot use or store sugar as well as a person who does not have diabetes. However, insulin can be manufactured outside the body as well as in it. And peo-ple who have an insufficient supply are given insulin. In this way they are able to live a nearly normal life. Their diet can be nearly that of a person without this disease. However, one with diabetes must be careful to avoid infectious diseases because he does not have the normal body resist-ance to germs and infections.

When a person produces too much insulin, the cells of the body burn up the energy supplies at a much faster rate than normal. As a result, his blood sugar falls, and he may develop headaches and feel tired and irritable. These things may change the personality of one who is otherwise very pleasant and well-adjusted. Of course, there are many things that can cause headaches; so it is only when the doctor has made a proper diagnosis that anyone would know that the personality is being affected by too much insulin.

Adrenal glands. The two *adrenal* (ăd · rē′ năl) *glands* are at the upper end of each kidney. Each gland is made up of two parts, the inner part called the *medulla* (mė · dŭl′ ȧ), and the outer part the *cortex* (kôr′ těks). These glands produce more than one hormone.

One hormone produced by the adrenal glands is known as adrenalin, or *epinephrine* (ĕp · ĭ nĕf′ rĭn). It is always being secreted in very small amounts by the medulla, or inner part of the adrenal gland. Whenever you become frightened or greatly excited, however, much larger amounts of it are released into your blood stream. The medulla is stimulated to secrete large amounts of epinephrine because of the nervous impulses it receives. The effects of this increased secretion have been studied carefully.

The secretion of epinephrine into the blood stream causes the action of the heart to be speeded up. A greater supply of blood sugar is released from the liver, where it is stored. At the same time, digestion is slowed and circulation of the blood to the skeletal muscles is increased. The blood has greater ability to clot, too. All of these changes would enable you to run faster, for example, or fight harder.

If epinephrine is secreted into the blood stream when it is not needed, a person may become fearful without understanding why. A person with too much of this chemical would become tense and

In emergencies your adrenal glands give you unusual strength and agility.

The Seventh Grade

Rates of growth are affected by the pituitary gland.

fearful. A constant anxiety is bound to change the average, or normal, personality for the worse. An anxious person worries too much, is difficult to live with, and is too tense to be happy and relaxed. This anxiety and tension will usually affect other persons who are in close association with the apprehensive one. Once again, you can see that personality might be affected by a body chemical.

Other functions of the adrenals. Recently, it has been found that one or more of the hormones secreted by the adrenals is necessary for the good health of the joints. A certain type of arthritis is caused if the adrenal glands do not produce enough of a particular hormone.

A lack of still another hormone produced by the adrenal glands has other important effects on the body. Too little adrenal cortex hormone causes one to lose body fluid. The blood pressure becomes low, and the person is unable to tolerate nervous tension.

Think for Yourself

Why shouldn't you eat when you are afraid?

The pituitary gland. This gland is located deep inside the head. It is attached to the central portion of the brain by a thin stalk. Because the *pituitary* (pǐ·tū′ǐ·těr′ǐ) *gland* partly controls the activities of many other glands, it is often called the master gland. The secretions of the pituitary gland have an effect on the secretions of the other glands.

For example, one of the most important functions of the pitu-

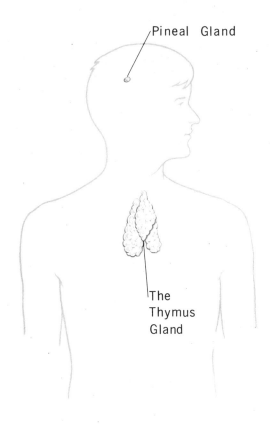

Pineal Gland

The Thymus Gland

itary gland is the regulation of the rate of growth through its effect on the thyroid gland. Secretions from the pituitary affect the secretions from the thyroid gland, which, in turn, has an effect on your growth. As you may know, there are other things that influence your growth, too. The kinds and amounts of food that you eat also have an effect.

A boy or girl who is not growing as much as he or she thinks is normal, might worry. On the other hand, those who get their growth in height early, especially girls, sometimes begin to worry because they think that they are going to be too tall. It should be remembered that, as a rule, girls get their full height sooner than boys. Also it should be remembered that usually the sooner a person attains his height, the sooner he stops growing. In other words, the tall girl in elementary school, for example, usually stops growing sooner than other girls, and is often only of average height when she becomes an adult.

It is well to know that most will grow to maturity regardless of whether they have an early or a late start. It is very seldom that any medical care is needed.

Pineal and thymus glands. The *pineal* (pĭn′ ė · ăl) *gland* is deep inside the head. As you have learned, we know very little about the function or functions of this gland. Since this gland is located deep inside the head, where it is well protected, this suggests that it may have an important function at some time in your life.

The *thymus* (thī′ mŭs) *gland* is located in the front of the chest. It

Mother and Dad show Betty's 7th grade friends how <u>they</u> looked in the 7th grade.

increases in size up to adolescence; then it decreases. Therefore, some think it may have something to do with growth at an early period in your life.

Tranquilizing drugs and mental health. Within the last few years tranquilizing drugs have become popular as a means of helping the tense, anxious personality by chemical means. It has been found possible, by using certain chemical substances, to tranquilize people who were so worried and tense that their mental health was seriously affected. To tranquilize means to calm. To tranquilize a person means to calm him, to reduce his worries and fears, and to make him feel more secure and relaxed. These drugs have been used by doctors to treat persons with mental illness, also.

The tranquilizing drugs have been useful in showing us that our personalities and mental health are affected by the chemicals within our bodies. In fact, the tranquilizing drugs have given doctors and research people a new way to study the problem of mental illness.

18

to determine your personality and mental health.

Maintaining glandular balance. Usually your glands function properly. If your body is damaged, or if it doesn't get all the things it needs to function properly, nature may bring about certain changes related to the production of body chemicals.

For example, when a part of a gland is lost, either through surgery or through disease, the part of the gland that is left may increase its production of hormones. Sometimes it enlarges in order to try to do the work that should be done by a whole or a healthy gland.

The glands are usually very efficient in secreting the proper amounts of hormones, also. In general, the amount of a hormone already in the blood has much to do with the amount of that hormone that will be secreted into the blood. In other words, too little of a certain hormone in the blood causes the gland which secretes this hormone to increase its secretion in order to make up for the deficiency, or lack. If there is too much secretion, that gland will tend to stop secreting until the bal-

However, it should be remembered that there is a danger in the use of such drugs. People should learn to solve their everyday problems by self-discipline and adjustment. Tranquilizers should be used only on the advice of a doctor. We call your attention to the tranquilizing chemicals only to show you how your personality and mental health may be influenced by a chemical substance. The chemicals that are produced in your own body are very important in helping

ance is correct again. Your glands usually maintain the proper balance among all the chemicals in your body, thus making it possible for you to develop normally and attain good mental health.

For the most part, these glands work smoothly and efficiently with the other organs of your body to keep you well and to help you develop physically, mentally, and emotionally.

Glands help to balance the wheel of your total activities, influence what you want to do.

Activities for Health

Everyday exercises. Did you realize that every time you move you exercise your body? There are two kinds of exercise—the kind that you engage in for the purpose of keeping fit and developing your body in desirable ways, and the kind that you engage in every time you move.

The first type of exercise is the kind that you usually think of as exercise. It may take the form of sports, games, or planned exercises.

Exercise 1, described below, is one that can help you to keep your body fit; it can also help you to stand and walk properly. Try it in front of a mirror if possible. By following carefully the suggestions for its correct performance, your body will derive the greatest benefit.

Exercise 1

Bring your feet together and stand about six inches from the wall behind you. Place the small of your back, your shoulders, and your head against the wall. Then move your feet back so that your heels are snug against the wall. If your back keeps coming forward, don't become discouraged.

If you can gain this position after three or four tries, you're making progress. Though it may be uncomfortable at first, this position will soon become natural to you if you repeat the exercise correctly each day.

The second type of exercise is the kind you engage in every time you move—when you go up or down stairs, pick up objects, or carry on other similar daily activities. If you do these routine exercises in daily activities properly, you will be helping to develop and strengthen your body. You will find it helpful to follow the suggestions which follow.

Exercise 2

To pick up an object from the floor, bend your knees and squat near the floor. Then, keeping your back straight, pick up the object without losing your balance.

Exercise 3

To lift something heavy, but not too heavy for your strength, squat close to the object to be lifted, keep your back straight, and lift slowly with the leg and thigh muscles. You will be able to keep your balance if you shift most of your body weight to the balls of your feet.

Exercise 4

If you are carrying books or other materials in one arm, let your back muscles do the work. Use your free arm to help you in balancing and to relieve some of the muscular strain.

If you are using two arms to carry something, hold the load close to your body. Always keep your body weight well distributed.

Exercise 5

While you are dressing in the morning, put on one sock or stocking as you stand on the other foot. Try to do this without losing your balance.

Exercise 6

When going upstairs, always keep your body as erect as possible. Keep your balance by shifting your weight to the balls of your feet. Go up the stairs without using the handrail. Your head, trunk, and supporting leg should bend slightly forward as you move upward. Your ankles, hips, and knees should be flexible and somewhat relaxed in order to make the climbing easy and free.

As you know, everyday exercises such as these can help you to develop and strengthen your body. As a result, you look better and you feel better, too.

Perhaps you have noticed that the better you feel, both physically and emotionally, the better you are in the games you play and the work you do. You work and play your best when you feel happy and well. You also work and play your best when you have had plenty of rest and when your body is well nourished with the right food, taken at regular times. Good nutrition and plenty of rest help you to build a strong body. They also help you to grow and to gain strength, so that you can use your muscles effectively in your everyday activities.

HELPS TO UNDERSTANDING

Points to Remember

1. Your mental health and your personality are affected to some extent by your body chemistry. Your personality development is affected also by your heredity, your environment, and the habits and attitudes that you have developed.

2. Secretions from the endocrine glands, called hormones, can affect the way you feel, think, and act. These secretions enter the blood stream directly.

3. The amount of hormones secreted by the various glands is not the same each day.

4. One who is mentally healthy can adjust to the normal and natural bodily changes caused by the secretions of the endocrine glands. He can control his emotions and direct his efforts to a desired goal.

5. Usually the endocrine glands work with amazing precision and efficiency to maintain a glandular balance in the body.

6. Your physical and mental development are affected to a certain extent by the hormones that are produced by the various glands of the endocrine system.

Questions to Discuss

1. What are some characteristics of a mentally healthy person? Can such characteristics be developed?

2. Why is the pituitary gland sometimes called the master gland? Where is it located?

3. Name some of the reasons why the proper functioning of the thyroid gland is essential for your health.

4. Why is it important that you get enough iodine in your diet?

5. What is basal metabolism, and what endocrine gland is closely associated with it?

6. What might happen if the parathyroid glands secreted too little hormone? What are some bodily effects that would be caused by a secretion of too much of the hormone produced by the parathyroid glands?

7. List the bodily changes that take place when one is greatly frightened or excited. Which endocrine gland is stimulated by such emotions to secrete more hormones?

8. Why is it thought that the thymus gland has something to do with growth?

9. In what ways have tranquilizing drugs been useful to doctors?

Some Things to Do

Make posters

1. Make posters that show the various endocrine glands and some of the functions of these glands.

2. Make posters that illustrate some of the characteristics of good mental health that were discussed in this chapter.

Have discussions

1. You might discuss the various ways of reacting to the same situation. Suppose that someone took another's coat by mistake. Which kinds of behavior would show a good adjustment? Which kinds of reactions would indicate a personality that was badly adjusted or immature?

2. Discuss the many objections to the use of tranquilizing drugs, except as prescribed by a doctor.

To Help You Learn More

Make a list of some ways in which you can help yourself develop emotionally and mentally. Consider especially the kinds of television programs you spend time on, the books you read, and the other habits you are developing.

Words to Remember

hormones	thyroxin
endocrine glands	pituitary
adrenal glands	iodine
epinephrine	pancreas

CHECKING YOUR UNDERSTANDING

Health words. The following words should be matched with the meanings given below them. The meaning for *hormones,* number *1,* is *b;* so *1b* should be written on your paper for it.

1. hormones
2. pituitary
3. pancreas
4. thymus
5. epinephrine
6. iodine

a. often called the master gland
b. secretions of the endocrine glands
c. secretes insulin
d. found in the front of the chest
e. secreted by the adrenal glands
f. an important part of thyroxin

Health facts. Write on your paper T after the number of each sentence below that is true and F after each that is false.

1. Most people have normal endocrine glands.

2. One should expect daily changes

in his body chemistry. Such changes have some effect on the way we feel, act, and think.

3. The thyroid gland affects the basal metabolism.

4. Basal metabolism is the rate at which the body makes heat and energy from the oxygen and food materials in the blood.

5. If the pancreas produces too little insulin the blood sugar falls, and one feels tired and irritable.

6. We know much about the pineal and thymus glands.

7. Other factors besides body chemistry affect mental health.

8. The brain is affected by secretions of the thyroid gland.

9. There is a very close relationship between the way you feel and the way you think.

Health not *rules.* Read the sentences below. On your paper write the number of each sentence that tells a health rule you should follow.

1. Make an effort to get along with others.

2. Face your problems and try to find a solution for them.

3. Do not use tranquilizing drugs.

4. Don't worry about your rate of growth; it is probably normal.

5. Consult a doctor if you have any physical problems. Do not try to diagnose glandular or other illnesses for yourself.

LOOKING AHEAD TO CHAPTER TWO

Do You Know?

1. Does your appearance have any effect on your personality and your mental health?

2. What things help give a person a good appearance?

3. What is poise?

4. Can poise be developed?

5. What are some good grooming habits?

6. What causes overweight?

7. How can you help yourself have good posture?

8. What does your posture tell others about you?

9. How often should you wash your hair?

10. What are some of the advantages of the early correction of facial defects?

2. Personal Appearance and Mental Health

You and Your Appearance

The importance of a good appearance. Dave and Bob were walking to school one morning when John, the new boy in their class, came along.

"Bob, this is John," said Dave. "He's in the seventh grade, too."

As Bob said "Hello" he thought to himself, "I think I'm going to like you."

Perhaps you, also, have felt that you were going to like someone from the start. When you meet a person for the first time, does his appearance affect your opinion of him? Probably it does.

Of course, you know that appearance was only one of the things that made Bob like John; but it is very important. The way you look can be either a help or a handicap to you in making others want you in their group. Just knowing that others like you gives you a good feeling about yourself, too, and helps you develop your personality in desirable ways. Do you see that a good appearance can contribute to your mental health?

In the following pages you will read about some of the ways in which your personal appearance

CENTERVILLE SCHOOL

affects you as well as the people around you. You will also read about some of the things you can do to improve it. Fortunately, there is much that you can do about the way you look.

▼

Check Your Appearance

▲

A new boy or girl who makes a good first impression when arriving at a new school usually has: (1) clean hands and face; (2) neatly combed hair; (3) clothes similar to those worn by others in his grade. As a class, see if you can add items to those listed above. Look in a mirror and decide what kind of first impression you would make.

Your appearance and the way you act. Have you ever been embarrassed by the way you looked? Did this affect your behavior in any way? Perhaps on a certain occasion, such as a party, you were embarrassed by your appearance. You may have felt that you weren't dressed properly. Perhaps everyone else was wearing a sport shirt and you weren't. Or maybe your hair didn't look "right." You didn't feel comfortable; and for this reason you didn't have much fun. You may have thought, "This isn't a good party."

Really, the party may have been a good one; but from your point of view it didn't seem to be. When you aren't comfortable, or when you feel that you don't "belong," it is harder for you to be natural and friendly.

The way you think and feel helps to determine the way you act. As you have seen, your appearance can affect the way you feel and, to a certain extent, the way you act and adjust to others. An attractive appearance and good grooming by themselves will not, of course, cause a person who is selfish, thoughtless of others, or unkind to become at once a fine, thoughtful,

well-adjusted person. But a good appearance can help the average person to develop self-confidence in his relationships with others.

What is poise? When Dave introduced John, the new boy, to his friend Bob, he was showing social poise in that situation. He was being considerate of the feelings of the new pupil.

Do you know someone who always knows what to do and say and who always seems to feel at ease with others? Maybe it is your scout leader or some other adult whom you have known for some time who has much *poise* (poiz), or the ability to feel confident and at ease in social situations. You may be wondering if you will ever feel as *confident* (kŏn' fĭ·dĕnt) and self-assured as he does.

The development of poise. As you may recall, everyone has his own rate of physical growth. For example, there may be as many as seventy pounds difference in weight between the heaviest and the lightest members of your class. There can also be much variation in height.

In much the same way, people differ, too, in the rate at which they develop emotionally and so-

TO HELP BUILD SELF-RESPECT

BE HONEST AND FAIR

MAKE A GOOD APPEARANCE

BE PROMPT

BE WILLING TO WORK HARD

DO YOUR BEST

HAVE GOOD MANNERS

cially. For a few, the development of poise seems to be swift and easy. Most people, however, need quite a long time in which to develop this feeling of assurance.

Repeated experience in meeting and talking with others is valuable in helping you to acquire poise. A good, healthy attitude toward others, as shown in consideration for their rights and feelings is also very helpful, as you have seen in the case of Dave and his friends. A healthy attitude toward yourself, as shown by the respect you have for yourself, may be your most valuable help in gaining more poise. This very important quality

of self-respect can be built up in many ways. Making a habit of always doing your best, of keeping your word, and of being fair and honest—all these are helpful. A good appearance, too, can help you to develop poise.

Think for Yourself

Are you taking some care to see that your appearance is pleasing? Do you take advantage of the opportunities offered in your school to meet and talk with others?

Improving Your Appearance

SLEEP

GROOMING

SUNLIGHT

MENTAL ALERTNESS

EXERCISE

CLEANLINESS

HAPPY TIMES

OATS

MILK

PROPER FOOD

Some things that help you have a good appearance

What makes a person attractive? Carol and her best friend Betty were talking. "I wish I were as pretty as Ann," said Carol. "She always looks nice, no matter what she wears. Some people have all the luck."

"I wouldn't say it's all luck, Carol," said Betty.

Betty was right. When anyone is especially attractive, it isn't all just luck. It's true, of course, that you inherit certain characteristics; but there are any number of things you can do to improve the characteristics with which you were born.

What things do you notice about a person's appearance? As you may recall from the list you made, as suggested on page 27, many different things were listed. A pleasing smile, shining hair, and good posture are often part of a good appearance. So also are a good complexion and a figure that is neither too fat nor too thin. You will probably agree that all of these things, and others not named, are important; each contributes to your appearance.

The importance of habits. Most of the qualities listed in the para-

for play   for school   for parties   for housework   for street

CHOOSE CLOTHES APPROPRIATE FOR THE OCCASION

graph above are partly, at least, the rewards of following good health habits. There are many others. An alert, "glad-to-be-alive" look, for example, is one of the benefits to be gained from developing and using the proper health habits.

Usually good looks and good health go together; and instead of just wishing for better looks and better health, isn't it more sensible to try to improve your health habits, and not just moan about your luck?

Essential to a good appearance, also, is good *grooming*. Good grooming habits, including proper attention to hair, teeth, nails, and hands, should be practiced until they become a natural part of your everyday living. The careful selection and proper care of your clothing is an important part of your appearance, too.

Controlling your weight. Do you keep a record of your weight? You may have noticed that you feel better when your weight is about right for you. You certainly look better, and your clothes look better on you.

Although there are exceptions, overweight usually is caused by incorrect eating habits. As you probably know, when you eat too

Alternately bend knees to chest

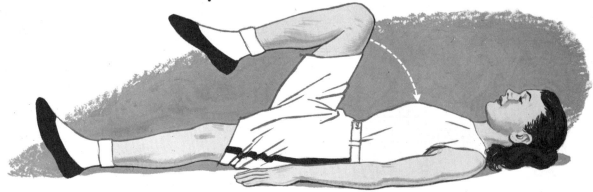

to strengthen abdominal and back muscles

much, or more than your body uses, the amount that is left over is stored as fat. This fat adds to your body weight.

If you are thin, it may be that you are not eating all the foods that you need or you aren't eating enough of them. Eating an additional small meal just before going to bed can sometimes help you in gaining weight. Whether you are overweight or underweight, it is important to eat a balanced diet that includes all the things you need for the proper functioning of every part of your body.

Why have good posture? You may have noticed how posture affects the way a person looks. It can either help his appearance or detract from it. Often it tells you something about a person, too—whether he is happy, confident, and energetic, or whether he is tired, unhappy, or discouraged.

Your posture not only can show others how you feel; your posture can help you feel the way you

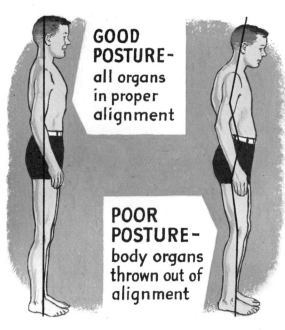

GOOD POSTURE— all organs in proper alignment

POOR POSTURE— body organs thrown out of alignment

Exercise with pole to strengthen back muscles

32 and 33, which show the proper standing and sitting postures.

Since you spend much of your time sitting, you should be especially careful of the way you sit. When you are sitting correctly, the long back muscles should be at work holding your trunk erect. Your abdomen should be flat. Your feet should be flat on the floor, about three inches apart in parallel position. Your chin should be at right angles to your neck. If you are sitting in the proper position, all the bones should be in proper alignment and you should feel no undue pressure on any part of your body.

want to. For example, assuming an erect posture and "standing tall" can help you feel more confident.

Your posture also can affect your physical comfort. Have you ever noticed how much better you feel when you "straighten up" after having sat in a cramped position for some time? Now is a good time to form the good posture habit if you have not already done so.

Standing and sitting postures. You can tell whether you have good posture by looking at yourself in a full-length mirror. Your ear, shoulder, and hip should be in a straight line. It may also be helpful to study the illustrations on pages

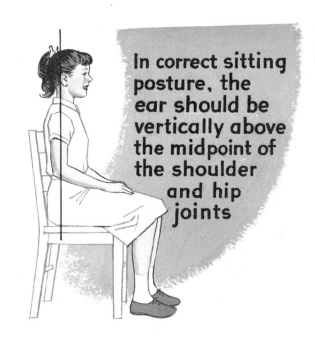

In correct sitting posture, the ear should be vertically above the midpoint of the shoulder and hip joints

WASH HAIR REGULARLY

BRUSH HAIR BRISKLY

CHOOSE A NEAT, BECOMING HAIRCUT

Maintaining good posture. In order to have muscles that are strong enough to help you have a good posture, it is important that you eat the right foods. You should also exercise the muscles of the back and abdomen. On pages 32 and 33 you will find some exercises that will help you to develop these muscles. Making a conscious effort to maintain good posture at all times will help to develop strong muscles, also.

Try This

Give yourself a posture check. Then plan to develop the muscles that need to be strengthened by exercise.

Taking care of your hair. "I can't do a thing with my hair." How often have you heard that! Boys as well as girls like to keep their hair looking its best. People are concerned about the appearance of their hair because it is such an important part of their appearance.

Although it is essential to keep your hair clean, it shouldn't be washed every day or it will become too dry. Probably once a week is about as often as is necessary. The time of year may help to determine how often your hair needs to be washed. In summer you may need to shampoo it oftener than once a week, and in winter perhaps every ten days is often enough. The important thing is to keep your hair clean.

Brushing your hair often will help you to keep it in good condition; the proper diet also is helpful; and, of course, you will want to find the hair style that is most becoming to you.

Probably the best thing to do is to experiment with various styles until you find the one or ones best suited to you. This is especially important for girls, but boys, too, need to give some thought to the kind of haircut they get. When you are trying to decide whether a hair style is right for you, be sure to look at yourself from all angles— front, back, and sides.

Improving your complexion. How do you feel when your face "breaks out" just when you want to look your best? You'll just have to accept the fact that your skin may not always look the way you would like it to. It may help you to know that some difficulties with your complexion are normal for most boys and girls of your age or a little older, when your bodies are developing so fast.

However, you can expect that, for most of you, time will take care of the difficulties. Meanwhile, you can help yourself have a better complexion. If you follow good health rules, you are likely to have a better-looking skin than you otherwise would have. It is, of course, very important to eat a well-balanced diet and to keep your skin clean. If you are having a great deal of trouble, it is best to see a doctor about your skin.

Your teeth, nails, and hands. Proper care of your teeth, nails, and hands is essential to a good appearance. Cleanliness is basic to their proper care.

Your teeth should be brushed often. They should be brushed after each meal and at bedtime. If it is not possible to brush them after each meal, at least rinse them with water.

Your nails should be clean and filed. The cuticle should be kept pushed back, too. When you wash your hands, push the cuticle back with a towel as you dry your hands.

Trying too hard. When you are well-groomed and well-dressed, you should look "naturally" attractive. You should also look comfortable and suitably dressed for the weather and the activity you are engaging in. Looking "natural,"

BRUSH CLOTHES OFTEN

HANG WITH SHOULDERS WELL SUPPORTED BY HANGERS

SHINE SHOES AND KEEP HEELS STRAIGHT

of course, does not mean looking sloppy or carelessly groomed. It means avoiding an artificial look, or grooming that is considered "overdone" or in bad taste.

For example, extreme hair styles, clothes that are too highly styled, or the use of make-up be-fore you are old enough, are not in good taste. Also, they may give the impression of one who is trying too hard and is thinking too much about himself. A normal amount of concern about one's appearance, however, is essential for the devel-opment of good mental health.

Overcoming Your Handicaps

Taking care of defects. Usually all that a person needs to do to make himself attractive is to form good health and good grooming habits and take an interest in the selection and care of his clothes. Sometimes, however, more funda-mental changes may be needed.

Some people are born with de-fects of the face that can be corrected, or at least greatly im-proved, by medical and surgical science. You should know that most facial defects can be improved or completely corrected. Therefore, if you have a physical handicap, or *defect*, such as crossed eyes or very crooked teeth, there is no need to become discouraged.

Adjusting to handicaps. There are some kinds of defects that cannot be corrected. Some people who were born with such handicaps or who acquired them after birth have learned to overcome them and make a good *adjustment* to life. Probably one of the best examples of a person who made a good adjustment to severe physical handicaps is Helen Keller. Though not born blind or deaf, she lost both sight and hearing before she was two years old. She overcame her handicaps by accepting what couldn't be changed and by making the most of her life. Not only did she learn how to talk; she also gave lectures, wrote books and articles, and made many other valuable contributions in helping other blind people with their problems.

Sometimes handicapped people exaggerate the importance of their handicap. As a result of their exaggeration, they develop a sense of inferiority. Sometimes they become sullen and antisocial and use their handicaps as an excuse for not taking a normal part in group activities.

Helen Keller

Since most defects or physical handicaps can be improved, however, or even completely corrected, the sensible thing to do would be to have the correction made, if at all possible. If the defects are such that they cannot be corrected or improved, they must, of course, be accepted. They should not be exaggerated out of their true importance, however.

Crooked teeth. "Your teeth are straightening nicely," said the dentist to Mary Jo as he tightened the braces a little. Mary Jo didn't like the braces, but she knew that many of her friends had them, too. She was glad to hear that her crooked teeth would be straight again.

A pleasing smile, showing healthy teeth, helps the appearance of this girl.

Crooked teeth and poorly fitting teeth should be corrected in order to prevent dental decay as well as to help develop an attractive appearance. A dentist who specializes in the correction of crooked and poorly fitting teeth is called an *orthodontist* (ôr'thȯ·dŏn'tĭst).

The earlier this kind of work is done, the better. Sometimes the dentist can pull out certain teeth in a badly crowded jaw. This leaves more room for the teeth that have been shoved into crooked positions. In a few years these teeth can straighten out, to a remark-

able degree. At other times, the dentist may use wires or bands to straighten crooked teeth.

If you have teeth that you feel self-conscious about, or which you think are too crooked, you should ask your dentist about their correction. If he thinks that your teeth should be straightened, he will talk to your parents about it, and make recommendations.

Defects of the eye. Many babies have eyes that are slightly crossed. As the muscles grow, the eyes usually straighten. However, sometimes the muscles do not develop properly, and the child may be cross-eyed or walleyed. These kinds of defects can now be corrected by eye surgery.

Muscle imbalance is the result of one eye muscle being weaker than the corresponding muscle on the other side of the eyeball. When the surgeon makes a correction of this kind of defect, he shortens the weaker eye muscle. This gives the weaker muscle a stronger pull, thus balancing the pull of the stronger muscle. The eye muscles are on the outside of the eye, where the surgeon can reach them quite easily. The operation to correct muscle imbalance is not a dangerous one, but it can greatly change a person's appearance.

A drooping eyelid is one that hangs down over the eye more than is normal. It may be caused by paralysis of a nerve. The doctor cannot make this nerve well again; but he can shorten certain supporting tissue in the upper eyelid that results in a better lifting of the lid and a more normal appearance.

Other defects at birth. Sometimes babies are born with other facial defects. Such defects include harelips and cleft palates. These conditions that are present at birth can be completely corrected by surgery during the early months of life, and they can be greatly improved later in life.

When babies are born with a *cleft palate*, the upper part of the roof of the mouth has not joined together properly. This leaves an opening, or crack, in the roof of the mouth. Another defect which is sometimes found at birth is *harelip*. Harelip is a condition in which the two sides of the lip have not joined together properly, so that there is a split in the lip.

Advantages of early correction. Defects such as harelips and cleft palates prevent a person from learning to speak properly. It is also very difficult for a baby with a cleft palate or a harelip to get the proper nourishment. Often, also, infections from the mouth will spread into the nose and throat area, or from the nose and throat into the mouth.

A person with these difficulties needs medical and surgical care; but he also needs acceptance by other people. Often he becomes very shy and retiring, and tries

THE HANDICAPPED CHILD MAY BE SHY ABOUT TAKING PART IN GROUP ACTIVITIES

not to speak because of his speech defects. Sometimes he is so ashamed of his appearance that he does not want to take part in any activities with other children.

Although cleft palate and hare-lip can be greatly improved even in later years, it is better to correct them as soon as possible because of the harmful effects of this kind of defect on speech and personality.

Think for Yourself

Why should you know about the importance of early correction of facial defects even though the problem does not now concern you personally?

Activity for Health

Bowling. Bowling is one of the most popular sports in America. It is easy to understand why this is so: bowling can be enjoyed by young and old; one can bowl alone or with others; and it is excellent exercise. Since bowling is so popular, it will be to your advantage to learn how to bowl, thus adding one more way in which you can participate in group activities, as well as knowing how to play a game that you can enjoy now and for many years to come.

The object of the game is to roll a ball down an alley at least thirty feet long and to knock down as many as possible of the tenpins that are placed at the end of the alley. The pins are arranged on points about twelve inches apart, in a triangular shape, with the point of the triangle facing toward the player. A foul line is drawn thirty feet or more from the front pin. The ball is bowled from behind the foul line. Most bowling lanes or alleys are about four feet wide.

In official games the balls weigh from ten to sixteen pounds and may not be more than twenty-seven inches in circumference. The balls have two or more holes in them at various angles, into which you can put your thumb and fingers. The tenpins also are of a certain size and weight. They are fifteen inches high and weigh not less than three pounds nor more than three pounds, eight ounces.

When you are learning the game, however, you can substitute other equipment. You can use a softball instead of the regulation bowling ball; for an alley, you can mark off a lane about four feet wide with chalk lines on any hard, smooth surface, such as a driveway or a sidewalk. You can use Indian Clubs for tenpins, if you wish. Or you may wish to practice rolling your ball down an alley without using tenpins.

Before you begin to bowl you must learn to co-ordinate the movements of your hands, arms, and shoulders with hip, leg, and foot movements. To develop good rhythm and good footwork, you should practice certain movements without a ball. As these movements are practiced and brought under control, you should become a skillful bowler. Here are some of the things you can do to learn how to bowl with ease and assurance: (1) Walk to the foul line. As you do so, swing your bowling arm rhythmically in pendulum style. Push an imaginary ball forward to start, then back for power, and follow through with a thrust toward the tenpins. (2) Practice your footwork. Take four steps: start with the right foot and end with the left, with your toes pointed straight at the target about four inches back of the foul line. Take your time. Rushing spoils your sense of timing. Practicing

the rhythm of the steps before you try to use the ball is important.

After much practice without using the ball, you will be ready for your first game. Line yourself up at a starting spot towards the right side of the alley. (Always start from the same spot.)

Hold the ball in front of you with both hands, resting it on your left palm so as not to strain your right arm. Insert your thumb deeply and comfortably into the thumb hole; then insert your fingers. Keep your eye on the space, or pocket, between the number one and number three pins as you take your starting position, or *stance.*

As you take your four steps you should:

1. Push the ball forward and away from your body in a down position.

2. Swing your right arm backward in a pendulum motion.

3. Hold your ball at the top of the backswing, ready to start its forward trip toward the target.

4. Continue your forward march, swing your arm through, and release the ball.

If you have moved correctly, your left foot and right arm should be at the line at the same time.

Most bowling alleys are well-kept establishments, suitable for family gatherings. Often instructors are available to give expert advice to the new bowler.

Your thumb should be straight up, as if you were shaking hands, as you follow through with your right arm. The left arm should be extended backward, like a wing, for best balance.

With practice, and lots of it, you should be able to master these simple beginner-bowler actions and do them almost automatically.

Common faults among beginners are throwing a lofted ball, one which hits the alley with a bang, and throwing the arm away from the body.

1. Throwing a lofted ball is usually caused by holding the ball too loosely, with the fingers not in- serted completely into the holes, and by throwing rather than roll- ing the ball.

2. Reaching out and throwing the arm away from the body, usually sends the ball into the gut- ter. A smooth, pendulum-arm motion will give the ball the proper direction and speed.

Scoring is something you will need to study, perhaps with the help of your teacher or parents. A perfect score is 300 points. A frame is like an inning in baseball. A game consists of ten frames. You can earn a strike if you knock down all the pins with the first ball of each frame.

HELPS TO UNDERSTANDING

Points to Remember

1. Your appearance has an effect on the development of your personality and on your mental health.

2. Poise is the ability to feel at ease in social situations. Your appearance can help you to develop this feeling of confidence.

3. Usually good health and good looks go together.

4. Good health habits and good grooming habits contribute much toward a good appearance.

5. The careful selection and proper care of clothing are important to a good appearance.

6. Many facial defects can be corrected completely. Most can be greatly improved at least.

7. Facial imperfections such as harelip, cleft palate, or muscle imbalance of the eyes should be corrected as soon as possible because of their harmful effect on mental health.

Questions to Discuss

1. Give examples of some situations in which your appearance may have a great effect on your feeling of self-confidence.

2. What are some of the things that affect your appearance?

3. In what ways can your posture affect the way you feel and act?

4. Discuss some of the things you can do to improve your posture.

5. Explain this statement, "It is possible to try too hard to have a good appearance."

6. What is meant by the terms walleyed and cross-eyed?

7. Is there a connection between your diet and your appearance? Explain your answer.

8. How is it possible to control your weight?

9. Why is it especially important to have a harelip corrected as soon as possible?

10. What is a cleft palate?

Some Things to Do

Keep records

1. Make a weight graph and keep a record of your weight over a period of a year.

2. Make a grooming chart that can be checked daily. Include such items as the care of teeth, nails, and hair.

Collect pictures

1. Gather pictures that would be suitable for display on a bulletin board. These pictures could show clothing that is appropriate for various activities.

2. Collect pictures showing exercises that are designed to help you develop and keep good posture. Display the best pictures on the bulletin board.

To Help You Learn More

Find in a good book about manners the correct etiquette for various situations in which people of your age might often find themselves, such as attendance at games, dances, parties, and the like. Get a group together and give a series of playlets that illustrate the correct etiquette in these situations.

Words to Remember

poise	harelip
cleft palate	cross-eyed
adjustment	posture
walleyed	orthodontist
muscle imbalance	defect

CHECKING YOUR UNDERSTANDING

Health words. On your paper write the word or words that fit best with each definition given below. Choose from words in the section *Words to Remember*.

1. adapting oneself to something or someone in a satisfactory manner

2. a dentist who specializes in the straightening of teeth

3. a feeling of ease in social situations

4. a condition in which the upper part of the mouth has not developed properly

5. the way you hold your body

6. an imperfection

Health facts. Read the sentences below. On your paper write T for each sentence that is true and F for each sentence that is false.

1. Your personal appearance affects your mental health.

2. Correction of a harelip is especially important because of its effect on speech as well as on appearance and physical and mental health.

3. Crooked teeth may be straightened only one way.

4. When an eye surgeon corrects a muscle imbalance of the eyes, he shortens the weaker eye muscle.

5. A person with facial defects needs medical and surgical care as well as acceptance by other people.

6. In order to be well groomed, one should avoid an artificial look.

7. Teeth should be brushed immediately after eating.

8. Poise can be developed in many ways, but it usually takes time to develop this feeling of confidence.

9. People grow at differing rates.

Health rules. Arrange the words in each group below so that they make a health rule. Write each rule on your paper.

1. defects possible be should as Facial early corrected as.

2. weight for Control your appearance health and.

3. hair, Keep nails teeth, groomed carefully and.

4. be should teeth straightened Crooked.

5. good poise A appearance to contributes.

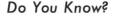

LOOKING AHEAD TO CHAPTER THREE

Do You Know?

1. What should you do if you see a tornado cloud?

2. Why should you avoid telephoning during an atomic emergency?

3. What are some of the health problems people face during a flood?

4. Why should you boil water for a time after a flood or similar emergency?

5. How can you help to make your home safe in case of an atomic emergency?

6. What does the word Conelrad mean?

7. What should you do if you are outdoors when you hear a Take Cover signal?

8. What is meant by contamination of water?

3. Keeping Safe In Emergencies

Being Prepared to Act

The importance of being prepared. Mr. Olds, the fire chief, was talking to the class about what to do in case of fire. "The most important thing," he said, "is to know ahead of time what you should do; then keep calm enough to do it."

"If you know what should be done in a fire or, for that matter, in any emergency," he continued, "you won't waste time and energy in useless or unwise action."

The advice given by Mr. Olds is certainly sound. Being prepared for an emergency may even save your life and the lives of others around you at some time, too.

No one likes to think that he will ever be involved in such disasters as fires, floods, or tornadoes; nor does he expect that he ever will be. However, being confident that you know what you would do in such *emergencies* (ẻ·mûr′ jĕn·sĭz) can save you needless worry.

In this chapter you will learn of some ways in which you can help yourself and others if an emergency situation should arise. You will read also about some of the things that your community and the civil defense authorities are doing to protect you in emergency situations.

▼

**Have a
Discussion**

▲

You may wish to discuss in class the things a person should know in order to be able to help himself and others in case of a fire at school. You might use the chalkboard to show the route that should be taken from your classroom in a fire drill, for example. As a class, you may wish to list reasons why fire drill instructions should be carried out exactly and immediately.

Kinds of emergencies. There are many kinds of emergencies one may have to face at some time in his life, even though no one expects to meet them. No one, for example, expects a fire to break out in his home; yet you understand how important it is to know what to do if a fire should strike. You learned about this in an earlier grade.

You should be prepared for other emergencies, too, though it may be hard for you to realize this now. For example, you may live in an area where tornadoes rarely occur; however, some day you may live in a different part of the country, where tornadoes are common. Or, you may be visiting in an area when a tornado strikes. Then you would need to know what to do to keep safe.

In this chapter you will learn how you can guard your health and safety in different kinds of emergencies — those caused by floods, by tornadoes, by hurricanes, by earthquakes, and even in emergencies caused by nuclear explosions. What you learn will be valuable to you in these and in similar emergencies.

Health and Safety During Floods

Flood warnings. Conditions that can cause a flood are often apparent well in advance of the danger itself. For this reason, there is often time for warning of flood danger to be given. Sometimes it is even possible to prevent floods, or at least to lessen their effects by taking action after a warning is given. Things that can cause floods, such as heavy rainfall in a river valley or the rapid melting of snow along the headwaters of a river system may take place hours or even days before the streams reach flood stage.

At other times, however, a combination of factors may cause a flood without much warning. Severe and sudden floods may be caused by a combination of unex-

pected warm weather and heavy rains coming very early in spring, when the ground is still deeply frozen and cannot absorb the extra moisture.

Unless the floods come very suddenly, there will be flood warnings broadcast by radio and television stations. The broadcasting stations receive this information from the weather bureau and pass it along to the public at once. You may have heard these warnings telling people that the flood waters are rising in certain areas and will soon reach another area.

Paying attention to warnings. Everyone should understand the importance of following instructions that are given by health and other authorities at times of floods or other emergencies. Delay in carrying out their instructions may be dangerous.

Some people do not *evacuate* (ė · văk′ ů · āt), or leave, their homes when ordered to do so because they want to stay and protect their belongings. They endanger their lives in an effort to save their homes and possessions. It is unwise to try to take all of your belongings with you if you have to leave your home; but you should be sure to take warm clothing and other articles that are important for your health and comfort if it is at all possible to do so. Before you leave the house, all electrical appliances should be disconnected and the gas should be shut off. If you do not need to leave your home, try to keep informed by radio as to conditions in the area. Helpful information about the water supply, gas, and electricity may also be broadcast.

Try This

Fill a container with water from a pond or river. Look at a few drops of it under a microscope. Boil the water for twenty minutes and then look at a few drops under a microscope. How has its appearance changed?

To make water safe for drinking, chlorine is often used. The liquid chlorine in these tanks is changed to a gaseous state before it is forced into the raw water.

Guarding your water supply. Those who do not have to leave their homes should realize that the water supply may have become *contaminated* (kŏn · tăm′ ĭ · nāt′ ĕd), or made unsafe to drink, because of the entry of bacteria or waste matter as a result of flood conditions. The safeguarding of the water supply is an urgent problem in any emergency situation; but it is probably more acute during floods than during most other types of emergencies.

For this reason, a stronger *chlorine* (klō′ rēn) solution than usual is often added to the available water supply during flood emergencies. In addition, people are usually warned that they should boil their drinking water. Sometimes public authorities ask neighboring communities to send in a supply of pure water. Large milk cans or milk tank trucks are often used to transport the water.

Danger of typhoid fever. During almost every large flood some people hear the rumor that everyone must be immunized immediately against typhoid fever. It is true that there is a possible danger of an outbreak of this disease. However, by boiling water it is possible to avoid the danger. Usually it is not possible, or necessary, for all people to be immunized against typhoid fever during floods. Such immunization requires three injections, at least one week apart, plus an additional time for immunity to build up. If immunization is necessary, the health authorities will advise the public of the need.

Think for Yourself

Why it is unwise to pay attention to rumors that everyone needs immunization against typhoid fever when there is a flood?

The problem of food. During a flood emergency, food is another problem that needs attention, both by the individual and by the health authorities. Both must understand that much food may have become contaminated because of the flood. Additional food may have to be sent into the area. People who have a supply of canned goods on hand for emergency use may be able to use these supplies; but almost all other food that has been touched by the flood waters is at least potentially dangerous.

Remember, also, that the loss of electric power during times of flood may cause the spoiling of food in refrigerators and freezers even in those areas that are higher than the flooded land.

Contaminated food is so dangerous that it must be destroyed, either by private citizens or by public health and other authorities.

After the flood. As you can understand, there will be many health problems after a flood. As a result of flooding, many homes may have become unsafe. Foundations may have been undermined. Other parts of buildings may have been damaged. Such buildings must either be repaired or torn down.

Many small animals may have been drowned in the flood, too, thus attracting flies in great numbers and adding to the ease with which diseases may be spread. Often health authorities use DDT or other chemicals to spray or dust areas where flies are breeding.

All *debris* (dĕ·brē′) should be removed as soon as possible. In cities, instructions often are broadcast as to what you can do to help the authorities in their cleaning up activities after the flood.

51

It is important that you continue boiling your drinking water until notified by the health authorities that it is no longer necessary to do so. You should also continue to take precautions with your food, being sure that it has not become contaminated from flood waters or spoiled from lack of proper refrigeration.

When Tornadoes Strike

What a tornado is. If you live in the midwestern or southwestern part of our country, you may already know something about tornadoes since it is in these areas that these violent windstorms are most likely to occur. However, tornadoes can occur in any part of the United States.

A tornado is the most violent type of windstorm — even more destructive than a hurricane in the area it touches, though it doesn't cover as great an area as a hurricane. A tornado is usually formed in connection with a thunderstorm and is usually followed or preceded by rain or hail. The tornado cloud itself is dark and funnel-shaped. The wind in the funnel of the tornado cloud itself may reach speeds of as much as five hundred miles an hour, though the storm itself usually travels across country at about twenty-five to forty miles an hour, usually in a northeasterly direction. Tornadoes follow a very irregular path, striking one house but skipping the next, or hitting one whole block but leaving the next untouched.

Tornado alerts. Since the path of a tornado is irregular, it is impossible to know ahead of time just where one will strike; but it is possible to predict that one is likely to form in a certain area because of atmospheric conditions there. The warnings by the weather bureau are a sort of admonition to keep your eyes open and be aware of the possible danger of a tornado. You should learn to recognize the dark funnel-shaped cloud so that if you see one you can get to a shelter in time.

Taking shelter. If you see a tornado cloud, you should take shelter immediately. The safest place during a tornado is underground. Storm cellars have been built by many families that live in parts of the country where tornadoes are common. These underground shelters are safe. The southwest corner of a basement in a well-constructed wooden or concrete house, or any concrete or steel-structured building may be used as protective shelter if there is no underground shelter available. If you are outside, either in a car or on foot, when you see a tornado cloud, get to a ditch, cave, ravine, or any place that is low and out of the wind.

Think for Yourself

If you are inside a building during a tornado, why should you stay away from windows?

After the tornado. As in the case of floods, there are many things that are likely to require your attention after a tornado has passed. You should take certain precautions to protect yourself. For example, it is wise to be very careful about entering homes that have been struck, as they may be unsafe. Do not touch loose wires, but report such damage to the light and power company, or to the nearest police station. Also report any injuries to a hospital or Red Cross disaster station.

As in other emergency situations, it is important to be cautious

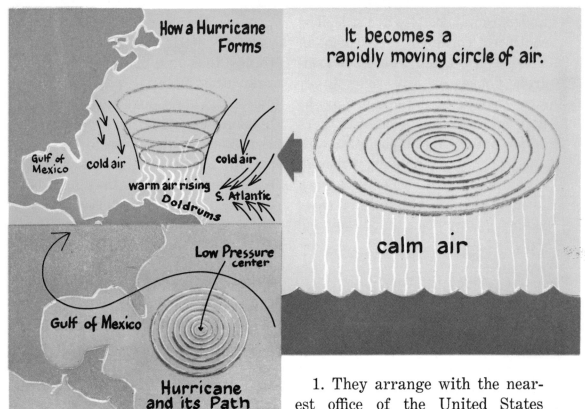

How a Hurricane Forms

Gulf of Mexico   cold air   cold air

warm air rising   S. Atlantic

Doldrums

It becomes a rapidly moving circle of air.

calm air

Low Pressure center

Gulf of Mexico

Hurricane and its Path

about food and water. It is a good idea to boil your drinking water even though you may not have been told to do so. Frozen foods should be watched, also, to see whether they are in good condition, as the electric power may have been interrupted long enough to have affected them.

Community measures. To be prepared if a tornado should strike, many communities in tornado belts follow procedures such as these:

1. They arrange with the nearest office of the United States Weather Bureau to be notified when local conditions are favorable to the formation of tornadoes.

2. They arrange with nearby towns to be notified when a tornado is sighted.

3. They have a special system of signals for letting the people in the community know when a tornado is coming.

4. They tell the people about safe places of refuge, such as storm cellars, in their neighborhood or in the community.

Safety During Hurricanes

What a hurricane is. If you live in Kansas or some other state far from the Atlantic Coast or the Gulf of Mexico, you may never encounter a hurricane unless you happen to be visiting in a place where one strikes; but it is well to know what hurricanes are and what to do if you should ever find yourself in an area where one is expected.

Hurricanes are violent windstorms that move in a circular pattern over large areas of either land or water. Usually hurricane winds blow with greater force when over water. The winds within the circular pattern of the hurricane can reach speeds of from seventy-five to more than one hundred miles an hour; but the speed at which the storm itself moves across the country is much less, as little as ten to twenty miles per hour. Hurricanes are usually accompanied by rain, thunder, and lightning. Sometimes hurricanes cause huge waves that flood cities situated along a coast line.

Most of the hurricanes that strike the United States are formed over the South Atlantic Ocean near the equator, where there is normally little wind. Hot air rises over the ocean, forming strong updrafts, and as this air rises, cooler air rushes in to take the place of the hotter air. The rotation of the earth gives a circular motion to the mass of air, which picks up speed as it travels and spreads out into larger and larger areas.

Hurricanes are the second most violent type of windstorm found in the United States. The most violent, as you know is the tornado. Hurricanes do more damage than tornadoes, however, because they cover a larger area and they last longer. For example, a single hurricane in New England caused almost the same amount of damage as that caused by all the tornadoes in this country in a period of twenty years.

Warnings in time. Fortunately, hurricanes can be *detected* (dĕ· tĕkt' ĕd), or discovered, well in advance of the time they strike. Thus you have time to prepare for them and to get to shelter if you are outdoors. It is essential to pay attention to warnings of this kind.

The United States Weather Bureau maintains stations that can tell where hurricanes are forming and in which direction they are moving. They give this information to the broadcasting stations, together with advice about what precautions should be taken.

Meteorologists employed by the weather bureau can tell when a hurricane is developing by the movement of winds and other conditions in the upper atmosphere. Information about the upper atmosphere is obtained by radar and by specially equipped aircraft. When the wind *velocity* (vĕ · lŏs' ĭ · tĭ), or speed, of a tropical storm increases, large waves are formed on the surface of the water. These large waves cause a shaking of the earth's surface below. The shaking of the earth below can be measured with the same instruments that measure earthquakes.

Leaving the danger areas. When the people in a community are warned that a hurricane is approaching, they can move to higher ground and safer places. They can get away from low-lying beaches or other places that may be swept by high tides or storm waves. This is very important, since most of the deaths caused by hurricanes result from drowning. People who live along low coast lines are in special danger. Warnings are usually given far enough ahead of time so that all the people in a community can go to safe places. The radio should be kept on for the latest information about what should be done.

Making preparations. Between the time of the warning and the actual approach of the hurricane, there is time for many things to be done. Medical services can be organized and sanitary crews can get ready to protect or repair the water or sewer systems, and so on. Water can be stored in sterilized cooking utensils, jugs, bottles, and even in the bathtub.

Those who do not have to evacuate their homes — those who live in areas up out of danger from flooding — can use this time to board up their windows or put storm shutters in place. The outside doors should be securely braced, too. There should be one window left unshuttered or fixed in such a way that it can be opened from the inside. This window should be on the side of the house

There is always danger from gas leaks and "live wires" after severe storms. Citizens should co-operate with crews of experienced workers in cleaning up.

which is away from the direction from which the hurricane is approaching.

Everything that might blow away or be torn loose should be stored inside or fastened securely. This would include such things as garbage cans, garden tools, signs, porch furniture, or awnings. If blown through the air, such articles can cause serious damage.

Be sure to keep your radio on and listen for late warning and advice. If the center, or "eye," of a hurricane passes directly over your home, there will be a lull in the wind lasting from a few minutes to half an hour or more. Stay in a safe place. Remember that the wind will return suddenly, perhaps with more violence than before, and from the opposite direction.

Think for Yourself

Why does the wind come from the opposite direction after the "eye" of a hurricane has passed over your house?

After the storm. It is a good idea to tune in your radio to find out what you can do to help in the "clean-up" that must follow a hurricane. In cities, instructions may be given as to how to collect limbs of fallen trees, for example, and pile them along the curb to make collection easier. As you know, you should be careful not to touch any loose or dangling wires and avoid entering structures that were damaged by the storm until you are sure that it is safe to enter them. Special precautions should be taken to avoid fires, since the water service may be shut off because of the storm.

As in other emergency situations, it is wise to boil your drinking water for a while even after water service has been restored. Do not empty any water that you may have stored until you are sure that there is safe water again.

Protection During Earthquakes

What causes earthquakes. There have been earthquakes in many different parts of our country, though more have occurred in the western states than elsewhere. Although it is not known exactly what causes earthquakes, it is believed that the tensions and pressures that are built up inside the earth may cause a shifting of the earth along two sides of an earthquake fault, or break.

Earthquakes are measured by classes from one to twelve, according to their intensity. A Class 1 earthquake is a feeble shock not felt by the average person. A Class 12 earthquake is one of peak intensity that causes great disturbances, makes craters in the earth, and causes landslides. Earthquakes of Class 6 or over are felt by almost everyone in the area affected.

Safety when an earthquake strikes. It is very difficult, if not impossible, to predict when earthquakes will take place. It is possible to know the regions in which they are most likely to occur, however.

A great danger is that of being hurt by falling objects. Most of the people who are injured or killed in an earthquake are hit by falling objects. Many people run out of their homes into the street at the first indication of an earthquake. They should stay inside their homes and take shelter under some protecting furniture or under some strong structure such as a doorway.

A well-constructed building will usually survive the strongest earthquake. Some of the houses that were close to the earthquake

Much of the damage done by an earthquake is costly. The picture shows part of a road destroyed by an earthquake.

fault in the famous San Francisco earthquake of 1906 remained in useful condition for many years afterward. The *hazards* (hăz'ẽrdz) of an earthquake are usually such things as collapsing roofs, walls, and other unsafe parts in a poorly constructed building.

After an earthquake. As you have learned in this chapter, it is a wise precaution in any disaster situation to be very careful of your drinking water to be sure that it is safe. Water mains are often broken during an earthquake, so this precaution is important. Immediately after an earthquake, the gas should be shut off, since there is danger of gas escaping from damaged or broken gas pipes. In cities where earthquakes occur often, there should be facilities for fighting fires with chemicals, since all public utilities may be cut off for several days. As you know, you should avoid going into buildings that have been damaged, and you should not touch loose or dangling wires.

Nuclear Explosions

An unlikely emergency. The terrible *devastation* (dĕv' ăs · tā' shŭn) that would result from a large-scale nuclear explosion makes it very unlikely that any of us will ever have to meet this kind of emergency. However, if there ever should be such an explosion, knowing what to do could save your life or help you to avoid serious injury. Everyone should know about what the Civil Defense and other authorities are doing to provide all possible protection in case of such an emergency. The government is carrying on research all the time to find better methods of protecting you from radioactive fall-out as well as from other effects of a nuclear attack.

The warning system. The Civil Defense authorities have set up a warning system that is to be used by each community in case of a nuclear attack. Most large communities have held practice drills using these signals.

There are two kinds of warning signals. The ALERT SIGNAL is a steady blast on some type of siren or whistle that will produce a sound loud enough to be heard throughout the community. This blast lasts for three minutes. When you hear such a steady signal, you should be alert for a second warning, if it should prove to be necessary.

The second warning is the TAKE COVER signal. It is a wailing tone from a siren or whistle of sufficient size and volume to be heard throughout a community. In some communities the TAKE COVER signal is a series of short blasts of three minutes. This signal means "Take shelter immediately."

Radio frequencies. When people hear an alert signal, they should turn on a radio to 640 or 1240 kilocycles. These are known as *Conelrad* (kŏn′ ĕl · răd) frequencies. Conelrad is an abbreviation for "Plan for *Con*trol of *El*ectromagnetic *Rad*iations." As you see, the word Conelrad is made up of the first syllables of several of these words. These frequencies are the ones the Civil Defense authorities would use to broadcast information if the need arose. At such times, there will be no broadcasts on any other frequencies, and it may take a few minutes before the Conelrad stations begin to broadcast. Be sure to keep tuned in.

Try This
Tune in your radio to the Conelrad frequencies. Try to find both. Ask your parents if you may mark these two spots.

Following directions. If a warning comes during school hours and if there is time enough, the Civil Defense authorities will probably give instructions over the radio for all pupils to go to their homes.

If there isn't enough time for the pupils to get home, several different things may be done. The pupils may remain in the school, either in a shelter, in a basement, or in the classroom. Or they may go to a shelter in the community. The important thing is that everyone realize the importance of following instructions quickly and with the utmost exactness.

During this time of alertness many things must be done. Electric switches should be turned off, except those that are used for emergency communications. All doors and windows should be closed. Window shades should be drawn, and if there are curtains, they should be drawn, in order to help control the shattering of glass should an explosion occur. Ventilators and air inlets from the outside should be closed. If the pupils have identification tapes, they may then apply the tapes to themselves. The teacher will take a roll call to be sure that all are present.

Taking cover. If it should happen that a Take Cover signal comes without a previous alert, or if it comes when you are outdoors, it is important that you take cover immediately. If possible, get to a shelter of some kind. If this is not possible, lie face down on the ground behind any kind of cover that can be reached. If you are in a car, lie down or crouch down on the floor of the car, close your eyes, and cover as much of your body as possible. Be sure to close your eyes to protect them against any nuclear flashes from the explosion.

When you "take cover," you are trying to protect yourself against

Conelrad
640-1240

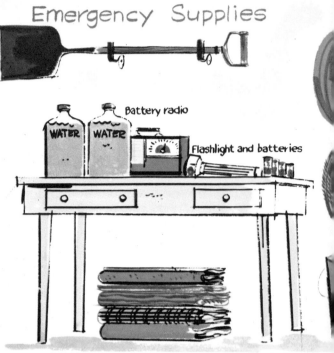

Emergency Supplies

Battery radio

WATER   WATER

Flashlight and batteries

blast, heat, or *radiation*. This means getting into something or under something.

Protection against fall-out. Radioactive particles that fall to the ground after a nuclear explosion give out penetrating rays that are very dangerous. Exposure to such rays could make you sick, or even kill you. You can't feel or taste fall-out. You can't hear it; and often you can't see it. Your Civil Defense authorities have instruments for detecting it. Radioactive particles decay in time, and they can be safely removed in various ways.

You can protect yourself against the particles by following the instructions of your local authorities. They will tell you when it is safe to go outdoors. They will also tell you just what you should do. There is one thing you can do immediately, without waiting for instructions. When you are inside, you can remove any outer garments that may have been contaminated. You can take a bath and put on fresh clothing. Then wait for instructions of the authorities as to what else you may do.

Household safety. There are certain things that you can do to help

Emergency Kit

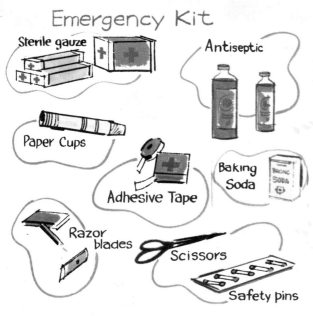

Sterile gauze

Antiseptic

Paper Cups

Adhesive Tape

Baking Soda

Razor blades

Scissors

Safety pins

keep yourself and your home as safe as possible in case of a nuclear explosion. Some of these things should be done long before there is any emergency; others you could do after the alert signal has sounded.

You should decide where you would go for shelter in your home if you didn't have time to get to a large community shelter. Those who have storm cellars for protection against tornadoes can use these. In many cases the basement would provide good protection.

Every home should have a survival supply kit stored in the shelter. This kit should include emergency supplies, including first-aid equipment, food, and water. There should be enough food and water for two weeks, and you should be able to pack a three-day supply quickly if you were required to evacuate your home on short notice. The other necessary supplies should be assembled in the shelter or packed in advance, also.

In case of an explosion, there would be danger from fires resulting from heat, blast, and radiation. Your home should be free from fire hazards such as piled-up papers or open paint cans.

You can help eliminate sparks by doing these things after an alert sounds: (1) Shut off the electricity or disconnect all electrical appliances; (2) Turn off any gas-range burners or room heaters; (3) Smother any fire in the fireplace and close the chimney damper; (4) Shut off any oil-supply valves on an oil burner; (5) Close all windows and doors to keep out fire, sparks, and radioactive dusts.

When an alert sounds, tune in your battery-operated radio to a Conelrad frequency to receive the latest information from the Civil Defense authorities. Do not use the telephone for this purpose. The lines should be kept open for real

A well-balanced emergency supply of food...

Fruits and juices.. vegetables, soups.

Canned milk, meat and fish, instant drinks.

Baby food, raisins and chocolate, dried fruit, packaged cereals.

emergency calls. Failure to cooperate in this way could hinder the defense activities and might endanger your life and the lives of others as well.

Someone in the family should be trained in first aid. The same precautions that you learned in connection with food and water in emergency situations apply to nuclear explosions, too. There is one exception. The safest water after a nuclear explosion is the bottled kind. Boiling doesn't remove much radiation, though it does reduce the bacteria count.

Safety in other kinds of emergencies. As you have seen, there are certain basic principles that apply in each of the emergency situations that were discussed in this chapter. For example, it is always wise in any emergency situation to boil drinking water or to use a purifying chemical to make sure that it is safe. Food should be watched carefully, also, to make certain that it is still in good condition. One should always be careful not to touch loose or dangling wires. You can think of other principles that were discussed which would be helpful to you in almost any emergency.

Try This

Think of several situations in which a knowledge of the basic principles you learned about in this chapter would be helpful to you in keeping yourself safe in emergencies.

Activity for Health

Run, throw, and catch test. This is a test of speed, skill, and accuracy—a contest to see if you can improve your own record as well as to see who makes the best record. In the relay games you played when you were younger, you learned the rules about a starting line, touching a goal line, and following through on all the requirements for the game. You will follow similar rules in this test. It will help you find out:

1. How well you can run, and how fast.

2. How well you can throw and catch a basketball.

3. How much you remember about the rules and requirements of any race and how much agility, muscular control, and skill is demanded of you.

To prepare for the test, stretch a rope or place a bamboo pole about 15 feet long between two jump standards, or posts, about 8 feet high. The rope should be 8 feet above the ground, or as near the top of the standards as possible. Stretch the rope taut. For girls, draw a base line 30 feet from the rope and parallel to it. The base line for boys should be 40 feet from the rope. A basketball and a stop watch are needed. In order to make sure that each contestant may have the same fair chance, your teacher or some other person should act as starter, while a second person keeps an accurate record of each contestant's time.

At a signal from the starter, a contestant runs from behind the starting line, throws the basketball over the rope, catches the ball, and then returns to touch the starting line with his foot. Three successive trips are made. When a contestant returns to the starting line after the first and second trips, it is not necessary for him to cross the line, but he must touch it. He may throw the ball over the rope from in front of or from behind the rope.

If the ball is not caught when it is first thrown over the rope, it must be recovered and the throw repeated until a fair catch is made. It is a fair ball if it goes over the rope without touching it and is caught and held. The contestant may not touch a wall, the rope, or any other object during the event.

If you are to do your best in this test, you will need to be in good physical condition. You can make sure that you are in good physical condition, as you know, by getting plenty of rest, by eating plenty of body-building and energy-producing foods, and by getting a proper amount of exercise.

For accurate records, use a stop watch. Time the test in minutes, seconds, and tenths of a second from the starting signal until the contestant crosses the line after completing the three trips. The trips must be made in succession. The one who completes the test in the shortest time, without making any errors, receives the highest rating and is called the winner.

This test should be given only when the needed skills have been practiced and achieved by a large part of your group. If you are a fast runner, accurate at throwing and catching, and have a positive mental attitude, you should measure up well on this test. If you are weak in one of the required skills, a regular schedule for practicing the skills of running, throwing, and catching will be helpful. Time scores in this test for your age may range from 17.1 to 22 seconds. If you are very skillful and accurate, your score will be low.

HELPS TO UNDERSTANDING

Points to Remember

1. You can take better care of yourself in an emergency if you know ahead of time what should be done in order to keep safe.

2. Every family should have an emergency first-aid kit, as well as an emergency supply of food.

3. It is important to follow the instructions of the health authorities or other community leaders during emergencies.

4. The safest place during a tornado is underground.

5. The safeguarding of the public water supply is difficult during any kind of emergency situation, but it is an urgent problem during floods.

6. The *Alert Signal* for a nuclear emergency is a steady blast on a siren or whistle for three minutes.

7. The *Take Cover* signal is a wailing tone of a siren or a whistle, or a series of short blasts for three minutes.

8. Conelrad frequencies (640 or 1240 kilocycles) are assigned to the Civil Defense authorities for use during a nuclear emergency.

9. Although earthquakes cannot be predicted, it is possible to predict the places where they are most likely to occur.

10. Although hurricanes bring great destruction, they can be detected well in advance of their arrival.

Questions to Discuss

1. Why do floods sometimes come without warning?

2. What are some of the kinds of emergencies that everyone may have to face at some time or other?

3. What kinds of foods should be in an emergency supply?

4. Why is it often a wise precaution to boil water during and after an emergency such as a flood or a tornado?

5. Tell of some precautions often taken by communities in tornado belts.

6. What are some of the dangers of eating foods that have been stored in a refrigerator during a flood?

7. Discuss the methods used to detect hurricanes.

8. Why are hurricanes more destructive than tornadoes in our country?

9. Why is it unsafe to enter a building that has been damaged during an earthquake?

10. Name some ways in which you can protect yourself against fall-out.

11. If you are outdoors, far from shelter, when you hear a *Take Cover* signal, how can you best protect yourself?

Some Things to Do

Write safety slogans

1. Write slogans to help you remember what to do in tornadoes, hurricanes, floods, and earthquakes.

2. Make up slogans that tell things you should do to keep safe during a nuclear emergency.

Make posters

1. Make posters showing what to do after receiving hurricane warnings.

2. Make posters showing things to be done to make your home safe during a nuclear emergency.

3. Show the supplies that would be useful during a nuclear emergency.

To Help You Learn More

1. Make a survey of your home to see whether there are things that should be done to make it safer from danger of fires.

2. Plan a household drill as preparation for a possible nuclear emergency. Assign tasks to various family members. After the practice, talk over with the family ways in which you could improve the plans.

Words to Remember

emergencies	Conelrad
evacuate	detected
contaminated	velocity
debris	devastation

CHECKING YOUR UNDERSTANDING

Health words. On your paper write the word that fits best with each definition below. Choose from those listed in *Words to Remember.*

1. leave a home or dwelling

2. speed

3. radio frequencies

4. ruin

5. spoiled or polluted as by the entrance of bacteria

Health facts. On your paper write T for each sentence that is true and F for each that is false.

1. Chlorine tablets may be used to purify water.

2. It is important to be able to recognize a funnel-shaped cloud.

3. It is impossible to predict the path that will be taken by a tornado.

4. Hazards in earthquakes are such things as collapsing roofs and walls and falling objects.

5. Hurricanes can be detected ahead of time by the weather bureau.

6. Since public utilties may be shut off for several days following an emergency such as an earthquake, chemicals that can be used to fight fires should be available.

7. If you are outdoors, away from a shelter, when you hear a *Take Cover* signal, lie face down on the ground behind any available cover.

Health rules. Read the sentences. Then write on your paper the numbers of the sentences that tell the right thing to do to keep safe.

1. Take shelter immediately when you see a tornado cloud.

2. Mark the Conelrad frequencies on your radio.

3. Do not risk your life in order to save furniture or personal possessions during a flood.

4. Learn to recognize the *Alert* and *Take Cover* signals.

5. When you hear an *Alert* signal, telephone the Civil Defense office nearest you.

6. Never touch loose or dangling wires.

7. Stay under strong, protecting furniture if you are indoors during an earthquake.

LOOKING AHEAD TO CHAPTER FOUR

Do You Know?

1. Why is exercise especially needed by young people?

2. Is there such a thing as an athletic heart?

3. How can you protect yourself against accidents when taking part in sports?

4. How can you improve your physical endurance?

5. How are good sportsmanship and personality development related?

6. Does a slow pulse indicate an efficient heart?

7. Does physical activity increase blood pressure?

4. Exercise and Health

What Physical Activity Does for You

The need for exercise. If you have ever watched young kittens or puppies at play, you probably have noticed how active they were and how much they seemed to enjoy being active. Such young creatures not only enjoy exercise; they need it. It is essential for their proper growth.

Almost everyone enjoys physical activity. Young people, especially, need much physical exercise to promote their growth and the proper development of their muscles and nerves.

In this chapter you will learn about how the bones, the muscles, the nerves, the heart, and other parts of the body work together to make it possible for you to move your body. You will also learn about the ways in which physical activity affects your physical growth and development as well as the development of your whole personality.

▼

**Demonstrating
Lung Capacity**

▲

A member of your class may wish to demonstrate lung capacity by exhaling air into balloons. Two balloons should be used. The demonstrator should blow up the first balloon by exhaling air from his lungs into it after having taken a normal breath. The second balloon should be blown up after the demonstrator has taken a very deep breath and exhaled into it.

Notice how much more air the second balloon contains. What conclusion can you draw about the ability of lungs to expand?

Physical development and co-ordination. As you may know, if you didn't exercise, your body wouldn't develop properly. Perhaps you have had an experience that has proved this to you. If you have ever had a broken arm, you may have worn a cast on it for a while. When your arm was free again, you found that it was weak until it regained its normal strength through exercise.

Your arms as well as other parts of your body are developed and strengthened by exercise. You also need to exercise in order to develop the *co-ordination* (kŏ·ôr′dĭ·nā′shŭn) or smooth, efficient working together of all the parts of your body. And after such co-ordination has been fully developed, physical activity helps you keep yourself fit.

Many parts of the body are involved in any vigorous physical activity. For example, to be a good athlete, you will need good muscles. Equally important are good bone structure, a nervous system that enables you to have co-ordination in movement, an excellent heart and circulatory system, and a good respiratory system.

Physical activity requires the co-ordination of all of these parts of the body. You can understand that this is so when you stop to think about what would happen if any of them did not work properly. Think what would happen if the nervous system stopped sending messages to the muscles; or if the lungs stopped working, or the heart did not pump the blood.

Building physical endurance. You may know someone who has especially good *endurance* (ĕn·dūr′ăns), or the ability to work or play effectively for long periods without getting too tired. Perhaps you, yourself, have good endurance.

It has been found that regular physical activity can improve endurance. Though endurance, or stamina, is especially important to an athlete, it is also helpful to one engaging in almost any activity; and it is an indication of good health. Endurance can be helpful to you, both at school and at home. It can be helpful to you all your life. If a person worked in a laboratory, for example, he could work longer and better if he had good endurance. In almost any activity you can mention, it is useful to have good endurance.

Skills in everyday activities. As you may remember from your study of the first chapter, you exercise your body every time you move. Such movements as walking, going up and down stairs, lifting and carrying objects, pushing, and pulling—all of these movements can be carried out in such a way that you not only avoid straining your body but help to develop and strengthen it.

You have learned about some of these activities and how they should be performed. When you use the right muscles you feel less fatigue, and you can engage in these activities more efficiently. You feel more confident, too. Standing, sitting, and walking properly also give others the impression of one who is self-confident and poised.

Effects on personality development. Did you realize that participation in sports can have an influence on your mental health and the development of your personality? The ability to relax is important for good mental health, as you may know. Taking part in sports can help one to relax mental tensions. Even watching games such as baseball or football helps one attain the relaxation that comes with recreational activities.

In addition, learning the skills that enable you to take part in various sports can help you develop poise in social situations. Knowing that you are able to take your place in a group helps to give you a feeling of confidence. There are other benefits to be gained from participation in group activities and team games, too.

One of the most valuable of these is the ability to get along well with others. As you play in a group, you learn much about the others in that group, and you begin to understand them better. You learn, for example, that though one person may have developed great physical strength, another may have developed greater skill, or *dexterity* (dĕks·tĕr'ĭ·tĭ), in his movements. Another can think especially quickly and well. You respect each for what he has accomplished; and you also learn to help those with less skill, strength, or mental ability.

To be a good team member, you must learn to respect the feelings and rights of others. You must control your actions, if not your feelings, for the good of the team. You learn to do what is best for the group, even though you can't play the position you prefer, or be

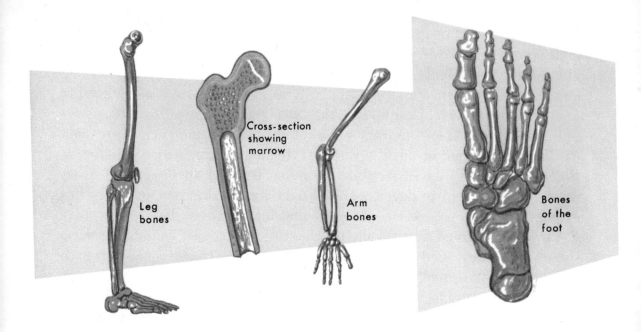

Leg bones

Cross-section showing marrow

Arm bones

Bones of the foot

captain of the team. You and the other members of your team soon realize that you can get the most accomplished by working together smoothly.

In addition, games and other forms of physical activity offer a healthful, wholesome means of using part of your leisure and of getting some of the exercise you need to keep fit. Knowing at least one sport that you can enjoy alone, if it becomes necessary, and others that you can enjoy in groups, will be helpful to you, both now and in the future.

Physical Activity and the Skeletal System

The bones and their work. If you stop to think about it, you will realize that your bones perform a very important function. Without your skeletal system, you couldn't move as you do. Without bones, you would be like a jellyfish; you could not run, jump, or walk.

You can move various parts of your body because many of your bones are fitted together at movable joints. The bones are connected with each other across these joints by muscles and tendons.

The bones also serve as the framework, or support, of the rest of the body. They help to give shape to the body and protect the softer parts, such as the heart, lungs, and brain.

This framework of the body, called the *skeleton,* is made up of about two hundred bones. The skeleton may be thought of as having three main parts — the skull, which contains the brain and gives form to the face; the trunk, which encloses the organs in the chest and abdomen; and the extremities, or the bones of the arms, hands, legs, and feet.

Think for Yourself

Why do you think the brain is enclosed so well by bone?

What your bones are made of. Your bones contain cells, blood vessels, fat, and cartilage. This is all living animal material. There is also some nonliving, or mineral material, in your bones, mostly calcium and phosphorus. This material is what makes them strong.

Your bones are constructed in such a way that they provide the greatest amount of strength with the least weight. Most bones are nearly hollow, and their centers are filled with a soft, lightweight substance called *marrow* (măr′ ō). If you have ever broken a chicken bone and noticed the sponge-like material inside it, you have seen bone marrow. The marrow in your bones is similar to that found in a chicken bone. Some bones have to be stronger than others because of the work they do in the body. The cortex, or hard outer layer, of these bones is therefore thicker, or denser; but the bones are still light in weight.

Except at the joints, the bones are covered with a membrane of connective tissue called the *periosteum* (pĕr′ ĭ · ŏs′ tē · ŭm). To it are attached the tendons of the muscles and the ligaments of the joints. You will read more about the joints and muscles later in this chapter.

How your bones grow. At birth and for some time thereafter a baby's bones are soft. They are composed of more animal matter and less mineral matter than the bones of older children or adults. As growth takes place, increasing amounts of mineral deposits, chiefly calcium and phosphorus, are added to the cartilage, through cell action, and the bones become harder.

As you can see, the bones of younger people, being softer, would not be so easily broken as those of older people. The bones of older people also take longer to mend when they are broken.

Though your bones grew at a faster rate when you were younger, they are still growing rapidly. The rate of growth, however, may vary greatly. For example, some people attain most of their growth in height much earlier than others.

For strong bones, you need a well-balanced diet, enough rest, and plenty of activity in the air and sunshine. These good health rules apply equally well to the rest of your body. The proper amounts of calcium, phosphorus, and other food substances are important for the growth and health of bone tissue, as well as of the other tissues of the body. Certain foods, especially whole milk, are rich sources of calcium and phosphorus.

Think for Yourself

What bones of the body need to be very strong?

Kinds of joints. The kinds of movements that can be made by the various parts of your body are partly determined by the joints. Some joints permit your bones to move freely, others permit movement only in certain directions, while others do not permit any movement at all. The joints between the flat bones of the head, for example, do not permit any movement. Your lower jawbone, however, is movable. Joints between the vertebrae of the spine permit very slight movement. Other joints, such as those at your elbows, knees, shoulders, and hips, allow greater movement.

Joints are protected and supported by *ligaments* (lĭg′ȧ·mĕnts). These tough, yet flexible, bands of

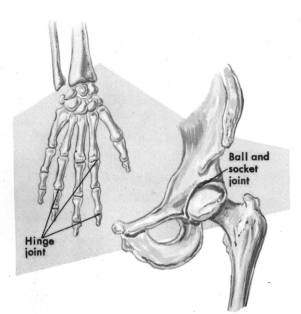

Ball and socket joint

Hinge joint

tissue help to keep the bones from being pulled out of position. Ligaments also limit the direction of movement at the joint.

The joints that permit you to bend parts of the body, such as those at the fingers, elbows, and knees, are called hinge joints because they move like a hinge on a door.

The joints that let you move bones in several directions, such as those at your shoulders and hips, are called ball-and-socket joints. In a ball-and-socket joint, the rounded end of one bone fits into a depression in another bone. There is a membrane which partly lines the space between the bones in certain joints—the freely movable ones. This membrane secretes a fluid that keeps the joint moist. This fluid is needed for the same reason that oil is needed in machinery.

You can see that joints make it possible for you to move your body and parts of it in various directions. Whenever joints are injured, your ability to play or engage in sports may be temporarily interrupted, and sometimes seriously impaired.

Muscles and Exercise

What muscles are. Muscles are bands of long, thin cells. They usually end in a long cord, or band, forming the tendon. These fibrous bands connect the muscles to the bones or other parts of the body. The tendons transmit the mechanical force of the muscle to the bone, or other part, causing it to move.

Muscles vary in size and shape, according to the work they do and where they are located in the body. In addition to their function in movement, muscles help to hold bones in place and to give shape to the body. When muscle cells are exercised, they tend to become larger and this, of course, affects the shape of the body.

How your muscles work. As you have learned, the kinds of movement that you can make are determined, in part, by the various kinds of bones and joints. The muscles and their points of attachment to the bones or other parts also affect the kinds of movement that can be made.

Some muscles join one bone to another; other muscles join bone to skin; and still others, such as

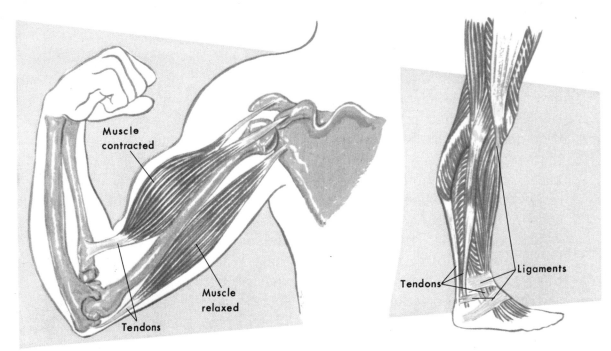

Muscle
contracted

Muscle
relaxed

Tendons

Tendons

Ligaments

some of the muscles in the face, connect one part of the skin to another. By means of such muscles in your face, you are able to show various expressions. Such muscles also are used in speaking and singing.

You are able to move the various parts of your body because your muscles have the ability to contract and relax. You have all felt the large muscle in your upper arm. As you hold that muscle and bend your elbow by raising your forearm, you can feel the muscle become shorter, though its total volume remains the same. The middle part becomes thicker and

harder. This is called *contracting* the muscle. When a muscle is contracted, it shortens the distance between the points where the muscle or tendons are attached to the bones, thus causing movement.

Now if you straighten your arm, you can feel the muscle on the upper side of your arm become longer, though the total volume of the muscle remains the same. It is just in a different shape. The middle is thinner and softer than it was before. This is called *relaxing* the muscle.

Muscles usually work in groups. When one group of muscles contracts, another group relaxes.

Again feel your upper arm. As you bend your elbow, the band of the muscle on the upper side of your arm becomes short and hard, but the one under your arm becomes longer and softer. Now as you straighten your arm you can feel the top muscle band become longer and the bottom one become shorter.

There is much yet to be learned about the many adjustments that take place in the body during exercise. We do know something about the effects of muscular activity, however. We know that when your muscles contract, there is a chemical reaction which produces heat and burns, or oxidizes, the food materials that are in the muscle cells. This food material is supplied to the muscle cells from the blood. In this way the energy from the oxygen and the food materials is turned into mechanical energy. Only about 20 to 30 per cent of the energy is turned into mechanical energy, however; the rest is dissipated as heat.

The heat that is produced when your muscles are contracting helps to maintain normal body temperature. You know that if you become chilled you often shiver. This means that some of your muscles are contracting, thus producing heat. Shivering is one way in which your body can help to maintain its temperature of approximately 98.6° Fahrenheit.

We know, too, that muscle contraction also causes a greater production of wastes and increases the need for these wastes to be carried away. More oxygen is needed, too. As oxygen is used up, more is needed by the muscle cells.

Food materials and oxygen are always being carried to the muscle cells through tiny blood vessels. Waste products are also carried away from the muscle cells through tiny blood vessels. When you exercise, you help your body circulate oxygen and food materials to the cells more rapidly.

Nerve and muscle co-ordination. No movement of your body would be possible without your nervous system. You will learn more about the work of the nervous system in another part of this book, but here it is important to know that during physical activity your brain directs your physical effort.

The voluntary muscles are the principal ones used in exercise, and they are under your conscious control; that is, they are under the direction of your brain. Thus, when someone throws you a ball, your brain receives the message that the ball is coming. Your eyes, ears, and other sense organs carry this information to the brain over various nerves. The brain decides what to do and then sends out a message to your arms or legs that permits you to move into position to catch the ball. This working together of the nervous system and the muscles is known as coordination. You can see that your muscles depend upon the nervous system to direct them.

Exercise and the Circulation of the Blood

The work of the circulatory system. As you remember from your study of the circulatory system, it is the work of this system to carry oxygen and food materials to the individual cells and also to remove waste products from the cells. Everything that goes to the cells and everything that is carried away from them is carried by the blood. The heart may be thought of as the pump for the operation of the circulatory system.

When a person takes part in vigorous physical activity, the heart and circulatory system begin to function with greater intensity. As a result, a greater supply of oxygen is carried to the cells and waste products are removed from them more rapidly.

In an earlier book you learned about the structure of the heart and the circulatory system. You know that the heart is a hollow organ that might be thought of as a bag of muscle. It is near the center of your chest cavity, behind the breastbone. It is divided into two large parts, or chambers, each of which is divided into an upper and a lower chamber. Blood flows into the *auricles* (ô′ rĭ · k′lz), or upper chambers, from various body parts, including the lungs. Blood is pumped out of the *ventricles* (vĕn′ trĭ · k′lz), or lower chambers, by the contraction of the muscles.

The right ventricle pumps blood that has come back to the heart from the body into the lungs, where a fresh supply of oxygen is obtained. From the lungs the blood enters the left auricle, and thence to the left ventricle, which pumps the blood that has fresh oxygen in it to all parts of the body.

Arteries and veins. Blood vessels

that carry blood away from the heart are called *arteries* (är' tĕr · ĭz). Since the blood in the arteries has just left the lungs, it contains much oxygen. The large arteries leading from the heart divide again and again to form a network of smaller vessels that reach out to all parts of the body.

Capillaries

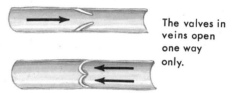

The valves in veins open one way only.

Lying close to the tissue cells are tiny blood vessels called *capillaries* (kăp' ĭ · lĕr' ĭz). It is through the thin walls of the capillaries that food materials and oxygen are exchanged between the cells and the blood.

After the blood has gone through the capillaries, it returns to the heart through vessels that are called *veins* (vānz). This blood returning to the heart is carrying carbon dioxide and other excreted materials from the cells. The blood doesn't take all the carbon dioxide away from the cells, however. A certain amount of carbon dioxide remains in the cells, as it is necessary in helping to control the rate of respiration, or breathing.

The veins return the blood to the heart, much of the time against the pull of gravity as, for example, the blood in the legs. Because the veins have one-way valves in them,

the blood can flow in only one direction—toward the heart.

When a person exercises, the contractions of the muscles help to push the blood back toward the heart, because of this action of the one-way valves. This greatly helps the heart to do its work.

Try This

To prove that there is some carbon dioxide in the lungs, blow through a glass tube or soda straw into a glass tumbler which has a teaspoon of limewater in it. Did the water turn a milky color? When carbon dioxide combines with limewater, the water becomes a milky color.

The pulse. You can tell how many times your heart contracts

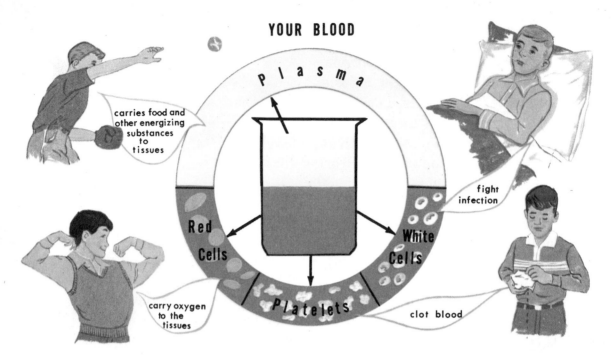

YOUR BLOOD

carries food and other energizing substances to tissues

Red Cells

carry oxygen to the tissues

Plasma

Platelets

fight infection

White Cells

clot blood

per minute by feeling your *pulse*. In an adult, the pulse during normal everyday activities is usually about 70 to 80 contractions per minute, but in children it is higher. Women tend to have a higher pulse rate than men, too, usually ten to fourteen more beats per minute. When the body is at rest or asleep, the pulse is somewhat lower.

A slow pulse, such as 50 or 60, or even slower seems to indicate, in most cases, a heart that is superior in mechanical efficiency; that is, the heart is able to pump more blood with fewer contractions. This means that a person with a slow heart rate can usually

exercise for a longer period of time without getting tired. In other words, he has more endurance.

The blood. Blood is made up of a fluid called the *plasma* (plăz′mȧ), and a number of different kinds of cells. These blood cells are called red corpuscles, white corpuscles, and blood *platelets* (plăt′lĕts). The red corpuscles carry oxygen to the body cells. The white corpuscles help the body to fight infections. The blood platelets help the blood to clot in case a blood vessel is broken.

The blood plasma is a thick, yellowish liquid that is mostly water. It carries many things in it; some of them are dissolved and some are suspended in the plasma. You know that food materials and oxygen are carried in the blood. So also are various other substances, including secretions from the endocrine glands. The blood carries these substances to and from the various body cells.

Blood plasma also helps to regulate body temperature. This is especially important during vigorous physical exercise. When a person exercises, his muscle cells, as you recall, produce heat and waste products. The waste products are carried away in the blood plasma and the heat is thrown off through the skin as the blood vessels near the skin dilate and expand. As heat is lost through perspiration, there is a cooling effect on the inside of the body.

Because the red blood corpuscles carry oxygen to the muscle cells, they are especially important during physical activity. There must be plenty of red blood cells and they must be healthy red cells, able to carry enough oxygen to keep one's muscles well supplied as he takes part in vigorous sports.

Blood pressure. When the heart contracts, blood is forced out into the arteries. The force, or pressure, of the blood as it pushes against the walls of the blood vessels can be measured. It is called blood pressure. As you probably remember from your earlier study, the heart rests between contractions. Every time the heart contracts, the blood pressure goes up, and every time the heart relaxes, or rests, the blood pressure goes down.

Blood pressure when the heart is contracting is called *systolic* (sĭs · tŏl′ ĭk) *pressure*. When the heart is resting, the blood pressure is called *diastolic* (dī′ ăs · tŏl′ ĭk) *pressure*. Since the heart contracts approximately three-eighths of the time and relaxes almost five-eighths of the time, you can see that more than half the time the blood pressure is at its lower level.

The arteries are elastic and they expand when more blood is pumped into them by the contraction of the heart. If the arteries become hardened, as is often the case in very old people, the vessels lose their elasticity. The blood then presses against the walls of the vessels with greater force. The pressure thus becomes higher.

Physical activity increases the blood pressure temporarily. This is a normal thing and is necessary to enable one to do vigorous work or engage in strenuous physical activity. Other things besides physical activity can elevate the blood pressure temporarily. Excitement, for example, can raise blood pressure.

It is only when the blood pressure remains high much of the time that it becomes a health problem. When the blood pressure is high much or all of the time, an added strain is placed on the heart, blood vessels, kidneys, and other organs.

The Lungs and Exercise

The work of the lungs. You have already learned about the structure, or anatomy, of the respiratory system. You know that there are air passages within the lungs. The membranes separating the air passages are very thin and are filled with tiny capillaries. As the blood comes from the heart through these small capillaries, the red corpuscles pick up oxygen from the air in the lungs.

When not physically active, a grown person usually breathes about sixteen or more times per minute. Not all of the air in the lungs is expelled, however, when one breathes out, or exhales. There is always some air in the lungs. As you remember from the experiment on page 71, the lungs also have the capacity to expand greatly. The amount of air taken in during physical exercise may be increased as much as seven times in very great exertion. The rate of breathing also increases. The greater the physical exertion, the greater the need for oxygen. The lungs help supply the needed oxygen.

The respiratory system works with the circulatory system to supply oxygen to the body cells and to

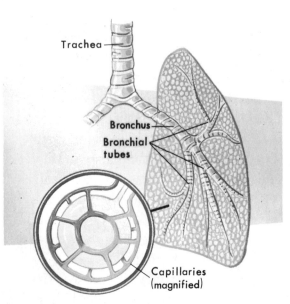

Trachea

Bronchus

Bronchial tubes

Capillaries (magnified)

remove carbon dioxide from them. There must be an abundant and easy exchange of oxygen and carbon dioxide if a person is to continue vigorous activity.

Effect on endurance. Strenuous physical activity over a number of years helps to develop the respiratory system. As a result, one who takes part in such activities develops a bigger chest, with more lung space and more breathing power. Perhaps you have noticed that athletes, singers, and others who use their lungs vigorously have larger chests than most people.

Injuries from Sports

Kinds of injuries. When a person takes part in physical activities and various sports, there is, of course, a chance that he may injure a muscle, a bone, or some other part of his body, since all strenuous physical activities call for the movement of the body at a faster speed than usual. These kinds of injuries do not happen so often that they spoil the fun of taking part in sports. It is important, however, to remember that when there is pain following an injury, one may need medical attention. Therefore one should pay

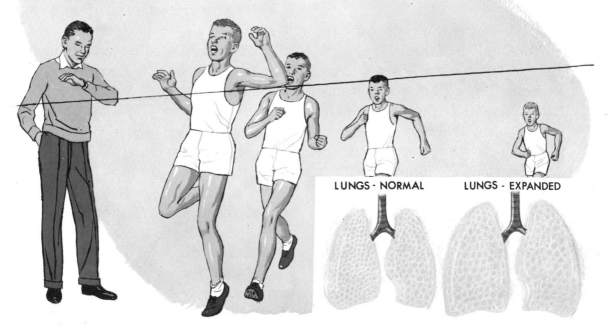

LUNGS - NORMAL   LUNGS - EXPANDED

Protective gear for games

ankles in such a way that the chance of injury is reduced.

Even with protective equipment, it is important to play the game according to the rules, and in a way that will help prevent injuries. Rules for a sport are intended to help protect the players against injury as well as to give order to the game. If the players break rules and begin to play wildly, there is a much greater chance that someone will be injured.

Each sport has its own kinds of hazards, or dangers. If you can learn what these special hazards are, you may be better able to help prevent accidents. A fundamental

attention to the warning and have an examination of the injured part. Failure to do so may be serious. For example, a person may think that he merely has a turned ankle, when he actually has a broken bone in the foot.

Prevention of injuries. Much can be done to prevent injuries from games and sports. For example, one should use protective equipment, such as a catcher's mask or a football helmet. Other means of protection can be used, too. Tape can be applied to the rule is that you should develop some skill in a sport before you try to engage in the more difficult phases of it. For example, you should not try to ski down a long, steep hill until you have had enough instruction and have developed enough skill to do so with safety. You should not engage in vigorous competition in a sport until you have gained enough skill in it to conduct yourself safely and at the same time help to protect other players.

Activity and your heart. Some years ago many people, and some doctors, believed that if you exercised too much, you would develop a kind of heart disease known as *athletic heart*. Now we know that this is not true. If a person has a normal heart, he can engage in all kinds of vigorous physical activity without any injury to his heart. In fact, the heart becomes stronger from the exercise because, like any other muscle, it needs exercise. It is only when there is something wrong with the heart that strenuous physical activity should be avoided; and even those with mild heart disease can usually engage in mild sports and physical activities in moderation. They must, of course, be guided by their doctors in the kinds and amounts of exercise they take.

Because it is important to know whether you can take part safely in sports and physical activities, you should have medical examinations regularly, including, of course, an examination of your heart. Some schools require medical examinations for all the boys who plan to be on the school teams; and many schools have medical examinations for all pupils to make sure that they are in good physical condition.

Activity for Health

Flag football. You have already learned some of the skills needed for playing soccer and modified forms of football, such as how to kick a ball correctly. You also have practiced running, throwing, and catching. Now you can use and continue to improve in these and other skills by playing flag football, which is a safe adaptation of regular football for your age group. The difference between the two games is that in flag football an opponent downs the ball-carrier by pulling a flag from his belt instead of tackling him. The object of the game is to pass or carry the ball across the goal line of the opposing team. The other team tries to prevent the ball-carrier from advancing to its goal line.

This is a team game calling for much close teamwork and fair play. It is best suited to boys. Any number may play and practice informally the skills it calls for, but seven to eleven players on a team is usually the number used in informal competition. For official games seven players may be chosen.

You can be guided by the diagram on this page in marking an outdoor playing field. The diagram shows how the field is marked off and the starting positions of the players. The game may be played on a field 60 yards long and 30 yards wide, or as large as 80 yards long and 40 yards wide, depending upon the experience and ability of the group. The diagram here shows the smaller dimensions. The end lines measure 30 yards and the sidelines 60 yards.

You will not need goal posts. Ten yards from either end line, measure and draw a goal line parallel to the end line. A center line parallel to the goal lines divides the field into two parts. The field is marked off in 10-yard zones. These lines should be parallel to the end lines.

Each player needs two flags, or pieces of cloth, 4 to 6 inches wide by 18 to 24 inches long. A knot is tied in each flag 4 inches from one end and 16 inches from the other. The short ends are tucked under a player's belt so that the knots are up against his belt and the long ends hang down over his hips. Instead of tackling a ball-carrier to stop his progress, an opponent downs the ball-carrier by pulling a flag from his belt. This stops the

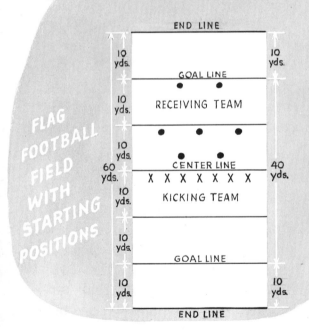

FLAG FOOTBALL FIELD WITH STARTING POSITIONS

END LINE

10 yds.　　　　　　　　　　　10 yds.

GOAL LINE

10 yds.　　RECEIVING TEAM

10 yds.

60 yds.　　CENTER LINE　　40 yds.
X X X X X X X

10 yds.　　KICKING TEAM

10 yds.

GOAL LINE

10 yds.　　　　　　　　　　　10 yds.

END LINE

play, and the ball is "dead". The ball is also "dead" if a player touches the ground with any part of his body except his hand or foot.

Playing time is divided into four quarters of ten minutes each. A two-minute rest is allowed between quarters and a ten-minute rest between halves.

At the kickoff, the two teams line up in the positions shown on the diagram, with the kicking team 10 to 20 yards behind its center line. The football is held with its tip perpendicular to the ground while the kicker kicks the ball as far as he can toward the goal of the opposing team. A fair distance would be 20 yards. If the ball goes out of bounds, it should be kicked again from the same line. After two out-of-bounds kickoffs, the opposing team is awarded the ball at midfield.

The team receiving the ball has four trials, or downs, to advance the ball to the next zone, moving toward the opponent's goal from the point where a player received the ball. The number of yards in a zone depends on the size of the field used. In the field illustrated in the diagram, one zone is 10 yards. If the offensive team fails to advance the ball to the next zone in four attempts, the ball goes to the other team at the point where the ball was declared dead on the fourth down. The second team then has four tries to advance the ball one zone.

A touchdown, scoring six points, is scored when a team advances the ball over the opponent's goal line. A try for point after a touchdown counts one point, but it must be made by running or passing. When a ball becomes dead in the possession of a player who is behind his own goal line, the opposing team scores a safety. A safety counts 2 points. After a safety, the opposing team puts the ball in play by a place or drop kick 20 yards from the goal line.

A running play cannot start by a direct pass from center. The ball must be lateraled to the person who will run with it. Every player on an offensive team is eligible to receive passes, and may throw a pass from any point behind the line of scrimmage.

You can see that your value to a team may depend upon your ability to throw or catch the ball accurately, so you may need to perfect your skills of throwing and

catching. You may need to learn, for example, how to catch the ball while running. If you are the receiver, you must remember to keep your fingers and arms relaxed and ready to "give" slightly as the ball is caught.

You can readily see that flag football calls for mental alertness if you are to anticipate a play and be ready for it. It also calls for endurance. You know that you can help build endurance by eating the right foods, by sleeping the right number of hours, and by exercising in the fresh air.

This vigorous team game also calls for teamwork and qualities of mental health such as fairness, co-operation, and the willingness to accept the decisions of the referee. You can increase your usefulness to your team by talking over the fine points of the game with your teacher and with others who know the game well.

Flag football calls into use the co-ordination of all your large muscles and demands quick thinking for safe play. By improving the tone of your muscles, it aids in the natural, well-rounded development of many parts of the body. It is also fun to play flag football when safety rules are observed in the game.

HELPS TO UNDERSTANDING

Points to Remember

1. Young people and children need exercise to aid their growth and the proper development of their muscles and nerves.

2. Physical activity helps adults to keep fit.

3. The respiratory system, the skeletal system, the nervous system, and the circulatory system are all involved during vigorous physical activity.

4. If you walk, lift, push, pull, and perform similar everyday activities in the right way, you help strengthen your body and you also avoid straining it.

5. Taking part in team games has a wholesome effect on personality development.

6. Bones contain cells, blood vessels, fat, and cartilage. They also contain mineral materials which make them strong.

7. As growth takes place, increasing amounts of mineral deposits are added to the cartilage, through cell action, and the bones become harder.

8. Joints help to determine the kinds of movements you can make.

9. Muscles vary in size and shape, according to the work they do.

10. The heart works harder during vigorous physical activity.

11. The blood pressure is raised temporarily by physical activity.

12. The lungs expand greatly during strenuous physical activity. The rate of breathing also increases.

Questions to Discuss

1. Why are the bones of older people more easily broken than those of younger people?

2. What is the relationship between physical activity and endurance?

3. Explain some of the changes that take place in the body during physical activity.

4. What are some of the functions of ligaments?

5. Why should one drink sufficient quantities of milk to have strong bones, as well as to have a healthy body?

6. What makes your bones light in weight, yet strong?

7. How does shivering help the body to maintain its normal temperature?

Some Things to Do

Write sentences

1. Write rules that tell some things that you can do to protect yourself as well as others when you play games on the school grounds.

2. Write sentences that tell of the hazards connected with various sports, and then give some suggestions as to how accidents may be avoided.

Make collections

1. Make a class collection of pictures of athletes wearing protective equipment as they participate in sports.

2. Get permission from the proper authorities to bring to class samples of protective sports equipment used in your school.

To Help You Learn More

1. Find out what activities are included in the Olympics. Tell the class what you have found out.

2. Keep a scrapbook of items concerning your favorite sport, including pictures of famous athletes, newspaper articles on the sport, and other similar items.

3. Choose a sport about which you know very little, and find out how to play it. Perhaps you can get someone to teach you how to play it.

Words to Remember

vertebrae	ventricles
auricles	dexterity
capillaries	endurance
tendons	ligaments
skeleton	marrow

CHECKING YOUR UNDERSTANDING

Health words. Match the following words with the correct meanings given in the list. Word 1 matches c, so write 1c on your paper for it.

1. dexterity
2. auricles
3. endurance
4. vertebrae
5. skeleton
6. marrow
7. ventricles
8. capillaries

a. stamina
b. lower chambers of the heart
c. skill
d. tiny blood vessels
e. upper chambers of the heart
f. the bones of the spine
g. the bony framework of the body
h. substance found in bones

92

Health facts. Write on your paper *T* after the number of each sentence below that is true and *F* after each that is false.

1. Even the most vigorous physical activity does not harm a normal heart.

2. Regular physical activity can improve endurance.

3. Ligaments support and protect the joints and help to keep bones from being pulled out of place.

4. All body joints permit bones to move.

5. The membranes separating the air passages in the lungs are very thin and are filled with tiny capillaries.

6. When muscle cells are exercised, they tend to become larger, thus affecting the shape of the body.

7. You can move parts of your body because your muscles have the ability to contract and relax.

8. The heart of an adult beats approximately 70 to 80 times per minute during normal everyday activities, though women tend to have slightly higher pulse rates than men.

9. The heart, like any other muscle, becomes stronger with exercise.

Health rules. Arrange the words in each group below so that they make a health rule. Then write each rule.

1. right Use muscles lifting, the when walking, pulling, or pushing.

2. physical intervals Have at examinations regular.

3. games rules to Play prevent accidents according the to.

LOOKING AHEAD TO CHAPTER FIVE

Do You Know?

1. Does your diet have any effect on your teeth?

2. What are dental caries?

3. How many primary teeth did you have?

4. How many permanent teeth will you have?

5. How do teeth decay?

6. Does your dental health have any effect on your general health?

7. What are the three main parts of a tooth?

8. How should your teeth be brushed?

9. When are the best times to brush your teeth?

5. Your Dental Health

Your Teeth and Your Health

Learning about your teeth. Bill and Don were talking about the dental examinations their class had just had. "Did you have any cavities, Don?" asked Bill.

"Just a small one," said Don. "Last time I didn't have any."

"I don't have any cavities," said Bill. "But I have to have X-ray pictures taken of my teeth. It's time for my regular visit to the dentist, anyway."

"What's an X ray for?" asked Don.

"I don't know, exactly," said Bill. "But I'll find out tomorrow when I go to the dentist's."

Your dentist uses X rays and other equipment to help him take care of your teeth and gums. He has certain responsibilities for your dental health. But you, also, have some responsibilities for keeping your teeth and gums in good condition. There are things that you should be doing to safeguard the health of your teeth and gums.

There is a close relationship between the condition of your teeth and mouth and your general health and well-being. For this reason it will be to your advantage to learn as much as you can about your teeth and how to take care of them.

94

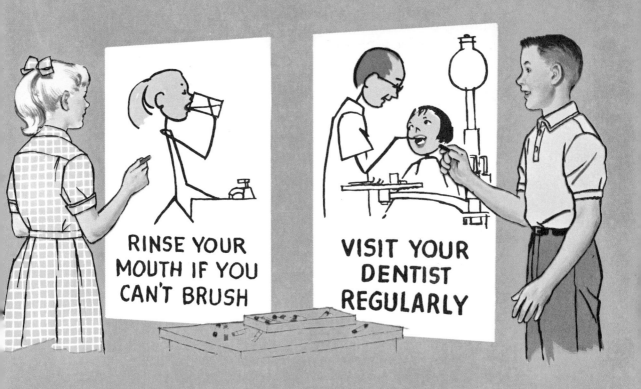

RINSE YOUR
MOUTH IF YOU
CAN'T BRUSH

VISIT YOUR
DENTIST
REGULARLY

Make a Survey

You may wish to make a survey of the dental habits of the members of your class and then make a chart for display in the classroom. You could find out: (1) when the members of the class brush their teeth; (2) what tooth powder, toothpaste, or other *dentifrice* (dĕn′ tĭ·frĭs) they now use; (3) how much candy or other sweets they usually eat; and (4) how often they visit the dentist. After you have read this chapter, you could discuss ways in which the members of your class could improve their dental habits.

How valuable are your teeth? At one time or another, all of you have probably noticed someone's smile as being particularly attractive. "What a beautiful smile," is frequently said of an attractive girl, for example. Boys, too, are better-looking if they have a pleasant smile and clean, well-cared-for teeth.

Though other qualities are important, your appearance does play a part in the development of your personality, and clean, attractive teeth add greatly to one's smile and to one's appearance in general. Teeth also have an effect on the shape of your face. Did you know that the shape of your lower jaw as it developed was affected by the way your first teeth came in and the care they received?

Your speech, too, is affected by your teeth. The loss of even one

Early care of the teeth can prevent many trips to the dentist later in life.

tooth, if it is in a certain position in your mouth, can greatly affect your speech. You may remember having had some difficulties of this kind during the time when you were losing your first front teeth.

To some extent, then, your personality is affected by your teeth. Anything that affects your appearance and your speech is certain to have some effect on you. Your general health is closely connected with your dental health, too. Any infection in the mouth, just as in any other part of the body, must be eliminated or it may cause illness.

You need teeth to prepare your food for digestion. Teeth are needed to bite, chew, and grind food so that it can be digested properly. The food you eat should be chewed and ground into very small pieces so that they will mix well with the digestive juices in the mouth and stomach. Unless the teeth are able to prepare the food for digestion properly, poor nutrition or indigestion may result.

Though your teeth are durable and with care can last a long time, even for a lifetime, they are subject to decay; and if the *enamel* (ĕn·ăm′ ĕl), or hard, outer covering of the tooth, is destroyed, it is not replaced by the body. This is another reason why it is to your advantage to learn all you can about your teeth and gums and how to take care of them properly.

Structure and Development of Teeth

Your first teeth. Most people have fifty-two teeth, altogether, during a lifetime. Twenty of these teeth are primary, or first, teeth. The remaining teeth, thirty-two, are your permanent teeth.

Some refer to the first teeth as *deciduous* (dĕ · sĭd′ ū · ŭs) *teeth* because they fall out and others, the permanent teeth, take their places. The first teeth are also called baby teeth, or primary teeth. The diagram on this page gives the names of the first teeth.

You probably got your first tooth when you were about six months old, though you had the buds of your first teeth inside your gums when you were born. A large proportion of the crowns of these teeth had already been formed. You had all your first teeth by the time you were two and a half or three years old.

Your permanent teeth. By now, most or all of your first teeth have been shed and have been replaced by permanent teeth. The first teeth were not shed all at the same time.

You began to lose them when you were about seven years old, or even younger, and this shedding may not yet be completed.

One interesting difference between the first teeth and the permanent teeth is that the roots of first teeth are absorbed in the jaws, whereas the roots of permanent teeth are not. When you lost your first teeth, it was just the crowns of the teeth that fell out.

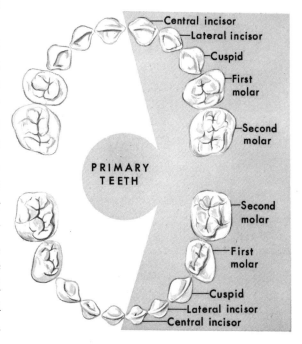

Central incisor
Lateral incisor
Cuspid
First molar
Second molar

PRIMARY TEETH

Second molar
First molar
Cuspid
Lateral incisor
Central incisor

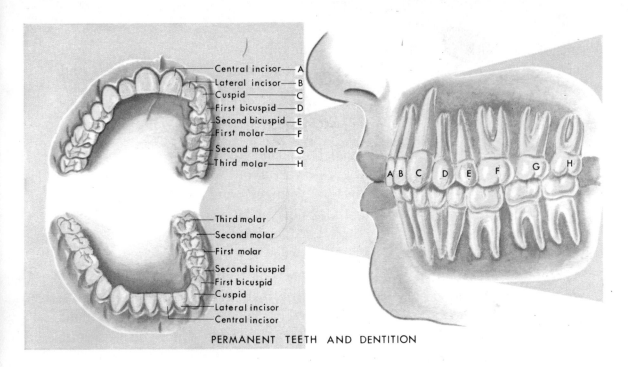

Central incisor — A
Lateral incisor — B
Cuspid — C
First bicuspid — D
Second bicuspid — E
First molar — F
Second molar — G
Third molar — H

Third molar
Second molar
First molar
Second bicuspid
First bicuspid
Cuspid
Lateral incisor
Central incisor

PERMANENT TEETH AND DENTITION

The crown of a tooth is the upper part—the part that you can see when the tooth has *erupted* (ĕ·rŭpt′ ĕd), or come through the gum. There are two main parts of a tooth—the crown, or upper part, and the root or roots. The place where the crown and root come together at the gum line is called the neck of the tooth.

The six-year molars were probably the first of your permanent teeth to erupt. They are often mistaken for first teeth because they do not replace any first, or primary, teeth.

You probably do not have all of your permanent teeth even yet.

Most likely, you do not yet have your third molars, or wisdom teeth as they are often called. Some people have their full set of permanent teeth by the time they are seventeen. Others do not have all their teeth, including their wisdom teeth, until they are twenty-one, or even later. Frequently, too, the wisdom teeth do not erupt fully. They may also be *impacted* (ĭm·păk′ tĕd), or wedged against another tooth in the jawbone.

Think for Yourself

Why do first teeth fall out easily, whereas permanent teeth must be extracted?

How Teeth Decay

Holes in the enamel. Probably you have had a *cavity* (kăv′ ĭ·tĭ), or hole, in one of your teeth. Most young people of your age have had at least one, and many have had more than one. When the dentist found the cavity, he cleaned out the decay and then filled the tooth. In order to understand what takes place when a tooth decays, you must know about the various parts of a tooth.

Enamel, dentine, and pulp. The enamel of the tooth may be compared to the hard, outer part of a kernel of corn. Enamel is very hard and is made up almost completely of calcium salts. Though it is able to stand a great amount of pressure, it is subject to decay. Under the enamel is the *dentine* (dĕn′ tēn), or the ivory-like material that makes up the body of the tooth. In the center of the tooth is the pulp cavity.

It is the pulp cavity that contains the nerves, arteries, veins, and lymphatic tubes. All of these enter the tooth through an opening at the base of the root. The root

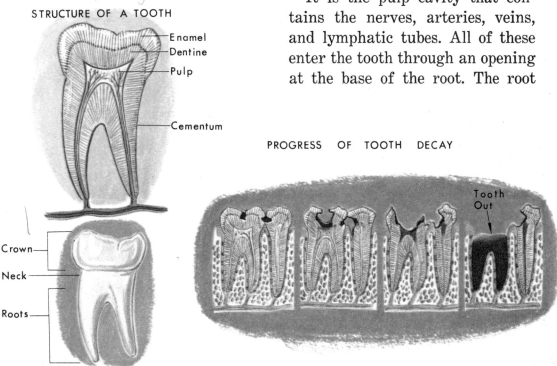

STRUCTURE OF A TOOTH

Enamel
Dentine
Pulp
Cementum
Crown
Neck
Roots

PROGRESS OF TOOTH DECAY

Tooth Out

These can cause tooth decay

too much of this...

too little of this.

itself is enclosed in a bonelike material called *cementum* (sė· mĕn′ tŭm).

What causes cavities. Dental *caries* (kâr′ ĭ· ēz), or decay in teeth, is caused by the action of acids that break down the enamel of the teeth. Bacteria are always present in the mouth. Some of these bacteria can make acids out of the food particles that are in your mouth. Although acids may

be formed by other foods, fermentable carbohydrates, chiefly sugar, are those that are most easily converted into acids.

These acids, if allowed to remain in the mouth, can destroy the enamel and cause cavities, or holes, in the teeth. This process is called decay. Decay starts in the enamel and, if not checked, spreads to the dentine, and finally to the pulp. When the decay reaches the pulp, there is usually pain, and often an abscess forms. Very often, too, the tooth has to be extracted.

However, there are things that you can do to help prevent decay of the enamel and if a cavity should develop, your dentist can repair the tooth and check the spread of the decay.

Try This

Use blue litmus paper to find out whether a substance contains acid. Let some litmus paper come into contact with the substance being tested. If it contains acid, the blue litmus paper will turn red. The following may be tested: toothpaste, lemon juice, orange juice, bicarbonate of soda, vinegar, and toothpowder.

100

Taking Care of Your Teeth

Brushing your teeth. You can help to prevent decay by keeping your mouth as clean as possible. When you brush your teeth, you remove food particles from your teeth. You also remove some of the acids that the bacteria may have formed from particles of sugars, carbohydrates, and other foods in your mouth.

The best time to brush your teeth is immediately after eating because you remove food particles before the bacteria in the mouth can act on them. Some people have formed the habit of brushing their teeth in the morning before breakfast because it makes their mouths feel fresher. But the most effective time to brush in the morning, of course, is immediately after breakfast.

Frequently, too, people form the habit of brushing their teeth before going to bed; but, as you know, it is far better to brush teeth in the evening just after dinner.

The size of your toothbrush is important, too. Use a toothbrush that is small enough so that it can reach all parts of your mouth easily. The bristles should be firm and give a flat brushing surface. After you have used your toothbrush, hang it up to dry, or place it in such a way that the bristles can dry before you use it again. Use a good dentifrice. There are many good toothpastes and tooth powders on the market. A combination of salt and soda is also satisfactory, or either salt or soda used alone.

Brush your teeth in the direction in which they grow, with downward strokes for the teeth in the upper jaw and upward strokes for the teeth in the lower jaw. The chewing surfaces should be thor-

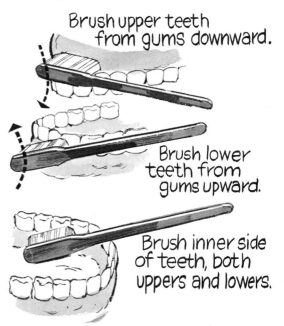

Brush upper teeth from gums downward.

Brush lower teeth from gums upward.

Brush inner side of teeth, both uppers and lowers.

oughly brushed with a scrubbing movement. Take several minutes and brush your teeth thoroughly.

Try This

Ask someone to time you when you brush your teeth. If you are brushing your teeth properly, you should have brushed for more than one minute.

What rinsing does. If you can't brush your teeth, it is helpful to rinse your mouth with water immediately after eating. There are many times, of course, when you can't brush your teeth; but you

can usually find a drinking fountain. Force the water back and forth between your teeth.

Rinsing gets rid of some of the food particles that may be in your mouth, as well as some of the acids that may have been produced. Those acids that remain will be mixed with water, too, thus making them more diluted and therefore less effective. Rinse your mouth not later than five minutes after eating, if possible. The length of time the acids stay in the mouth is a factor in the development of decay.

Think for Yourself

Why is rinsing or brushing the teeth immediately after eating especially helpful after sweets have been eaten?

Fluoridation of community water supplies. For a long time it had been noticed that people in certain areas had exceptionally good teeth. After careful study, it was found that people who had lived all their lives in communities where *fluoride* (floo′ ō · rīd) is naturally present in the water have fewer cavities than people living in areas where the water does not contain fluoride.

102

Two methods of using fluoride for teeth.

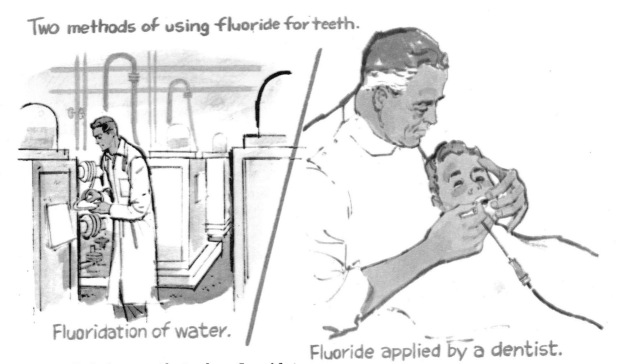

Fluoridation of water.

Fluoride applied by a dentist.

It is known that when fluoridated water is consumed during the years when the teeth are developing, it makes the enamel very hard and highly resistant to decay.

When very small amounts of fluoride are added to water that is naturally lacking in fluoride, the amount of tooth decay is greatly reduced. There is approximately 60 to 70 per cent less dental decay among children drinking such water from birth than among children drinking nonfluoridated water. In communities which have decided to add fluoride to the water supply, the public health departments and the water depart-ments work together in supplying fluoridated water for the community.

Fluoride is added to the water in very small quantities, usually one part of fluoride to a million parts of water. Fluorides are added to the water in much the same way as other substances are added.

Watching your diet. You know that what you eat has an effect on your general health—that there is a close relationship between what you eat and how you feel. What you eat also affects your dental health.

A diet which permits good general health is adequate for good dental health. It should include meats, vegetables, fruits, milk, eggs, butter, and whole-grain cereals and breads. Vitamin D, which is essential to the development of bones and teeth, is especially important when the teeth are forming.

In addition, you should limit the amount of fermentable carbohydrates, especially sugars, in your diet. As you have learned, sugars are very easily converted into acids by certain bacteria in your mouth. Since this is so, you would expect people who eat large amounts of sweets to have many cavities. This fact has been confirmed by research.

Certain kinds of foods should be eaten raw, too. Eating firm, crisp foods exercises the jaw muscles. It also helps clean the teeth. Evidence seems to indicate that teeth become harder when food is chewed well and vigorously. When teeth are compact, or harder, they seem better able to resist the acids that are found in the mouth.

Benefits from milk. You know that milk is a very nutritious food. Not only does milk give you calcium and phosphorus, which are used in the making of healthy bone tissue; it also supplies other materials that are needed for the teeth. It is particularly important to have these minerals while the teeth are developing. It is usually recommended that a growing child drink three to four glasses of milk a day.

Regular examinations. You probably know that you should visit the dentist regularly, just as you should go to the physician for medical checkups at regular intervals. In most cases, it is recommended that you see your dentist every six months. Those having special treatments usually will need to go oftener, of course.

If you visit the dentist regularly, he can find irregularities of growth or other difficulties in time to take measures to prevent further damage. By the use of X-ray pictures, for example, he can find tiny cavities too small to be seen with the eye.

What your dentist does. Your dentist does many things to help you take good care of your teeth. He not only finds and treats cavities and takes care of your teeth and gums; he also tries to prevent tooth defects and dental disease. Dentists are interested in learning the newest and best ways that have been discovered to take care of your teeth. Articles in professional journals, lectures, and meetings all play a part in keeping dentists well informed as to the latest findings of dental research.

One preventive measure that is often used is the application of a fluoride solution to the teeth. If you live in an area where the water is lacking in fluoride, your dentist may wish to use such a solution on your teeth to help prevent decay. Such treatments have been found to be most helpful during early childhood and youth.

Malocclusion. A condition in which the teeth do not come together as they should is called *malocclusion* (măl' · ŏ · klōō' zhŭn). This is a fairly common condition and one which often develops because the first teeth were not taken care of properly. If the first teeth are allowed to decay and fall out before the permanent teeth are ready to erupt, there will be a vacant space for a long time. The teeth around the vacant space will tend to slant toward the vacant space, and thus they will grow out of position. When the tooth below the vacant space is ready to erupt,

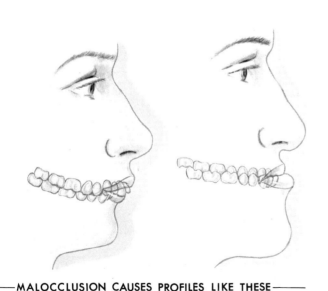

——MALOCCLUSION CAUSES PROFILES LIKE THESE——

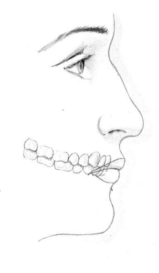

ORTHODONTISTS CAN CHANGE THESE
TO A NORMAL LINE LIKE THIS

But now she is glad she wore them.

Suzie didn't like her braces —

it won't have room to grow in properly; and it, too, will be out of position.

Sometimes the malocclusion is due to heredity. The jaw may be too narrow and teeth may not have enough room to grow in the proper positions. Occasionally, the permanent teeth come in too soon, before the jaw is large enough for them. In other cases, the first teeth are kept too long.

Malocclusion makes chewing difficult, as you can understand. Teeth that are badly crowded are harder to clean, too, and therefore are more subject to decay. Speech can be affected, too; and gum diseases and facial changes may result.

It is important that malocclusion be prevented if possible. With proper dental care, the first teeth can be retained until the proper time for them to be shed. If a tooth is lost too soon, the dentist may use a space maintainer to prevent primary teeth from growing in the places where the permanent teeth should erupt.

If malocclusion does develop, however, there are some corrective measures that can be taken. You learned about some of these in Chapter 2. An orthodontist is a dentist who specializes in the correction of teeth that are out of position and do not come together the way they should. Sometimes braces, wires, and bands are used to straighten the teeth. At other times, the dentist or orthodontist may remove teeth from a badly crowded jaw in order to give the other teeth room to straighten out. The dentist or orthodontist then watches the growth of the teeth carefully at regular intervals. You can help by keeping your regular appointments with him and by co-operating with him in every way.

Care of the gums. An important part of the dentist's job is taking care of your gums and the rest of your mouth. When the mouth becomes sore or inflamed, it is often because of an infection of one kind or another. If the gums become infected, it is very important that a dentist or physician be consulted at once. The earlier the treatment is begun, the more effective it will be. There are various means by which the doctor or dentist can cure such mouth infections. Sometimes pockets of infection, or pus, form in the gum at the root of a tooth. Such a pocket is called an *abscess* (ăb' sĕs). The pocket may even penetrate into the jawbone.

There really is no need to have trouble with the gums. If the teeth and gums are brushed properly after eating so that the mouth is kept clean, there is little danger of the gums becoming diseased. However, neglected, inflamed gums may result in a more serious condition and even loss of the teeth.

In their early stages, these signs of poor dental health can be found by means of an X ray. For this and other reasons, therefore, regular X rays of your mouth may be helpful to the dentist.

You and your dentist. As you can see, the dentist has a great responsibility for the health of

X rays of the teeth are helpful to the dentist. He can find the cause of trouble that does not appear on the surface. The X-ray picture below shows the beginning of tooth decay between two molars (arrow).

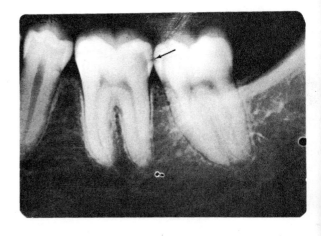

your teeth; but he needs your co-operation if your teeth are to be kept in the best possible condition. This means that it is important to keep regularly scheduled appointments and follow carefully his instructions in the daily care of your teeth and gums.

Activity for Health

Shuffleboard. This well-known game is played and enjoyed by all age groups. It is a good game for you to learn because you can play it all your life. At home it is family fun. On the sidewalk, in the gymnasium, or in a recreation room it will strengthen your ability to coordinate mind, eyes, and muscles to make deft, accurate movements with one hand.

You may buy the special equipment needed for shuffleboard or you can make it. Look about you for a smooth, flat surface of wood, stone, concrete, or asphalt and mark out a court, or playing space, 6 feet by 52 feet so that it resembles the diagram on page 109. There should be a 12-foot space between the scoring areas at the ends of the court—called the head and the foot.

You will need eight circular disks, 6 inches in diameter and between ¾ of an inch to 1 inch thick, four each of two different colors such as black and red. You also need four cues 3½ inches wide and about 5 feet long. The cues are shaped like a handle and have a head on one end cut to fit a disk. You use the cue to push the disk across the court.

The object of the game is to slide the disks onto the highest scoring areas of the court and to dislodge the opponent's disks and so prevent his scoring.

Two or four persons may play at a time. When two persons play, both players start at the head of the court and change to the opposite end of the court after all disks are shot by the two players.

Let us assume you have red disks and your opponent has black ones. You begin by sliding a red disk toward the foot of the court. Try to push it just hard enough to have it stop on a high number. Black plays next, pushing one disk in such a way that it may shove your red disk off the scoring area and leave his black disk in a position to score.

As you and your opponent take turns playing, you may be able to move one of your disks to a better scoring position by striking it with the disk you are then pushing. Such a move requires you to sight carefully and move deliberately. Take careful aim and push your disk at just the right speed.

After you have each had four turns—that is, after you have played one round—move to the foot of the court and count your score. A disk touching any line does not score. Subtract ten points from the score for each disk that lies within the 10-off area.

Play the second round from the foot of the court, black playing first from the left side. Play as many rounds as you need to reach the score you agreed upon before starting, such as 25 or 50 points.

In case of a tie, play another round.

In doubles play, two opponents play side by side at each end of the court. The red disk leads off. The opponents take turns playing until all their disks have been pushed. The scores are counted and the other two players play from the foot of the court. The partners' scores should be added together.

A disk removed from the court is not counted in the score. A disk must be removed if it does not cross the farthest dead line, or if it strikes any object other than another disk.

If the two teams obtain more than the required number of points in a single round, the team with the highest score becomes the winner. If a tie score is reached, another round is played, and the

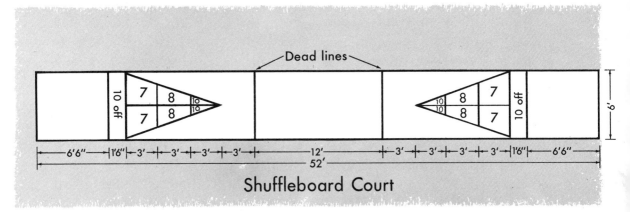

Shuffleboard Court

team having the highest score becomes the winner.

Keep in mind these points if you would become a good shuffleboard player:

a. Avoid the 10-off space.
b. Analyze and picture the move you want to make before you play a disk.
c. Take a long step forward as you push the disk.
d. Use your arm, trunk, and leg muscles with ease. Hold the cue in one hand.
e. Keep the cue in contact with the floor when pushing the disks.
f. Play fairly and as well as you can. If your disks are pushed out of their scoring position, accept the play you have made but try to do better next time.

This is a game which requires both skill and strength. To play well, you must also have muscle control. Practicing will help you develop skill in co-ordination. Good health habits, including the proper diet, sleep, and regular exercise will help you develop muscular strength, mental alertness, and social poise that help you play a good game.

HELPS TO UNDERSTANDING

Points to Remember

1. Your teeth, though very durable, are subject to decay; and if the enamel of the tooth is destroyed, it is not replaced by the body.

2. First, or primary, teeth, also called deciduous teeth, fall out and permanent teeth take their places.

3. The roots of the first teeth are absorbed in the jaws.

4. Often the wisdom teeth do not erupt fully, or they are impacted.

5. Decay in teeth is caused by the action of acids on the enamel of the teeth.

6. Some of the bacteria that are always in your mouth can make acids out of the food particles that are in your mouth.

7. Your dental health is very greatly affected by your diet.

8. Sugars and fermentable carbohydrates are the foods that are most easily converted into acids in the mouth.

9. Brushing the teeth removes food particles from the mouth and also some of the acids that may have been formed.

10. When it isn't possible to brush your teeth immediately after you eat, it is helpful to rinse your mouth with water.

Questions to Discuss

1. In what ways are dental health and general health related?

2. Why should any irregularities in the development of teeth be corrected as early as possible?

3. Can the condition of your teeth affect your nutrition? Explain your answer.

4. Explain the relationship between the shape of your face and the way your first teeth developed.

5. How was it discovered that fluoride in water seemed to help prevent dental decay?

6. Explain the various ways used by the orthodontist to straighten crooked teeth.

7. Why are six-year molars often mistaken for first teeth?

8. What part of the teeth contains the nerves, arteries, veins, and lymphatic tubes?

9. Where does decay of a tooth start?

10. Name at least three ways of helping to prevent tooth decay.

Some Things to Do

Write captions

1. Find pictures which show proper care of the teeth. Write captions for them.

2. Write descriptions of pictures that would show how irregularities in tooth development can be corrected or prevented. Write captions for such pictures.

Make plans

1. Think about the ways in which you can improve the care of your teeth. Consider the kind of daily care you give them, your diet, your dental examinations, and any corrective treatment that may be needed. Plan to improve your present program, if it is necessary to do so.

2. Mark on a calendar the date when you should visit the dentist again. It should be no longer than six months to a year after your last visit.

To Help You Learn More

1. Prepare a report on the qualifications and training a dentist must have. Be ready to give your report before the class.

2. Make menus that contain foods to help you have good teeth.

Words to Remember

dentifrice	impacted
enamel	cavity
deciduous	fluoride
erupted	malocclusion
abscess	dentine

CHECKING YOUR UNDERSTANDING

Health words. Match the following words with the correct meanings given in the list. Word *1* matches *b*, so write *1b* on your paper for it.

1. enamel
2. dentifrice
3. deciduous
4. erupt
5. impacted
6. cavity
7. fluoride
8. dentine

a. break through
b. the outer covering of the teeth
c. toothpaste or tooth powder
d. a hole in a tooth
e. a chemical
f. wedged against another tooth
g. the first teeth to appear
h. the bone-like substance which makes up the greater part of a tooth

Health facts. On your paper write *T* for each sentence that is true, and *F* for each that is false.

1. Dental decay is caused by acids in the mouth that destroy the enamel of the teeth.

2. There are always some bacteria in the mouth.

3. The enamel of the teeth is made up almost entirely of calcium salts.

4. People who eat large amounts of sweets often have many cavities.

5. A toothbrush should be small enough so that it can reach all parts of your mouth easily.

6. Brush your teeth in the direction in which they grow.

7. Malocclusion of the teeth develops very rarely.

8. There are thirty-two teeth in a full set of permanent teeth.

Health rules. For each health rule below, write on your paper the missing word or words. Choose from these words: dental, sugar, brush, rinse, advice, regular.

1. If you cannot _ _ _ _ _ your teeth, at least _ _ _ _ _ them.

2. Follow the _ _ _ _ _ of your dentist.

3. Be careful not to eat too much _ _ _ _ _.

4. Have _ _ _ _ _ examinations at _ _ _ _ _ intervals.

LOOKING AHEAD TO CHAPTER SIX

Do You Know?

1. Why must you have an almost continuous supply of oxygen?

2. Do you ever breathe out all the oxygen in your lungs?

3. What is meant by the composition of air?

4. What is smog?

5. Why is there more smog in some cities than in others?

6. What are some of the things that pollute air?

7. What can you do to help prevent air pollution?

8. What is overbreathing?

9. How does carbon dioxide regulate breathing?

You Will Need

a shallow saucer   vaseline

113

6. Air and Health

The Respiratory System

The air you breathe. Have you ever been high up in the mountains? If you have, you probably noticed that the air seemed quite different from the air at lower levels. It is different, too. The air is "thinner" at high altitudes. It probably seemed hard for you to breathe. Later in this chapter you will find out why this was so.

The air you breathe has much to do with your health. Clean, wholesome air helps you to maintain your health. On the other hand, air that is filled with dust, germs, pollens, and chemicals can be very bad for you.

In this chapter you will learn something about the *respiratory* (rĕ·spīr′ ȧ·tō′ rĭ) *tract* and other parts of the body that are related in some way to the breathing process. You will also learn something about the composition of the air and its effects on you and your health.

AIR POLLUTION— A MODERN PROBLEM

SOME USES OF AIR

▼

Make an
Observation

▲

At home ask permission to use a saucer and some vaseline. Put a thin smear of vaseline over the saucer and set it outdoors in a place where it will be out of reach. Let the saucer stand for twenty-four hours and then bring it to school. Show the class the things that have been collected from the air. Look especially for pollens, dust, and other small things that may have fallen out of the air.

If there is a microscope in your science room, ask your teacher to let you use it to look more closely at the pollens or other objects that your saucer and vaseline may have collected. What conclusion do you reach about the air around you?

Why you breathe. Without oxygen you could not live long. You must have oxygen in almost continuous supply, since you can't store much of it in your body. Oxygen is needed to help supply the body cells with the energy they need. Oxygen is used in the *oxidation* (ŏk′ sĭ·dā′ shŭn), or burning, of food materials that are supplied to the cells by the blood, thus producing the needed energy. The oxygen is taken from the air and passed on to all the cells of the body by the blood.

You need more energy at some times than at others; but you always need some energy to carry on body processes such as the beating of your heart, the digestion of food, and breathing.

One of the major purposes of the respiratory system, then, is to provide the necessary oxygen to the body cells. Not all the oxygen that you take into your lungs is kept in the body, however. Some of it is given off when you exhale, or breathe out.

Besides supplying oxygen, the respiratory system carries away carbon dioxide from the cells. Not all the carbon dioxide is given off. There must always be some carbon dioxide in the body because this substance plays a key role in the regulation of breathing. Carbon dioxide is found in all living things, and it is not harmful as long as it is mixed with enough oxygen.

The vital process of furnishing oxygen to the cells and carrying carbon dioxide away from them is called breathing, or *respiration* (rĕs′ pĭ·rā′ shŭn). In addition to supplying oxygen and carrying away carbon dioxide, the respiratory system also performs other services. It helps to regulate body temperature by releasing heat and moisture from the lungs when air is exhaled. The movement of the muscles involved in breathing also helps the heart and circulatory system to move blood in the large vessels of the chest cavity. You need air to sing, speak, and make other sounds, too.

The Anatomy of the Breathing Apparatus

Chief parts. Do you know all the parts of your body that belong to the breathing apparatus? The chief, or principal, parts include the nose, the pharynx, the trachea or windpipe, the bronchial tubes, and the lungs, including the air sacs and the capillaries inside them. The chest and ribs, which shelter the lungs, are also a part of the breathing mechanism. So also is the *diaphragm* (dī′ à · frăm), which separates the chest and lungs from the abdominal cavity.

Route of air. Let's follow the path taken by the air on its way to the lungs by looking at the picture in column two. Air enters your lungs through the openings of the nose called the *nostrils* (nŏs′ trĭlz). Inside the nostrils are fine hairs, which help to filter particles of soot, dust, and pollen. There are also hairlike projections of membrane in the nostrils called *cilia* (sĭl′ ĭ · à). They, too, help to filter and warm the air before it goes into the lungs. The wavelike motion of the cilia helps push foreign matter out of the nose.

The mucous-membrane lining of the nose secretes a sticky fluid which also helps to trap dust and germs before they reach farther into the air passage to the lungs. The whole pathway to the lungs is lined with mucous membrane and contains cilia. Notice that the nasal cavity and the mouth unite at the back to form the *pharynx* (făr′ ĭngks).

Everything that enters the lungs or the stomach must first pass through the pharynx. From here, food passes to the stomach through a food tube called the *esophagus* (ė · sŏf′ à · gŭs). Air passes through the pharynx to the *trachea* (trā′ kė · à), or windpipe.

At the upper end of the windpipe is the *larynx* (lăr′ ĭngks), or voice box. There is a flap of cartilage at the top of the voice box, called the *epiglottis* (ĕp′ ĭ · glŏt′ ĭs). This flap closes when you swallow, thus preventing food

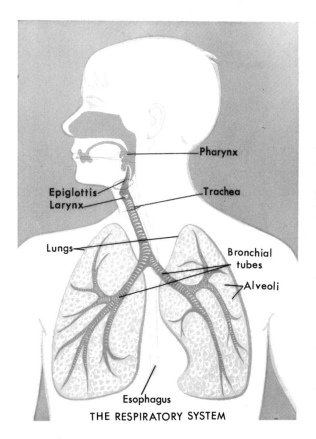

THE RESPIRATORY SYSTEM

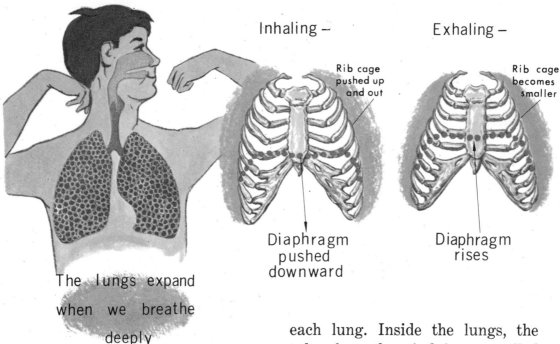

Inhaling –

Rib cage pushed up and out

Diaphragm pushed downward

Exhaling –

Rib cage becomes smaller

Diaphragm rises

The lungs expand when we breathe deeply

from entering the windpipe. The larynx is built of cartilage and it contains the vocal cords. When air passes over these cords, it causes them to vibrate, thus making different sounds. The degree of tension or the position of the vocal cords affects the sounds that are made. The airway to the lungs can be closed by the coming together of the vocal cords. They close automatically for just a moment after you exhale.

If you look at the illustration on page 117 carefully, you will see that the windpipe divides into two branches, or tubes, one going to

each lung. Inside the lungs, the tubes from the windpipe are called the *bronchial* (brŏng′ kĭ · ăl) *tubes.* These tubes divide again and again, becoming smaller and smaller, with each division ending finally at an air sac, or air cell. These sacs are very tiny and they have very thin walls.

Try This

Put your fingers on the front of your throat over your voice box and make a soft, humming sound. See if you can feel the vibration of the vocal cords.

Your lungs. If you will look at the illustration on page 117 again, you will see that the two lungs fill most of the space within your chest, or *thorax* (thō′ răks). There is a fine connective tissue which binds together the many tiny air sacs, or cells, and the bronchial tubes. A thin membrane, called the *pleura* (plŏŏr′ à), covers the lungs, and the same kind of membrane lines the cavity of the chest. The pleura is kept moist by a liquid which permits the two surfaces to move over each other without too much friction as the lungs expand and contract during the process of breathing.

The Process of Breathing

Muscles and movements. Perhaps you have noticed the way the chest of a sleeping animal rises and falls regularly when he breathes in and out. You make similar movements when you breathe.

When you inhale, or breathe in, your lungs expand, and some of the muscles which move the ribs contract in order to lift your ribs and chest and to push them up and out. The diaphragm contracts and pushes downward into the abdomen, thus making more vertical space for the chest. This movement forces the upper abdomen out. You can feel this movement by holding your hands over the outside of your stomach as air is inhaled. When you inhale, the increased size of the chest makes a partial vacuum, which helps to draw air into the various parts of the respiratory tract. When you exhale, or breathe out, the chest muscles relax, the chest cavity becomes smaller, and the diaphragm rises; thus air is pushed out of the lungs. People differ in the extent to which they use the diaphragm in breathing.

Internal and external respiration. The movement of the lungs and the walls of the chest as air is breathed in and out is called external respiration. All breathing, however, does not take place in the lungs. Part of the process goes on in the various tissues of the body. The exchange of oxygen and carbon dioxide which takes place both in the lungs and in the body cells is called internal respiration.

For a short time, air can be stored in the tiny air sacs within the lungs before it is carried to the body cells in the blood. The membranes separating the air spaces are very thin and are filled with tiny capillaries. As the blood coming from the heart travels through these small capillaries surrounding the air sacs, the red corpuscles pick up oxygen. At the same time carbon dioxide is discharged from the blood into the air spaces of the lungs. So also are moisture and heat.

The blood, with its fresh supply of oxygen, then returns to enter the left side of the heart. The heart then pumps this blood to practically all of the body. As the heart pumps the blood through the blood vessels, the oxygen is left wherever the body needs it. Thus respiration takes place both in the lungs and in the body cells.

The Control of Respiration

Supply and demand. In some ways, the body is remarkably efficient. It works with great precision and is able to adjust itself to varying conditions to supply what is needed. You may recall from your study of the endocrine system that the body tends to secrete as much of any hormone as it needs. In much the same way, each time the blood passes through the lungs, it tends to take up as much oxygen as is needed in order to enable the body to carry on the activities it is then engaged in.

Rate of breathing. The rate and depth of breathing are controlled almost completely by one of the nerve centers in the brain. This nerve center, in turn, is affected by the amount of oxygen and carbon dioxide in the blood. These substances in the blood either slow down or speed up the rate of breathing by their effect on this nerve center in the brain. The regulation of the rate of breathing is automatic. You do not have to think about it.

The activity of the body influences the rate of breathing. Usually only a small part of the lungs is used for breathing. During strenuous activity, however, such as participation in sports, the athlete may call upon his full lung capacity in order to get more oxygen; and the body then makes adjustments which make it possible to get the oxygen to the body cells. Oxygen is distributed to the body cells through a more rapid circulation of the blood, which carries the oxygen.

Overbreathing. When a person breathes deep and fast without there being a real need for the oxygen, however, he disturbs the natural balance of oxygen and carbon dioxide in the blood by supplying too much oxygen for the body to use. As a result, one can become quite dizzy, and suffer from a number of distressing symptoms.

As you recall, when a person exhales, he gives off some carbon dioxide, moisture, and heat. When he breathes deep and fast, without the need being present, he gives off more carbon dioxide than is necessary. As the amount of carbon dioxide in the blood falls, there is less stimulation to the respiratory nerve center in the brain; and as a consequence the whole breathing process is less efficient.

Red blood cells. The efficiency of the respiratory system and the rate of breathing are partly dependent upon the red blood cells, too. The red blood cells are the ones that carry the oxygen to all the parts of the body. The oxygen is carried by the hemoglobin in the red blood cells.

If there are not enough red blood cells, or if the red blood cells do not have enough hemoglobin in them,

BLOOD CELLS GOING FROM LUNGS TO TISSUES LADEN WITH OXYGEN

BLOOD CELLS RETURN TO LUNGS FROM TISSUES WITH LESS OXYGEN

there will be difficulty getting enough oxygen to the body cells, as you can understand. The heart and circulatory system may make adjustments in order to try to get enough oxygen to the body cells. The heart will tend to speed up. The rate of breathing will increase, also.

A person with too few red blood cells or with too little hemoglobin in them is said to be *anemic* (*a·nē′mĭk*). As you can understand, this condition should not be allowed to continue. If the body cells don't get enough oxygen, they can't do their work properly. A physician should be consulted in order to find out the cause of the anemia and to take steps to correct it.

Voluntary modifications. Though the rate and depth of breathing is largely automatic, as you have seen, you do have some control of your breathing. To a certain extent, and with effort, you can increase or decrease the rate and depth of your breathing. For example, you know that you can change the rate of your breathing when you swim, sing, or even talk and laugh. And, as you have seen, you are controlling your breathing when you overbreathe. You know that you can even hold your breath, for a time. Soon, however, the nerve center, stimulated by the carbon dioxide, assumes control, and breathing tends to become automatic.

Think for Yourself

If you had to think about breathing before you could take air into the lungs or expel it from the lungs, what could happen if you became absent-minded or completely absorbed in thinking about something else?

Air and Its Pollution

Composition of air. If you look at the diagram on page 115, you will notice that over 99 per cent of the air you breathe in is made up of oxygen, carbon dioxide, and nitrogen. The rest is made up of other gases, water vapor, and foreign matter, including such things as dusts, pollens, bacteria, soot, salt particles from the sea in some cases, and spores from plants.

The composition of the air is always essentially the same, though it does vary in the amounts of foreign matter and gases it contains, and in the amount of water vapor, too.

Air and comfort. The temperature of the air and the presence or absence of air currents have an effect on the way you feel. The pressure of the air also affects you. When the air is filled with moisture and is very heavy, you may not feel as well as usual. Especially when there is much moisture in the air, combined with very little air movement, you may feel uncomfortable. Very warm air makes your heart beat faster; and lack of air currents hinders the evaporation of moisture from your skin.

Oxygen and carbon dioxide. As you can see from the chart on page

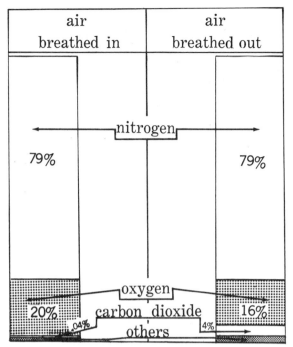

air breathed in	air breathed out
nitrogen	
79%	79%
oxygen	
carbon dioxide	
others	
20%	16%
.04%	4%

Adequate ventilation is important to health

123, the amount of oxygen in the air you take into your lungs is approximately 20 per cent of the total volume breathed in. The air you breathe out contains about 16 per cent oxygen, because you absorb some oxygen in your lungs.

The amount of carbon dioxide in the air you breathe in is approximately .04 per cent, whereas the air you breathe out contains approximately 4 per cent carbon dioxide. You might think, then, that if you rebreathed the same air over and over again, and each time it became more and more full of carbon dioxide, it would come to have too great a concentration of carbon dioxide in it. This is not often the case. Remember that you also breathe out some oxygen, too, when you exhale.

Usually there is sufficient oxygen in even a badly crowded and poorly ventilated room, though you are frequently uncomfortable, as you may recall from your own experience. The discomfort is due not to too much carbon dioxide or too little oxygen, but rather to the increased moisture in the air that is being breathed out, and to the lack of air movement. In such overcrowded rooms, the temperature of the air is also raised, thus adding to your discomfort; for, as you recall, heat as well as moisture is breathed out when you exhale.

Density of air. In the opening paragraph of this chapter it was pointed out that the air seems different at a high altitude; and it is true that the air is different, though its composition remains essentially the same. The air seems "thinner" because there are fewer molecules of air in the atmosphere at the higher levels and the molecules are farther apart. Air is made up mostly of gases. When the pressure in a gas is lessened, as it is at high altitudes, the gas expands. Thus the gases in the air expand. There is a greater and greater distance between the molecules the higher up you go. Hence, it is hard to breathe in enough air at high altitudes.

Kinds of dusts. Have you ever watched particles of dust that you can see in a ray of sunlight coming into a room? There is almost always some dust in the air, and most of it is harmless unless there is a very large amount, or unless you are allergic to it.

There are two broad classifications of dusts. Organic dusts are those that come from grains, furs, wools, wood, or anything from living materials. This kind of dust seldom produces any lung changes and is considered safe to inhale if there is not too much of it.

A second broad classification of dusts includes inorganic dusts, or metals. They are generally not harmful to any great extent unless the mineral from which they come is also poisonous. Mineral dust such as that from slate, soapstone, limestone, sand, granite, and marble may produce lung damage only if the dust concentration in the air is high and the dust contains silica in a powdery form.

Silica is the term used to refer to silicon dioxide, an element which is always found in combination with other elements. There are both crystalline and powdery, dust-like forms of silica. It is found in most of the minerals in rocks, and it makes up the largest part of sand. One who inhales dust containing silica usually must take it into his lungs for many years before damage is done. In this case, the silica that is present in these dusts may produce a scar tissue in the lungs. Asbestos dust will also produce scar tissue if one inhales enough of it over a long period. Many common dusts, such as limestone, cement, gravel, or marble have little or no silica dust in them and thus are not harmful, except for a slight irritation of the nasal membranes that they may cause.

Radioactive dusts. In Chapter 3 you read about some ways of protecting yourself, if need be, against the harmful rays of radioactive dusts from atomic and hydrogen explosions. You learned that it is very important to follow the instructions of your Civil Defense authorities and that you should keep tuned to your Conelrad stations for the latest information and advice. As in other emergency situations, it is wise to be very cautious and to follow carefully the instructions of the authorities. The Civil Defense authorities in your area will tell you when the atmosphere in safe and when you can venture outdoors again safely.

Size of dust particles. Just because you can see dust in the air or in a room does not mean that it is dangerous to health. The smaller the dust particle, the longer it is apt to stay in the air. This means that it is more likely to be breathed into the lungs.

The size of most dust particles that are carried in the air is less than one *micron* (mī′krŏn). A micron is about $\frac{1}{25,000}$ of an inch. Silica dust particles are one-fourth of a micron in size, and they require about ten hours to fall one foot in the air. A larger particle, one of about five microns, falls one foot in less than three minutes.

Pollens. At certain times of the year, and especially in certain places, the air may contain much pollen. Pollens are a kind of fine flour or dust, often yellow in color, that comes from the very small parts of seed plants. Flowers, trees, or other plant life may have pollens.

Some pollens are known as *allergens*. An allergen is a substance that can cause a person to have an *allergy*, or extreme sensitivity, to a substance. Many people, of course, are not bothered by pollens in the air. Those who are sensitive to pollens develop symptoms that resemble those of a cold. They are said to have hay fever. The affected one may sneeze, and the membranes of his nose may become badly swollen. He may be very uncomfortable. It is difficult to distinguish between hay fever and a cold, since the symptoms are very similar.

If the pollens are inhaled into the lungs, one who is sensitive to them may suffer from asthma. This is a disease of the respiratory tract in which it is very difficult to breathe.

Sometimes one who suffers from such allergies can obtain relief by being immunized against the pollens to which he is sensitive. There are other ways of keeping the effects of such allergies at a minimum. Keeping the bedroom window closed at night keeps pollens out of the bedroom, at least. Often air-conditioning devices that wash and filter air are helpful, too.

In some cases, people have moved to a different part of the country, where there are no plants that give off pollens to which they are sensitive. However, this is not always a final solution to the problem. The one affected may develop allergies to plants and flowers that are in his new environment.

Germs in the air. When the air you breathe contains germs, you may develop a respiratory infection. Some of the germs contained in the air may not be harmful, but some of them may be. Then, too,

germs do not live forever in the air. They need food and water, just as any other living organism does. Fortunately, too, sunlight kills most of the germs in the air.

The viruses are the smallest of the disease-producing germs in the air. They are so light in weight that they can remain suspended in the air longer than heavier germs. Most people have developed an immunity to many viruses and other microorganisms, however, because they have breathed these germs into their bodies so often.

Whether or not you become ill from breathing a virus is partly dependent upon the state of your own health. If you are not in good health, or if your immunity is low, you may become ill. Then, too, at various times, such as during an epidemic, you may become exposed to greater numbers of the offending virus.

It is wise, therefore, to keep in good health and to stay as far away as possible from a person who appears to be ill with a respiratory infection. You also have a responsibility to avoid spreading germs to others when you have a cold or some other disease caused by a virus.

Pollution of the air. There are other things besides germs in the air, too, that can be harmful. In recent years, many of our large centers of population have come to have a serious health problem because of air pollution. The air in such places has become polluted with chemicals from the exhaust fumes of automobiles, smoke from factories, incinerators, or burning garbage. This kind of air pollution is usually known as smog.

All air has some impurities in it; but the amount of such foreign matter in the air determines whether or not a condition known as smog will develop. Air pollution usually develops only in certain areas and under certain conditions. When the wind blows, it tends to sweep away the air which is saturated with chemicals. When the air rises toward the sky, it tends to move the chemicals away. In communities where there is little wind, or little or no vertical movement of the air, smog is likely to develop.

If the air is badly polluted, people can suffer from various discomforts and illnesses. Many people find that their eyes become irritated. Others develop headaches. Still others have swollen nasal membranes. A few may have difficulty breathing. Those who are the most distressed by smog are

AIR POLLUTION CAN BE CURED

usually the aged or those who have had chest or lung diseases.

Prevention of smog. Some of our larger cities have made an effort to control smog. In these cities public health officers make a daily analysis of the air. When they find that the air is being polluted and the weather is such that smog is likely to develop, the people are notified through radio, television, or the newspapers. The public is asked to co-operate in measures designed to cut down smog.

Sometimes people are asked to drive their automobiles as little as possible to reduce exhaust fumes until fresh winds come up and sweep the polluted air away. The authorities may ask that trash not be burned in incinerators during this period. Factories may even close down for a few days. Only with community effort can the formation of smog be prevented.

Activities for Health

Track and field activities. There are so many track and field activities, including running, jumping, and throwing, that you might think of them as an "athletics-for-all program." Though these activities are very popular today, they have a long history. Track and field events were organized in ancient Greece before 776 B.C. and were called the Olympic games.

Because this program is so broad, there is a place for everyone in it. Girls as well as boys can participate, and everyone, regardless of size, ability, or strength can take part in some way. To be successful, however, you must be willing to work hard, exercise patience, and build up your body with the proper food and rest.

Appropriate track events for girls include dashes and relays. A girl who enjoys running may wish to train herself to take part in the 50- or 60-yard dash or shuttle relays run according to standards set for girls. The field events for girls of your age are broad jumping, high jumping, and the throwing of a baseball or a basketball a certain distance. The standing broad jump is perhaps more suitable for seventh-grade girls than the running broad jump.

The common events for boys of your age are dashes, low hurdles, running broad jumps, high jumps, and relays. Requirements and standards for boys are different from those of girls; but both groups need to know the fundamentals and the practices expected in track and field events.

For all events, the warm-up is an important part of the training period. Before you practice running or jumping, you should jog around the track to relax and condition your muscles and to start the blood flowing faster into all parts of your body. To jog is to run slowly, high on your toes with the feet kept straight. This will help to develop strong, springy muscles. As you jog along, bend the arms at the elbows, and let them swing easily. Hands may be slightly closed but not clenched. If one muscle group is tense, the feeling of tension will affect other muscle groups. The warm-up will prepare the whole body for easy, flowing action.

The start of any event often makes the difference between a good record and a poor one. In running, for example, the crouch starting position pushes you off to a fast start.

At the command, "On your mark," take a comfortable position with your hands turned out on the starting line, as shown in the illustration. Place the front foot, which is the right, about 12 to 15 inches behind the line. Place the rear knee, which is the left, next to the heel of the right foot. If you are more comfortable and relaxed with these positions reversed, you should reverse them and keep to the reverse positions throughout your days of practice.

At the command, "Get Set," raise your hips so that your back is parallel to the ground. Keep these arm and leg positions for two seconds until the command *"Go"* is given. When you hear "Go," push hard with the rear foot. This will give you the force to move ahead with speed. Practice several starts, one after the other. It is important for you to do this well before you run the required distances. If you concentrate and work hard, you should become a fast performer.

After the start, and after you are well on your way down the track, try to lift your knees high. Move your arms, still bent at the elbows, back and forth along with the body, not out from the body. When you are near the finish line,

On your mark

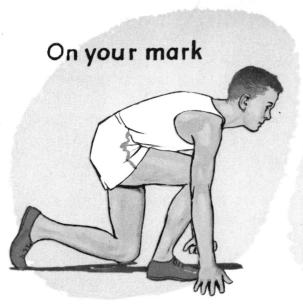

Get set ...

aim to run beyond it and keep up your speed. If you continue running for the extra distance, you should make a forceful finish.

If, after you have followed the instructions given above, you do not run easily, ask for help and suggestions from your teacher. Learning the proper way to run and practice daily will increase your ability to sprint, to run dashes, and to take-off correctly in the running broad and high jumps. It is important for you to do everything you can to improve your skill and increase your ability and confidence. To do well in any sport, you must believe that you have the ability to do so.

You take part in sports to have fun and to exercise. If you can win your share of the contests, you will have more fun. You increase your chances of winning by practicing proper health habits and training for the events you enter. The best sports training is nothing more than learning to take care of yourself every day by getting the proper food, rest, and exercise in the proper balance.

If you make progress more slowly than someone else, recognize this fact and go at your own pace, but do not let it discourage you. In the long run, the person who keeps trying often arrives at his goal before the one who perhaps has more sports ability but has not trained steadily or well.

Points to Remember

1. You must have an almost continuous supply of oxygen in order to help provide for the body's needs for energy.

2. One of the major purposes of respiration is to supply oxygen to the cells and take away carbon dioxide from them.

3. Although the cells give off some carbon dioxide, some remains in the blood stream. It helps to regulate the rate of breathing.

4. The pathway of air to your lungs is protected against the entrance of harmful substances by the mucous-membrane lining, by the cilia, and by the fine hairs in the nostrils.

5. As the blood is pumped through the blood vessels to all parts of the body, oxygen is left wherever it is needed.

6. The regulation of the rate of breathing is automatic.

7. Among the things that pollute the air are chemicals, pollens, dusts, and germs.

8. Severe air pollution, or smog, is likely to be a health problem only where there are many sources of air contamination and when there is little wind or movement of the air.

9. Air that contains a great many pollens may be harmful to the health of a person who is allergic to them.

10. Most dusts are not harmful to health, but they may cause some irritation of the nasal membranes.

Questions to Discuss

1. Why can you live longer without food and water than you can without air?

2. What is the difference between external and internal respiration?

3. How does respiration help to regulate body temperature?

4. How is the intake of air related to speaking and singing?

5. What are the chief parts of the respiratory system?

6. What is the function of the epiglottis?

7. Why is good muscle tone helpful to efficient breathing?

8. Why does overbreathing interfere with the efficiency of the respiratory system?

9. What relationship is there between the red blood cells and breathing?

Some Things to Do

Make reports

1. Find out what regulations your community has made to help prevent air pollution. Report your findings to the class.

2. Read about the problems in air pollution that are faced by some of the larger cities and the ways in which they have met these problems. Tell the class what you find out.

3. Find out and report to the class what plants in your community are often the cause of hay fever. Bring the plants to school, mount them on cardboard, and show them to the class when you make your report.

Write a paragraph

Write a paragraph on the importance of co-operating with the civic and health authorities in preventing smog.

To Help You Learn More

Find out what job opportunities are available for people who are interested in the prevention of air pollution. What training is necessary for these jobs?

Words to Remember

respiration	larynx
oxidation	epiglottis
esophagus	cilia
pleura	pharynx
trachea	thorax

 CHECKING YOUR UNDERSTANDING

Health words. On your paper write the words that fit best with the word meanings given below. Choose from words in the section *Words to Remember*.

1. food tube

2. thin membrane that covers the lungs and lines the chest cavity

3. flap of cartilage at the top of the larynx

4. the windpipe

5. fine, hairlike projections of membrane in the nostrils

6. the voice box

Health facts. On your paper write *T* after the number of each of the following sentences that is true and *F* after each that is not true.

1. Oxygen is used in the oxidation of food materials to supply energy to the cells.

2. You need less energy when you are asleep than when you are awake.

3. Heat and moisture are released in exhaled air.

4. Air can be stored in the tiny air sacs in the lungs for only a short time.

5. The physical activity of the body has no effect on the rate and depth of breathing.

6. Your heart beats faster when the air you breathe is very warm.

7. Air varies in the amounts of foreign matter and gases it contains.

8. Discomfort in a crowded room is usually not caused by lack of oxygen.

9. Inorganic dusts, if taken into the lungs over a long period, may be harmful to your health.

10. If you have too few red blood cells, or if your red blood cells are short of hemoglobin, your respiratory system will not work normally.

Health rules. Arrange the words in each group below so that they make a health rule. Write each rule on your paper.

1. develop   Take in   body part your to   sports.

2. breathing   Avoid   air polluted.

3. a as a   as   away person far Stay possible with   from cold.

4. in   way   to   every   Co-operate help the smog prevent   formation of.

LOOKING AHEAD TO CHAPTER SEVEN

Do You Know?

1. What are some characteristics of an intelligent person?

2. Can intelligence be measured?

3. Does heredity affect intelligence?

4. Can intelligence be increased?

5. What can you do to help protect your brain and your nervous system?

6. What kinds of things can harm your brain and your nervous system?

7. Do you have any responsibilites for the use of your intelligence?

7. Intelligence and Thinking

MUSICAL APTITUDE TEST
Tone Recognition

Tone Value	Right	Wrong
John	̶H̶H̶	II
Mary	̶H̶H̶ I	I
Don	II	

Your Brain and Your Nervous System

Some characteristics of intelligence. If you were to ask several of your friends to name someone who seemed to them to be very intelligent, they probably would name people who were outstanding, but for different reasons. One might name someone who can think especially quickly. Another might choose a person who can use words with great ease and accuracy. Still another might choose one who is very skilled in solving problems of various kinds.

In this chapter you will learn something about what intelligence is. You will also read about the structure of the brain and the nervous system. Finally, you will learn something about how to protect your own nervous system, and some suggestions for the development and improvement of your mental power.

Problem-
Solving Tests

▼

**Have an
Exhibit**

▲

Members of the class may wish to find samples or sample pages from intelligence, achievement, and aptitude tests. Samples might be put on the bulletin board or copied on the board. In some encyclopedias you can find examples of some of the tests used. As you read the chapter, you can identify each type of test and tell what it is supposed to measure.

What is intelligence? You may have guessed the reason why so many different qualities were thought of as belonging to an intelligent person. It is because all of these qualities, and others as well, are characteristics of a person who is very intelligent. Each of the qualities was probably developed to a different degree in the people who were described or referred to.

For example, the ability to think quickly and well is a quality that belongs to one who is very intelligent. So also is the ability to solve problems. There are others, too. The ability to behave in a reasonable manner when meeting new or unusual circumstances is one such quality. Being able to see relationships between various objects—to see in what ways they are alike and in what ways they are different—is another such quality. The ability to communicate ideas in words so as to express exactly what you mean, is another. There are some others, which you may be able to think of.

Can intelligence be measured? Although there is some question as to how well intelligence itself can be measured, there are some types of tests that are generally accepted as being able to measure intelligence with some degree of accuracy. Some tests are designed to measure intelligence in very young children, before they enter school and before they have learned to read. Others are designed for those who have learned to read. Most of such tests for young people of your age measure ability to understand and use words. The ability to do arithmetic problems is also tested. Some tests measure how well you can distinguish similarities and differences in various objects.

This type of test is called an intelligence test, though most of such tests also require a certain amount of achievement in order to take them, such as the ability to read and to use words. Other types of intelligence tests have been devised, however, which can be given to adults who can't read.

Intelligence tests are not to be confused with achievement tests, which measure how much knowledge you have gathered and remembered about various subjects. Intelligence tests are designed to measure the ability to think, not how much has been learned.

Individual differences. Just why some people are better able to do the things tested in an intelligence test is something not yet completely understood. We do know that people differ widely in the degree to which they have developed various abilities. For example, one may be particularly skilled in solving arithmetic problems, but not very skilled in expressing ideas in words.

This fact is not surprising, since people differ also in general appearance, in size, and in muscular development and co-ordination. People differ in athletic, artistic, and other special abilities, too. One may be able to play basketball very well, and another has developed skills that enable him to play a musical instrument. Another may have neither athletic nor musical ability, but can write well or paint beautiful pictures. There are tests that can be used to indicate what special abilities you may have. They are called *aptitude* (ăp′ tĭ · tūd) *tests*.

Development of native abilities. To a great extent, artistic and other special abilities seem to be inherited. Evidence seems to indicate that *inheritance* (ĭn · hĕr′ ĭ · tăns) has much to do with your native abilities, or those potential abilities you had at birth.

It is important to know, however, that native intelligence can be developed to different levels of potential. Intelligence can be developed to such a degree, in fact, that one born with less ability may, with effort, develop a mental power more effective than that of one with more native intelligence but with little desire to use it. The desire to improve his intelligence makes the difference.

To understand more about your intelligence and the way you think, it is necessary to know something about the structure of the nervous system, including the brain.

The Parts of the Nervous System

The two systems. The nervous system is divided into two major, or chief, parts. Together, they make up a complicated but very efficient network of communication inside the body. Though there are two separate systems, the nervous system is usually thought of and spoken of as a single system.

One part of the nervous system is made up of the brain, the spinal cord, and the nerves associated with them. It is called the *central nervous system*. It may be thought of as the more important of the two systems because it is concerned with voluntary (vŏl′ ŭn · tĕr′ ĭ) actions and with thoughts. Voluntary actions are those that you must think about; they are not automatic. The central nervous system does not work alone. It works very closely with the *autonomic* (ô' tổ · nŏm' ĭk) *nervous system*.

The autonomic nervous system is concerned with involuntary actions, or actions such as the beating of your heart, the digestion of your food, and your breathing. These functions go on inside your body without any thought on your part. Usually you don't think much about these bodily functions.

Though the main work of the autonomic nervous system is the regulation of the functions just described, it is influenced by the central nervous system, and it, in turn, has an effect on the central nervous system. The autonomic nervous system is closely related to the spinal cord in ways that you will learn about later.

Interdependence of the parts. The brain, though the center of one's intelligence, is not the only source of brain power. The brain depends for its information upon messages carried to it over the various *sensory* (sĕn' sổ · rĭ) *nerves*, or nerves that carry messages to it from the various sense organs such as the eyes and ears.

Without these messages from the world around it, the brain could not have the information it needs to do its thinking. Such information helps the brain make interpretations and decisions.

The Central Nervous System

The brain and spinal cord. The brain is a soft, spongy mass of tissue which is enclosed in the hard, bony cavity of the skull. It weighs, on the average, between two and three pounds, and is divided into two parts, which are called *hemispheres* (hĕm' ĭ · sfĕrz).

The spinal cord is made up of thirty-one pairs of nerves and the cord itself, which is protected by the spine, or backbone. The spine is composed of a series of ring-like bones called *vertebrae* (vûr' tĕ · brē). Nerves connect the brain and spinal cord with all the parts of the body.

Each spinal nerve is made up of both sensory and motor *neurons* (nū' rŏnz), or nerve cells. Messages sent over the spinal nerves pass in one direction only. Thus, the sensory neurons always run toward the brain and spinal cord. In the same way, motor neurons always carry the message, or

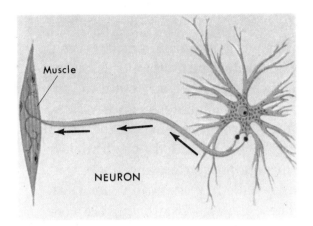

Muscle

NEURON

Cranial nerves. Twelve of the nerves of the central nervous system emerge directly from the brain or brain stem. These *cranial* (krā′ nĭ · ăl) *nerves* supply the head and face and some of the organs of the

nerve impulse, away from the brain and spinal cord. Motor neurons do not bring messages back to the brain.

In general, the spinal nerves carry messages to and from the spinal cord and the brain to the trunk and limbs of the body. These nerves vary in size and in length. The large *sciatic* (sī · ăt′ ĭk) *nerve* located in the thigh is almost one-fourth of an inch in diameter in an adult. The largest nerves usually follow the same course as the arteries in your arms and legs.

Try This

Imagine that you have stepped on something sharp with your bare foot. Trace the sensation through the nervous system from the foot to the brain. What kind of neurons carried the message?

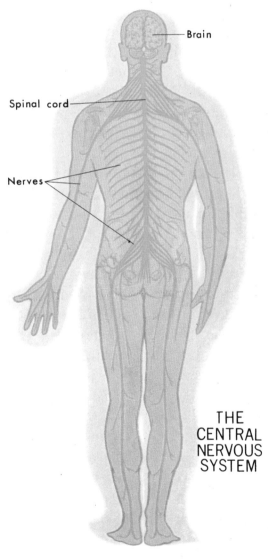

Brain

Spinal cord

Nerves

THE
CENTRAL
NERVOUS
SYSTEM

139

body. Some of the cranial nerves are sensory, some are motor, and some are both sensory and motor combined. The *olfactory* (ŏl · făk′ tô · rĭ) *nerves*, or nerves that enable you to smell, the *optic* (ŏp′tĭk) *nerves*, or nerves of sight, and the *auditory* (ô′ dĭ · tō′ rĭ) *nerves*, or nerves of hearing, are among the sensory nerves.

Neurons. The neuron, or nerve cell, is the basic unit of the nervous systems, both the central and the autonomic. The neuron has a network of branching nerve fibers. These fibers extending from nerve cells in all directions make it possible for messages to be carried to all parts of the body.

The nerve fiber has a clear, or transparent, covering over a white fatty substance. This covering protects the fiber and prevents the escape of the nerve impulse. The fatty substance insulates one nerve fiber from another, just as the wires of a telephone cable are insulated from each other.

The nerve cells have the special function of receiving and passing along nerve impulses, or messages. Because of this system of communications, it is possible for any neuron to contact many other neu-

rons. Each neuron, or nerve cell, co-operates with other cells of the body in order to carry out different activities. Messages can be transferred from one part of the brain and spinal cord to another through nerve cells and fibers that are called *association neurons*. These areas of the brain are connected with memory, reason, and the will. The memory of past experiences and actions is kept in the brain in these association areas.

Nerve impulses. All sensory nerve impulses originate as a message from one or more of the sense organs. The cause of the *stimulus* (stĭm′ ŭ · lŭs) may be chemical, mechanical, or electrical. It may also be caused by heat or cold.

Sensory nerve impulses are alike in character regardless of their source, but they differ in the stimuli which start them on their journey. For example, the nerve impulse starting from the eye travels to the visual center of the brain to produce sight. The nerve impulse from the ear sends its message to the auditory center of the brain to produce the sensation of hearing.

The motor nerve impulse is one that carries a message from the brain to another part of the body that is capable of movement.

The different parts of the brain have a relationship to various parts of the body. The visual center, for example, is located toward the back of the head. It is the place where nerve impulses from the eye are interpreted by the brain. Other parts of the brain are associated with other parts of the body. This helps to explain why, when a person has had some injury to the brain, a particular area of the body, such as the left leg, for example, may be affected, or paralyzed, and the remaining portions of the body may not be affected.

The Autonomic Nervous System

Two main divisions. Within the autonomic nervous system itself, there are two main divisions. These are called the *sympathetic* and *parasympathetic* (păr′ ȧ · sĭm′ pȧ · thĕt′ ĭk) divisions. Both of these divisions carry out the work of regulating the vital body processes that are carried on inside the body, such as digestion and the circulation of the blood. The activities of these body processes are increased or decreased according to body needs. The activities go on while you work or play, under the control of the autonomic nervous system.

If you look at the illustration on this page, you will see that the two main divisions of the autonomic nervous system lie in front of the spinal column. As you recall, this system sends fibers to the spinal cord, though it is separate from the central nervous system. It can work independently of the brain.

You will notice that the sympathetic nervous division lies along the front of the spinal column between the brain and the lower end of the spine. The parasympathetic

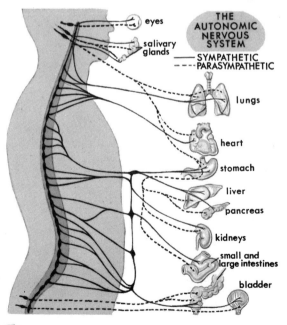

THE AUTONOMIC NERVOUS SYSTEM
—— SYMPATHETIC
- - - PARASYMPATHETIC

eyes
salivary glands
lungs
heart
stomach
liver
pancreas
kidneys
small and large intestines
bladder

division lies in the upper part of the neck and in the lower part of the spine, in the pelvic area.

These two divisions work together to regulate the work of the internal organs of the body, thus relieving the thinking part of the brain of these duties and freeing it to be active in the expression of intelligence. The two divisions of the autonomic nervous system tend to counterbalance each other. For example, one tends to speed up an activity such as the digestion of food. The other tends to slow down digestion. Usually these divisions of the autonomic system work well together, so that most of the time the bodily activities controlled by them go on without your being conscious of them.

The endocrine glands and the autonomic nervous system. The autonomic nervous system is closely related to the endocrine system. You may remember that strong feelings, such as fear, can stimulate the adrenal glands to secrete more epinephrine than they usually do; as a result of this stimulation by the epinephrine, the autonomic nervous system makes adjustments in the body. These adjustments help the body meet danger more effectively.

For example, the heart beat is increased, as a result of the stimulation by the epinephrine, thus sending increased amounts of blood into circulation. Increased amounts of sugar are also released into the blood stream from the liver, where it is stored. The digestive process is slowed down, and the blood supply to the skeletal muscles is increased.

Protection and Use of Intelligence

Getting the proper food and rest. There seems to be a relationship between proper diet and the ability to think well. One who eats a well-balanced diet seems better able to do school work. He can learn more easily, probably because he is less fatigued. A deficiency of the proper food also has an effect on the disposition. Such a lack makes one tired and irritable, and thus not as capable of using his intelligence properly. It may be that eating a poor diet for a long period will eventually damage the brain as well as other parts of the body; but even if intelligence is not harmed, it seems

You think better today if —

You had plenty of sleep last night

you ate balanced meals

to be harder to use intelligence if one is fatigued from lack of the proper food.

Getting enough rest is another way of helping your brain work more efficiently and protecting it. You may have had an experience of your own that showed you that you can't think well if you are too tired. After a good night's sleep, you should be able to think more easily and more clearly.

Think for Yourself

Do all the cells of the body need food in order to do their work? Are the brain cells different in this requirement?

The Vitamin B group. Ordinarily, if you eat a well-balanced diet, you will get enough of this very important group of vitamins. There are many vitamins in the B group, and they appear to be especially important for the health of nervous tissue. Fortunately, most people in our country eat a sufficiently well-balanced diet that they do not have a severe nutritional deficiency in this vitamin group. If a person eats a diet that is greatly lacking in B vitamins, he will have trouble remembering, and may even become greatly confused, as in the nutritional disease known as *pellagra* (pĕ·lā′grȧ). Nutritional deficiencies of this kind, if they last long enough and

143

are severe enough, can damage the brain.

Some people think that one can increase his intelligence by eating a diet that is rich in the Vitamin B group. Nothing has yet been proved in this matter. It is more likely that the opposite is true: intelligence can be harmed by lack of a proper diet, including the B group of vitamins.

Other ways of protecting the brain. The brain is affected by other things besides food and rest. Infections, accidents, drugs, and the like can have harmful effects on the brain.

Severe infections may cause inflammation of the brain. In some cases the inflammation is so great that it affects the personality. Accidents, too, may damage the brain and seriously impair the intelligence. Head injuries from automobile accidents are becoming increasingly frequent as the amount of traffic has increased.

Another source of harm is a prolonged, severe case of anemia, in which too little oxygen reaches the body cells, including the brain, over a long period. As you recall, all cells need oxygen; but the brain is especially sensitive to a lack of oxygen, and the intelligence may be hurt if the anemia is severe enough and continues long enough.

A severe lack of oxygen, from reasons other than anemia, can damage the brain, too. For example, a person who has suffered carbon-monoxide poisoning but has lived through the experience may have some permanent damage to the brain. When a person breathes in large amounts of carbon monoxide, the carbon monoxide combines with the hemoglobin of the red blood cells, thus preventing them from carrying oxygen to the cells.

Even foods to which a person is allergic can sometimes cause an inflammation of the brain, resulting in a severe headache and sometimes in extreme excitability and other unpleasant effects. During this time learning ability is impaired.

Drugs and alcohol. In a later chapter of this book, the subject of drugs and alcohol will be discussed more fully. Here it may be said that these substances also have an effect on the way you think. It is possible, too, that some permanent brain damage may result from the continued use of alcohol and drugs, especially when used in large amounts. When alcohol is taken over a long period, nutritional deficiencies may develop because one who drinks much alcohol frequently doesn't eat enough food or the right foods.

The immediate effect of alcohol and drugs on the brain, however, is very important. Alcohol and drugs have an effect on the brain so that when taken in certain amounts, one loses his ability to think as clearly as he normally does. There are other effects, too, which you will learn about in a later chapter.

Increasing your mental power. Do you want to increase your mental power? If you really want to make the most of your intelligence, you have already made a good start. As you have learned, an attitude of this kind is extremely helpful in the development of effective mental power.

Studies of highly gifted persons (those who were born with a great amount of mental ability) have shown that such highly intelligent people do not always develop the greatest mental power. Others, with less intelligence but with more spirit and determination, often surpass them in effectiveness, accomplishment, and in the intelligent direction of their lives.

Some succeed by hard work and determination.

Think about what you read.

Relate what you read to what you already know.

Attitude, then, is important. But it takes more than just a positive attitude and a strong wish to develop one's abilities. One who would develop his mental power must learn to discipline his thoughts and actions. If you make a study schedule, for example, and make yourself keep to it, you will be practicing a very helpful kind of self-discipline.

Developing some special ways of thinking are helpful, too, in increasing your mental power. When you are reading, for example, it is a good idea to try to relate what you are reading to something you already know. You might ask yourself in what ways this "new" knowledge adds to what you already know. Does it agree with something you have read elsewhere or learned about in some other way? If this "new" knowledge differs from what you have already learned, in what way or ways does it differ? In other words, develop a critical attitude toward what you read and try to fit it in with the knowledge you have.

Learning to look for the important, or key, statements in what you read is helpful, too. Some people jot down the main thoughts in a paragraph or on a page, as

Look for key
words and
key ideas.

Ask yourself,
"Why?"

they read. This may not be helpful to you; but you should look for the important idea in each unit.

It is certainly a splendid practice to try to be exact in the words you choose in order to express your precise thoughts. Form the habit of asking yourself, "Is this what I really wish to say?" To be able to choose just the right words, you must develop a vocabulary that will enable you to do so; and one very good way to do this is by reading widely and looking up new words in the dictionary.

Books, of course, are probably your biggest helpers in your plan to develop your mental abilities. Knowing how to find more infor-

mation in your library will be extremely helpful to you, too. In addition to books, your teachers, your parents, your friends, some radio and television programs— all of these can be sources of information and learning.

You can learn something from every experience you have, too, depending upon your attitude. Two people can have the same experience, and one can learn something from it while the other gains very little or nothing from it.

Perhaps you have never lost your childhood curiosity and the habit of asking "why." If you do have this habit, it can be very helpful to you. As you grow older, you may even find yourself going a step further and asking yourself, "Is there a more efficient way of doing thus and so?" Intellectual curiosity is a very good help in developing strong mental power.

So you see, it is in great measure up to you, whether or not you develop your abilities as much as possible, or even to near the "top" of your possibilities. Don't underestimate your ability. Most of us can do far more than we do. For most of us, it isn't the lack of ability that prevents us from accomplishing all that we might; it is often the lack of determination on our part. Once you have experienced a real achievement, and perhaps you have already, an achievement made possible by your disciplined, effective mental power, you will realize that living up to your abilities can bring you great satisfaction.

Activity for Health

Volleyball. Since there are only eight girls or six boys on a team in official volleyball, the game as explained here has been modified to provide fun for a larger group. As many as twelve or even more can play on each team. This game can be played indoors or outdoors on a court or in a space about 30 feet by 60 feet or 30 feet by 30 feet. A net or rope should be stretched across the width of the playing area, dividing the space into territory for two teams. The top of the net should be 7 feet from the ground.

Half of the players are on each side of the net. A volleyball or some other lightweight ball is used. A place 10 feet from the right back corner of each court should be marked off as the serving area. This serving area should be 3 feet long and at right angles to the end lines.

The object of the game is to keep the ball in the air as long as possible and return it over the net into the territory of the opposing team. This should be done in such a way that the opposing team cannot return the ball.

When you were younger you probably played a game called *Keep It Up*. That game was designed to teach you the skill called volleying, which you will need to use in volleyball. To volley a ball is to return a served ball by hitting it high enough to make it pass over a net and into the opposing team's territory.

As you can see from the diagram on page 150, the members of each team in volleyball have special positions on the floor. Each player has a number. During the game, when the opposing team wins the right to serve, players change their positions by rotation according to the plan shown on the diagram. You will want to study it to see how the players move in the direction of the arrows. Notice that the one who has just served takes the place farthest from the serving area when rotation takes place.

The game is started by a server who holds the ball in his left hand. Suppose the server is you. You stand behind the end line of the court in the serving area, holding the ball toward the right side of your body. Look at the ball, and then use the underhand serve as described here. This serve is easiest to control and should lift the ball high in the air as you serve it up over the net into the opposite court.

In the modified form of volleyball as described here, another player on the serving side is allowed to assist the ball once. An assist is a play to help the serve go over the net. In official rules an assist is not allowed. In official girls' rules the ball that clips the top of the net is served again. In boys' rules it is not, and the serve then goes to the opposing team.

A member of the opposing team should return the ball before it falls to the floor or ground. If the opposing team allows the ball to fall to the floor, your team scores a point. This means that only the serving team scores. In girls' official rules, the ball may be tapped twice by each of three players before it is returned over the net. In boys' rules, each of three players may tap the ball once. However, in the rules here, any player is allowed to tap the ball twice in succession and any number of players may tap it before it is returned over the net.

You continue to serve the ball until you or your team fails to return it to the opposing team. Then the opposing team serves. The ball changes sides when the ball fails to go over the net; hits the wall or goes out-of-bounds; strikes the wall or falls to the floor. Out-of-bounds means that the ball falls beyond the boundaries of the court.

The ball changes sides also if a server makes a foul. If the receiving team makes a foul, the serving team receives a point. The following are considered fouls: (1) touching the net; (2) tapping the ball more than twice in succession; (3) holding the ball; (4) pushing or holding the ball against the net. There are also other fouls listed in official rules.

When the ball changes sides, the players rotate as explained above.

Diagram showing rotation of players

Teams may play until one side scores fifteen points, or until the end of a time limit agreed upon by both teams. The winners must win by two points if playing for points. In other words, the opposing team must not have more than thirteen points when the winning team has fifteen.

As you play you will learn to use more skill and strategy. Learning to send the ball into the opponent's territory so close to the net that it can't be returned is called "spiking" the ball. Those nearest the net can "spike" a ball by jumping for a high ball, being sure not to touch the net or reach over it, and sending the ball over the net.

Practice in volleying a ball will be helpful to you. So will working together with the other members of your team. Building yourself up by practicing the good health habits you have learned about will help keep you in good condition. You can play better when you are alert and when you are rested from having had the proper amount of sleep. Eating the right foods in the right amounts helps to build up your strength, too. Volleyball is a vigorous game. To play well, you need to have strength as well as skill.

HELPS TO UNDERSTANDING

Points to Remember

1. Tests can measure intelligence with some degree of accuracy.

2. Achievement tests measure what has been learned. They are not to be confused with intelligence tests, which measure the ability to think.

3. Aptitude tests point out what special abilities a person may have.

4. People differ widely in the amount of their intelligence and also in the special abilities they possess.

5. Native intelligence, the intelligence a person is born with, can be developed to different levels of potential.

6. The central nervous system, made up of the brain, the spinal cord, and the nerves connected with them, is concerned with voluntary action.

7. The autonomic nervous system is concerned with involuntary action, such as the beating of the heart and the digestion of food.

8. The brain can be damaged by many things, including severe infections, head injuries, drugs, and certain types of disease.

9. Intelligent people have a moral obligation to use their intelligence in helpful ways.

10. You can help develop your mental powers by planning to do so and by exercising discipline in carrying out your plans.

Questions to Discuss

1. In what way do the sensory nerves assist the brain in making interpretations and decisions?

2. What is the main function of the spinal nerves?

3. In what way is the neuron, or nerve cell, the basic unit of both the central and autonomic nervous systems?

4. Give examples to support the statement that the different parts of the brain have a relationship to various parts of the body.

5. What are the two main divisions of the autonomic nervous system? How do they tend to counterbalance each other?

6. Explain the relation between diet and the ability to think well.

7. What group of vitamins seems especially important for the health of nervous tissue?

8. In what way can a severe case of anemia affect the brain?

9. What mental habits can one adopt that will help him increase his mental power?

Some Things to Do

Homework

1. Spend ten minutes trying to learn something difficult in the evening when you are tired. The next morning, after a good night's sleep, try to learn something just as hard or harder in ten minutes. Does the mind work better when it is fresh and rested?

2. See if you can make a small electric brain. Write to Science Research Kits, Inc., 108 E. 16 Street, New York 3, N.Y. for instructions and costs.

Keep a record

Keep a record of the foods you eat in a five-day period, then check your list to determine whether you got plenty of Vitamin B.

To Help You Learn More

Make a poster

Prepare to convince your classmates that they should increase their mental power. Make a poster on which you list a half dozen ways of developing one's native mental abilities, or list them on a section of the chalkboard. Enlarge on each way in a brief talk to the class.

Words to Remember

aptitude	neuron
autonomic	sensory nerves
cranial nerves	stimulus
hemisphere	sympathetic
intelligence	parasympathetic

CHECKING YOUR UNDERSTANDING

Health words. Selecting terms from *Words to Remember*, write words that fit the meanings below.

1. natural capacity or ability

2. a nerve cell with its network of branching nerve fibers

3. the power to know, to reason, to judge, to comprehend, to understand

4. connected with the cranium or skull

5. nerves that carry messages to the brain from the sense organs

Health facts. In doing this Fact Quiz, write on your paper the missing word or term that gives the sentence its correct meaning.

1. The brain, spinal cord, and associated nerves make up the _____ _____ _____.

2. The brain is divided into two parts, called _____.

3. The ability to solve problems is one sign of _____.

4. Messages can be kept in the brain as memories in the _____ areas.

5. The autonomic nervous system has _____ main divisions.

6. You can learn more easily if you eat a well-balanced _____.

7. The autonomic nervous system is closely related to the _____ glands.

8. Sensory nerve impulses originate as messages from one or more of the sense _____.

9. Vitamin _____ seems to be needed for building healthy nerve tissue.

10. A severe lack of _____ over a period of time may damage the brain.

11. A person who would develop his mental powers must learn to _____ his thoughts and actions.

12. You can help your brain work efficiently by getting enough _____.

13. The brain may be damaged by the use of _____ and narcotics.

LOOKING AHEAD TO CHAPTER EIGHT

Do You Know?

1. What is a communicable disease?

2. What communicable diseases most frequently appear in your age group?

3. In what ways is the human body equipped to keep germs from entering?

4. How does one develop a natural immunity to a particular disease?

5. How do antibodies fight germs and the toxins produced by them?

6. Why should one have a health examination at regular intervals?

8. Communicable Diseases

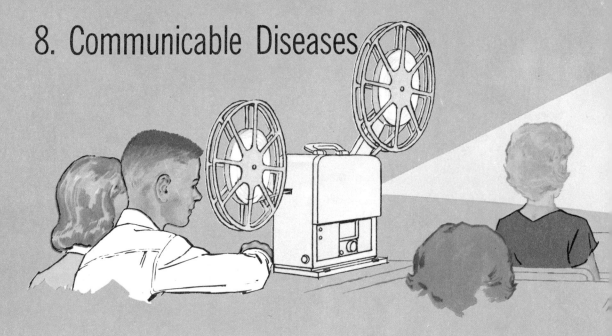

An Important Health Problem

An experience in common. Some members of the class were talking about the play that their class was going to give on the coming Friday afternoon. "I hope Jerry will be able to take his part in the play on Friday," said Jane.

"Why isn't he at school today?" asked Bob.

"He has a bad cold, so he has to stay at home until he feels better," replied Jane.

Jane might have added, "And so that he won't spread his cold germs to others, too." This is one very good reason for staying away from others when you have

a cold. Then, too, as you probably realize, you recover much faster when you stay at home and rest.

Having a cold is an experience that is common to all of us. And usually, as in Jerry's case, one who has a cold or some other illness is unable to do some of the things he wants to do.

No one likes to have to change his plans because of a cold, but many times it becomes necessary to do so. No one likes to be restricted in his activities after he has recovered from a serious illness, either; and this sometimes happens.

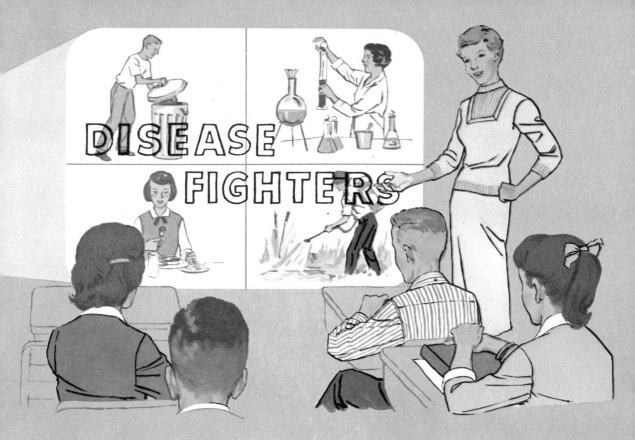

So you can see why it is important that you learn about *communicable* (kŏ·mū′nĭ·kà·b'l) *diseases*—what they are, how they are spread, what you can do to protect yourself against them, and what you can do if you become ill with one. It is equally important to know how you can protect others and also what your community and other public health authorities do to help keep them under control.

Make Your Own Record

▼

▲

Your class may want to make individual immunization records. Before you begin to make them, you may wish to discuss the kinds of information such a record should contain. You may be able to find samples of such records to bring to class. As you read the chapter, you will find more information to help you. The dates of immunizations and the lists of further ones needed are important items on such a record.

Major diseases in childhood and youth. A communicable disease is one that is caused by a germ and can be passed from person to person. Communicable diseases can be spread by means of water, food, or air. Animals, flies, and other insects can transmit disease germs.

On a world-wide basis, malaria, which is a disease that is spread by a certain type of mosquito, is considered the greatest health problem of all. This disease is not much of a problem in this country, however, because of the effectiveness of our public health program. The most serious communicable diseases that are frequently found in your age group, as well as among younger boys and girls, are influenza, pneumonia, streptococcus sore throat, rheumatic fever, tuberculosis, and poliomyelitis.

Influenza and *pneumonia* (nŭ · mō′ nĭ · à) are usually spoken of and grouped together in any discussion or report on communicable diseases. This is because they often occur in that order—a person may first develop influenza and then become ill with pneumonia. Of the two, pneumonia is usually by far the more dangerous.

Other communicable diseases often found among young people include measles, diphtheria, whooping cough, typhoid fever, and *dysentery* (dĭs′ ĕn · tĕr′ ĭ).

Losses caused by illness. As you can understand, it is important to try to prevent as much illness as possible. Illnesses can cause loss of much valuable time from school or work. Your health can be damaged permanently, too. Illnesses such as those mentioned can make it necessary for you to restrict your activities even after you have recovered from the illness. For example, if your heart were affected by rheumatic fever, you might have to restrict your physical activities somewhat after you recovered from the fever. It is possible to lose your life, too, if conditions are such that you aren't able to resist a disease, or if you don't get help in time.

In order to control communicable diseases, we must know how they are spread. Then we can take steps to protect ourselves and others against them.

Prevention and Control of Illness

How diseases are spread. In Chapter Six you learned something about the composition of the air. You learned that, in addition to oxygen, carbon dioxide, and other gases, the air contains varying amounts of foreign matter, including dusts, pollens, and germs.

The number of germs in the air varies from time to time and from place to place. Some of these germs in the air can be harmful to you if taken into the body in large enough amounts and if the body defenses are not strong enough to fight them.

As you recall, germs can be spread by people as well as in other ways, such as through food, water, and milk. Animals, flies, and other insects can carry disease germs, too.

For example, a certain type of mosquito, the *Anopheles* (à · nŏf' ĕ · lēz), is responsible for the spread of malaria. Only this kind of mosquito can carry malaria germs in its body. In fact, not even all Anopheles mosquitoes can carry the disease. Since the male mosquito doesn't bite, it is only the female Anopheles who gets the malaria germs into her body by biting a person who has this disease. Then, when "Annie" Anopheles, as she is sometimes called, bites another person, she transmits the germs to him.

Some controls. Since germs can be spread in so many ways, you may be wondering how anyone can avoid getting germs into his

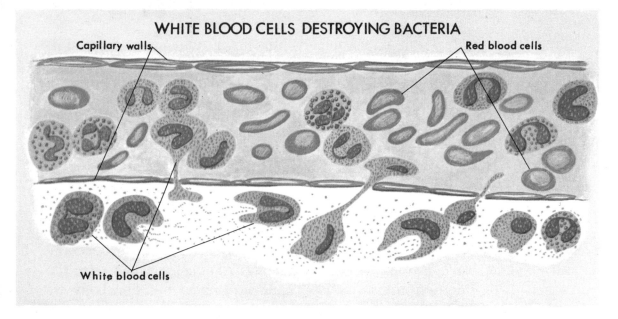

WHITE BLOOD CELLS DESTROYING BACTERIA

Capillary walls

Red blood cells

White blood cells

body and becoming ill as a result. But, as you recall, the body has certain natural defenses against disease-bearing germs.

Your body is covered with a protective covering, the skin. Germs can gain entrance into the body only through a break in the skin or through a body opening. Your body has certain defenses against the entrance of germs into the body as you breathe. At the entrance to the nose, and just inside the nostrils, are fine hairs that help to keep some germs from entering farther into the body. The mucous-membrane lining of the whole respiratory tract also helps to trap some germs by means of its sticky surface. And the cilia,

the fine hair-like projections inside the nose, try to push germs back toward the outside of the body with their wave-like motions.

You will recall that your blood contains white cells. It is the job of these cells to destroy germs. If they are needed, white cells can be produced by the body in great numbers. Usually they can fight infections successfully, if the body is in good condition and the infection is not too great.

In case of major infections, the body can fight germs in other ways, too. It can manufacture substances to help fight germs and the *toxins* (tŏk′ sĭns) or poisons, produced by the germs. These substances produced by the body are called *antibodies* (ăn′ tĭ · bŏd′ ĭz). After you have had an illness and have recovered from it, you are not likely to get it again for a while because your body still has these antibodies in it which it can use to fight the disease. You then have a natural *immunity* (ĭ · mū′ nĭ · tĭ) to that particular disease.

In addition to these natural defenses, there are other controls that can be used. You can protect yourself against diseases such as smallpox, whooping cough, tetanus. or polio, by being immunized against them. By the introduction into your body of dead or weakened disease germs, or other substance, your body can be stimulated to develop antibodies to fight these germs or substances. Then, if the true disease germs do enter your body, it will have antibodies with which to fight them.

There are also some medicines that are very helpful in fighting diseases, such as sulfa and the *antibiotic* (ăn′ tĭ · bī · ŏt′ ĭk) *drugs*.

Good health practices. There are things that you can do, too, that will help control the spread of communicable diseases. By practicing good health habits, you can help yourself to avoid becoming ill, and

thus a possible source of disease germs for others. Build resistance to disease by giving your body the materials it needs to build its defenses; that is, eat the right foods in the right amounts. Also be sure to get enough rest and sleep.

Health examinations at regular intervals give you information which you can use to help keep yourself in the best possible condition. You can also co-operate with your local health authorities

by following any instructions they may have concerning immunizations that may be needed.

If, in spite of all you do, you become ill, you can help control the spread of germs to others by observing a few simple precautions. You can cover your mouth when you sneeze or cough. And, as you have learned, you can be especially careful not to get too close to others when you are ill. You can be very careful to keep your hands clean. You should always wash your hands before you eat, in any case, in order to remove the germs from your hands before you touch food. You should also be careful to sterilize your dishes to protect others when you are sick.

Water supply. The public health authorities also do many things to prevent the spread of disease. One of the most important duties of your local health department is the safeguarding of your community water supply. Various ways are used to make the water safe to drink. Sometimes the water is filtered through fine sand or other substance. Sometimes chloride compounds are added to the water. A combination of these two methods is also used in some cities.

Whatever the method used to purify water, tests are made at regular intervals by the city or county health departments to make sure that the water is safe to use. Those who do not use the water supply of a city or town should make certain that the water they use is safe. They can do this by having it tested. Water from wells or other sources should be tested by the local or state authorities before it is used.

Boiling water for twenty minutes is a temporary measure to destroy germs in water, and one that is often used during times of emergency such as floods. At such times it is wise to take extra precautions such as these to make sure that your water supply is safe. Your local health or water department will usually notify you when they find it advisable that drinking water be boiled.

Pure milk. The safeguarding of the milk supply is another responsibility of the health authorities. At regular intervals dairies are inspected for cleanliness, and cows are examined to make certain that they are healthy. In addition, milk is pasteurized in order that harmful germs may be destroyed. In pasteurization, as you may remember, the milk is heated to 145° Fahrenheit and kept at that temperature for 30 minutes in order to destroy any harmful germs in it. Faster methods at higher temperatures are sometimes used. Then the milk is cooled quickly and kept cool to prevent the growth of more germs.

Food and food handlers. Health authorities inspect many places where food is served. Food handlers are also given examinations. This is done to make sure that those who serve or prepare food are in good health and that they follow certain sanitary measures, such as the frequent washing of their hands with soap and water. The preparation and storage of food and the washing and rinsing of dishes in sanitary ways is also checked.

Persons who serve food to the public are examined to insure sanitary conditions.

Think for Yourself

Why is the washing and rinsing of dishes in restaurants a matter of concern to public health authorities?

Other responsibilities. The disposal of sewage and garbage in sanitary ways is another responsibility of the health authorities. So also is the eradication, or destruction, of insects and rodents. You may have seen rivers or streams being sprayed with an oily substance that is used to control the breeding of mosquitoes. DDT and other chemicals are often used to control the breeding of flies.

Respiratory Diseases

Influenza and pneumonia. Since influenza and pneumonia are ranked among the five most serious diseases for young people in

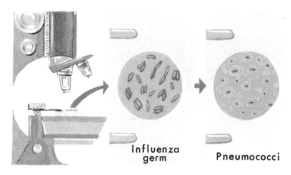

Influenza germ   Pneumococci

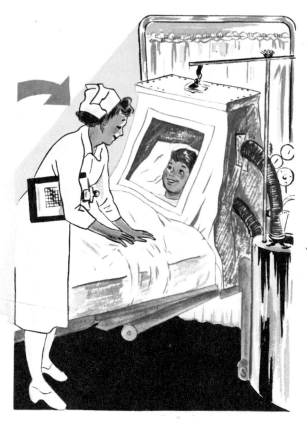

your age group, it is important that you know something about them.

Influenza is a disease that is caused by a kind of germ called a virus. A virus, as you may recall, is an organism that is very small and light in weight. Since viruses are so light, they stay in the air for a long time. Viruses are so small that they can be seen only with an electronic microscope. There is still much to be learned about viruses and their effects on the body.

There are several different viruses that can cause influenza. Influenza is a highly contagious disease, which is easily spread from person to person. This disease usually begins with a fever and symptoms of a cold, including aches and pains. The fever usually lasts from one to five days, and the nose and throat symptoms may be followed by a cough and difficulties in the chest.

Although one usually recovers from influenza, he may feel weak and tired for some time afterwards. The real danger from influenza, however, is that it may be followed by pneumonia. And pneumonia can be very serious. Statistics show that many more people die from pneumonia than from influenza.

Pneumonia. This is a disease in which the lungs become greatly inflamed. Chills and fever, pain in the chest, and coughing are some of the symptoms. Sometimes the *sputum* (spū′tŭm) contains blood and may look rust-colored.

Only a doctor can diagnose pneumonia in its early stages, and for this reason a doctor should be called when one has chills and fever. If a doctor is called early enough, he can control the pneumonia with antibiotics and other drugs. Since antibiotics are of no help in curing influenza, if a doctor gives such drugs to a person with the "flu," he is doing so in order to prevent the development of pneumonia.

There are a number of kinds of pneumonia. Virus pneumonia and *pneumococcal* (nū′ mŏ · kŏk′ ăl) *pneumonia* are by far the two commonest types. Several different kinds of viruses cause virus pneumonia. Pneumonia caused by viruses is usually milder than pneumococcal pneumonia. In pneumococcal pneumonia there is much inflammation, and fluid often collects in one or both lungs.

Streptococcus sore throat. The term "strep sore throat" is a common one, and one that you may have heard of. It refers to an infection of the throat which is serious because it may lead to serious illnesses if it is not treated in time.

Fortunately, *streptococcus* (strĕp′ tŏ · kŏk′ ŭs) infections of the throat can be treated successfully by the doctor with sulfa drugs and antibiotics.

If the "strep" throat is not treat-

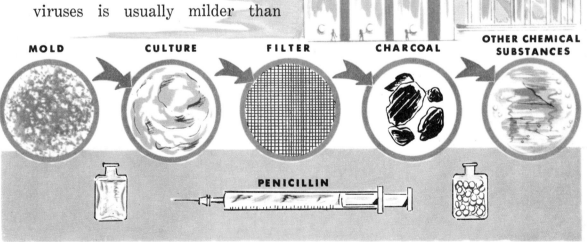

MOLD   CULTURE   FILTER   CHARCOAL   OTHER CHEMICAL SUBSTANCES

PENICILLIN

ed in time, however, *rheumatic* (rōō·măt′ĭk) *fever* may develop. It may be difficult for the doctor to diagnose rheumatic fever, and blood studies may have to be made. Since the antibiotics and sulfa drugs are not helpful to a person once rheumatic fever has developed, a long period of rest in bed is needed for recovery. It is easy to see why it is so important to get prompt treatment for a "strep" throat.

Not everyone who has a "strep" throat develops rheumatic fever. Whether or not he does, depends to some extent on heredity, it seems; but if rheumatic fever does develop, it may be followed by rheumatic heart disease. In this disease, the heart itself develops inflammatory changes and scar tissue may be formed, sometimes producing a permanent impairment of the heart.

Heart disease is not common among young people; but 90 per cent or more of the defective hearts found in young people are defective because of rheumatic fever.

Unfortunately, one can get rheumatic fever again and again; but one needn't if proper treatment is begun early enough for "strep" throat, as you have seen.

Sometimes rheumatic fever even leads to death. It is one of the five leading causes of death in your age group.

The common cold. Any discussion of respiratory diseases should include the common cold, not because it is serious in itself but because if taken care of, many other diseases can be prevented. As far as we now know, rest in bed is probably the best way to take care of a cold. As you know, in this way you also help to prevent the spread of germs to others. It may be that a cure for the common cold will be found soon. Research workers are constantly trying to find a remedy or preventive for this disorder.

Tuberculosis, Poliomyelitis, and Malaria

Tuberculosis, a communicable disease. You may know that *tuberculosis* (tŭ·bûr′kŭ·lō′sĭs) is not an inherited disease; that is, it is not passed from a mother or father to a child through any hereditary mechanism. It is important to know this. It is also important

164

to know that tuberculosis is very easily spread from person to person and that if you live in the same house with one who has tuberculosis, you are more likely to contract the disease than one who is not exposed to it so closely. Tuberculosis is usually spread from person to person by the sneezing or coughing of the infected person or by eating from contaminated dishes or utensils.

In recent years, the World Health Organization of the United Nations has called tuberculosis the second greatest health problem of the world, outranked only by malaria. It is still a major health problem in our country, too, though great strides have been made in the control of this disease.

Since there are few distinctive symptoms of this disease in its early stages, it is sometimes weeks or months before a person is aware that he has become infected with it. Although tuberculosis may affect other parts of the body, it is usually the lungs that are affected. People who have tuberculosis develop a fever that continues for a long time. They also develop a cough and bring up sputum. Sometimes there is pain in the chest and a loss of weight, though not always in the early stages.

A continued loss of weight, combined with other signs, could be an indication of this disease, though this is not always true. Tests must be made to make certain of a diagnosis of tuberculosis.

Some tests for tuberculosis. If a doctor suspects that a person may have tuberculosis, he usually gives a tuberculin skin test. A test material, *tuberculin* (tǔ · bûr′ kǔ · lǐn), is put into the skin. If there is swelling and redness within seventy-two hours, it is said to be positive. If there are no such reactions, it is said to be negative and the person can be sure that he does not have active tuberculosis, and never has had an infection of this kind.

Even in a positive test, there is a 99 per cent chance that the person does not have tuberculosis. Such a reaction may merely show that he is sensitive to a substance in the test material. A positive reaction may also indicate that the person has had such an infection in his body at one time but does not have active tuberculosis.

In the event of a positive skin test, however, further tests are usually made. A test of the sputum may be made at various intervals. The sputum is examined under a microscope to see whether there are tuberculosis germs in it. If there are no germs in repeated sputum tests, it is likely that the person does not have tuberculosis. However, used by itself, this is not a conclusive test. Used with other tests, it can be useful to the doctor. Sometimes an X-ray picture of the chest is made, also.

In some cases the doctor uses the patch test instead of the tuberculin skin test. In this test a strip of tape is put on the skin of the person tested. To the tape has been added thin filter paper which has been saturated with undiluted tuberculin. A negative test usually indicates no infection, but this test

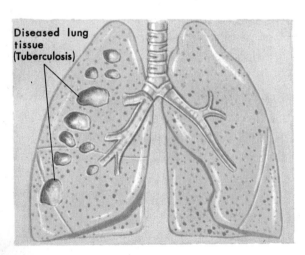

Diseased lung tissue (Tuberculosis)

is not quite so accurate as the tuberculin skin test described above. There are also various other tests for tuberculosis which can be used.

Think for Yourself

Why would there likely be more tuberculosis in a slum part of the city than in the less densely populated parts with better living conditions?

Treatment for tuberculosis. The treatment for one who is ill with tuberculosis consists of a long period of rest in bed, and administration of certain medicines. A diet that is rich in food essentials is important, too. Sometimes surgery is needed.

It may take a long time to cure an active case of tuberculosis; and even after a person is cured, he may not be able to do all of the same things that he did before he became ill. The earlier treatment is begun, the easier it is to cure the disease.

The National Tuberculosis Association. You probably already know something about the National Tuberculosis Association and its work. You may know that it is this nonprofit organization that sells the Christmas seals each year. You may also know that the money from the sale of the seals is used to help control tuberculosis.

The National Tuberculosis Association is a voluntary health organization that does many things to help control the spread of tuberculosis. It conducts a program of research to try to find better ways of treating tuberculosis and safer and more effective ways of detecting such illness. A program of educating the public in matters related to tuberculosis is also among its duties. It co-operates with other community health groups in these programs as well as in the *rehabilitation* (rē′ hȧ·bĭl′ ĭ·tā′ shŭn) of those who have recovered from tuberculosis. Those who have recovered from tuberculosis often must restrict their activities, at least for a time. They may need help in finding work that they can do and other kinds of help in making an adjustment to a restricted way of living.

Poliomyelitis. This disease, which is caused by a virus, is serious because it may affect some parts of the body permanently. Since the discovery of the Salk

vaccine (văk′ sēn), however, the number of cases of paralytic *poliomyelitis* (pō′ lĭ·ȯ·mī′ ĕ·lĭ′ tĭs) has been dramatically cut.

Poliomyelitis, or infantile paralysis, as it was formerly called, causes an inflammation of the nervous system, and especially of a certain part of the spinal cord. When the spinal cord is damaged by this virus disease, the person affected becomes paralyzed in certain parts of his body, usually in the legs. Sometimes, however, the paralysis also affects the chest or lungs. It may be necessary to put the patient in what has been called an iron lung in order to make it easier for him to get enough oxygen and to breathe more easily.

There is no paralysis in most cases of poliomyelitis, however. In fact, many people have had a very mild case of it and did not even know it. A person with a mild case of poliomyelitis might have a slight fever, a mild headache, and some feeling of nausea. Headache, as well as nausea and vomiting, is one of the early signs of polio. As you can see, it would be difficult for a doctor to diagnose poliomyelitis in its early stages, since the early symptoms of this disease are also the symptoms of other diseases.

Salk vaccine. It is well for you to make certain that you are protected against this disease, since there is no cure for polio, and since there is some danger of paralysis. None of the antibiotics or other drugs have been found effective against this disease.

It is possible for you to be well protected against polio. Three shots of Salk vaccine are recommended for the best protection. These shots have to be repeated every one or two years.

The National Foundation. The National Foundation for Infantile Paralysis was founded by Franklin D. Roosevelt to help fight poliomyelitis. This disease, often called infantile paralysis, was one that had been causing much crippling and some deaths in the United States.

The work of the National Foundation for Infantile Paralysis was mostly one of educating people in respect to poliomyelitis, of giving help to people who became ill with it, and of carrying on research to find out the cause of the disease and ways of preventing it.

The National Foundation for Infantile Paralysis organized the March of Dimes as a way of raising enough money to carry on the battle against poliomyelitis. You may know about the March of Dimes, because volunteer workers may have come to your door to ask if you wanted to give some money to the National Foundation. You may also have seen small containers that have been placed in stores to collect dimes from people who wish to help fight this disease.

It was money from the March of Dimes that helped carry on the research that produced the Salk vaccine against poliomyelitis. You are probably one of the many young people who have now been immunized with this vaccine against poliomyelitis. This would not have been possible if the National Foundation for Infantile Paralysis had not raised the money for the research that led to the discovery of the polio vaccine. Now it is possible for you to be well protected against this crippling disease.

Because the Salk vaccine should now give good protection against poliomyelitis, the organization has changed its name to the National Foundation and has enlarged its activities. It has started a new attack against arthritis, birth defects, and virus diseases. The National Foundation has selected these areas for study and research because each presents a serious health problem. Arthritis leads all other diseases in the United States as a cause of crippling. You learned something about birth defects in Chapter 2, when harelip and cleft palate were discussed. There are other kinds of birth defects, too, some of them even more serious than these. And virus diseases are still of major concern. There is much yet to be discovered about viruses and how they affect the body. It can be expected that in the future the National Foundation will continue to make great contributions to our knowledge in these fields.

There are other voluntary organizations that are concerned with finding out ways of preventing and combating various diseases. One of these voluntary, nonprofit organizations is the American Heart Association. There are many others.

The control of malaria. Although malaria is not a serious health problem in this country, as you have learned, it is a very serious problem in many other places throughout the world. Each year millions of people die of malaria, and the World Health Organization has named malaria its number one health problem.

Malaria can be described best as a disease of chills and fevers. These may be very severe, and various parts of the body, including the liver and the spleen, may be affected. Anemia and other complications can also arise.

Fortunately, malaria can be treated quite successfully with new drugs; but this disease is not easy to diagnose, and blood studies are necesary to make an accurate diagnosis. It is much better, however, to prevent the illness through control of the Anopheles mosquitoes, since this disease is spread by these mosquitoes. Usually mosquitoes do not fly far from the

place where they live. This means that you can help prevent the growth of mosquitoes around your own home.

As you may know, mosquitoes need water in which to grow and develop. When they cannot find water in which to breed, their numbers will decrease. Even rain water which may remain in old cans or other containers may provide a place for mosquitoes to live and reproduce. Therefore, if you find cans in which water from rainfall has collected, you should turn the cans over so that the water runs into the ground. If there are large bodies of water where mosquitoes may breed, the Public Health Department can treat these areas in various ways so that the mosquitoes cannot grow in them.

Public health program. The fact that malaria is not a widespread problem in our country is related to our excellent public health pro-

gram. A public health program for the control of malaria calls for many different kinds of activities.

Of great importance is the proper drainage of swamps and other places where water may be trapped. Drainage ditches are dug in order that water may be carried away from such places. You can see that drainage of this kind would take away much of the water that the mosquito needs for breeding. Where the water cannot be drained away, there are various means of treating it to prevent its use by mosquitoes. Sometimes it may be possible to fill in a mosquito breeding place with dirt so that water can no longer collect at that point.

Another important public health approach to the control of malaria is the spraying of individual homes with DDT or some other chemical that will kill mosquitoes. In addition to the spraying of homes with DDT, a dusting program with this same chemical can also be carried out in places where the mosquitoes are thickest. Remember that DDT is a poison. It is important that only people who know how to use this product safely do the spraying or dusting.

By measures such as these, public health officials can carry out an effective program of mosquito control. And mosquito control has proved an effective means of preventing malaria.

Other communicable diseases. There are many other communicable diseases from which people may suffer. In this chapter you have learned something about a few of them; but there are many others, including such diseases as measles, whooping cough, diphtheria, brucellosis or undulant fever, typhoid fever, tetanus,

trichinosis, and dysentery. There are still many others.

As in all communicable diseases, the best treatment, of course, is prevention. As you grow older, you will want to pay attention to whether or not there are diseases around you that you may catch, and take measures to protect yourself against them. You can do this by immunizations, in some cases, by practicing wise health habits, and by taking sensible precautions to avoid unnecessary exposure to communicable diseases.

Activity for Health

Paddle Tennis. This game is a good introduction to tennis. Since paddle tennis requires a smaller playing space than the standard game of tennis, and since its equipment is not so expensive, it is widely played today, both in schools and in recreational centers. The rules for paddle tennis are similar to those for tennis. It is a sport that can be enjoyed by players of all ages; but many people master it as the first step in learning to play tennis. Paddle tennis can be played either indoors or out on almost any kind of surface—wood, grass, cement, asphalt, or clay.

The court is marked like a tennis court. It is 18 feet by 39 feet and divided into two equal parts at the center by a net 2 feet 2 inches high. A tennis net should be used, but gunny sacks sewed together can be substituted for a net. A regular tennis ball is used, or a lightweight rubber ball the size of a tennis ball. Two or four paddles are used, depending upon the number of players. The paddles are made of plywood, 14¾ inches by 7½ inches. You can buy the paddles or you can make them.

Jumping standards may be used to hold the net, or permanent posts can be set in the ground one foot outside the outer lines of the court.

In a game of singles, two play, one on each side. In a game of doubles, four play, two on each side. The competing players stand on opposite sides of the net. The player who first strikes, or serves, the ball over the net is called the server. His opponent is called the receiver.

Note on the diagram that the section of the court near the net is called the service court. The object of the game is to serve the

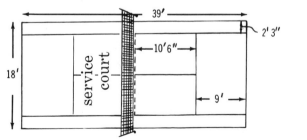

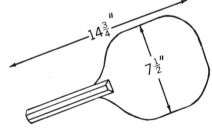

ball into your opponent's service court and to return the ball to any part of the opponent's court after the service.

If you are the server, you stand behind the end line of the right-hand court. Play begins when you toss the ball and strike it with your paddle before it touches the ground. You hold the paddle as though you were shaking hands with it. A good serve is one made into the proper court without a foul being committed. The proper court is the one diagonally opposite the server. Fouls include: (1) striking the served ball before it has bounced once; (2) touching the ball with any part of the body or clothing; and (3) touching or reaching over the net.

The method of scoring is a complex one and should be studied from a handbook. You will need to know the following facts, however:

One point is awarded to a side whose opponent fails to return a fair ball into any part of the opposite court or sends the ball outside the court lines. When tallying the score, the server's score is announced first. Each side's score is totaled separately. A zero score for either side is called *love*. A side's first point is called *15*, the second point *30*, the third point *40*, and the fourth point is called *Game*. If both sides have won three points, the score is called *Deuce*. In order to win, one side must then make two consecutive points.

Do not be too much concerned with your score until you have mastered the skills of serving accurately and returning the ball swiftly. Learn what makes a foul and a foot fault, and, from the very beginning, try hard to overcome foot faults. For example, if during a serve your foot touches or goes over the base line, it is a foot fault. It is also a foot fault to jump up with both feet during a serve. One foot must be kept on the ground.

A server may have two serves. If the first ball served fails to land in the opponent's service court, the server is then allowed one more attempt. A ball that touches the top of the net and then lands within the opponent's service court is called a *let ball*. A let does not count as an attempted serve.

When a served ball clears the net and falls within the opponent's service court, the opponent at-

tempts to return the ball into any part of the server's court. A service ball must bounce once before it is returned. As the volleying continues, the ball is played on the first bounce or on the fly. The ball is volleyed until it fails to reach an opponent's court. Play continues after a *let* ball during a volley.

Service is delivered alternately from the left and right side of the court, as each point is scored, with the same player acting as server throughout the game. Those who receive also alternate between the left and right sides of the court, as each point is scored, with the same player acting as receiver throughout the game.

In singles, the players alternate in service, with one player serving

for a complete game. In doubles, the receiver of the preceding game acts as the next server, and the partner of the former server becomes the receiver. After the service ball has been returned, either player on the team may continue the volley.

You can play a better game and you are a better partner when you are in good physical condition. Plenty of good, nourishing food and enough sleep and exercise help you keep yourself in good condition. When you feel your best, you are more alert mentally, too, thus helping yourself become a better player.

This game is not so strenuous as tennis, and thus it appeals to a wide age group and to those for whom tennis is too vigorous. Paddle tennis not only gives you an opportunity to learn the basic rules of tennis but also gives you good fun and recreation.

HELPS TO UNDERSTANDING

Points to Remember

1. A communicable disease is one that can be spread between persons or animals.

2. The real danger from influenza is that it may be followed by pneumonia. Pneumonia is one of the most serious diseases for your age group, but most cases can be controlled by antibiotics.

3. Malaria is not much of a problem in this country, but it is still the world's greatest health problem.

4. Tuberculosis is still a serious communicable disease in the United States and the second greatest health problem in the world.

5. A person who has a fever should ask a doctor for a diagnosis.

6. Prompt medical treatment of a "strep sore throat" is a good way to prevent rheumatic fever.

7. The best protection against poliomyelitis is to be vaccinated against the disease.

Questions to Discuss

1. What is a communicable disease?
2. How does the mucous membrane of the respiratory tract help to keep germs out of the body?

3. What are antibiotics?

4. What is natural immunity?

5. How can the body be immunized against such diseases as smallpox?

6. How can you go about protecting yourself from rheumatic fever?

7. Do most people who have poliomyelitis recover from the disease without suffering paralysis?

Some Things to Do

Take inventory

1. Ask your parents to help you make a list of the diseases against which you have been vaccinated and the year in which you were last vaccinated. Should you have a booster shot for any of these diseases?

2. Ask your parents to arrange with the family doctor for you to get a booster shot for diphtheria, tetanus, "polio," or whooping cough.

To Help You Learn More

1. Pretend you are going to a foreign country. Find out what immunizations you would need to feel safe in

that country, and what ones you would need to re-enter the United States.

2. Read about the invention of Salk vaccine. Try to report experiences that some of the scientists had as they worked on this problem.

CHECKING YOUR UNDERSTANDING

Health words. Match the following words with the meanings given after them. Word *1* matches c, so write *1*c on your paper for it.

1. antibodies
2. communicable
3. immunity
4. antibiotics
5. rheumatic
6. virus

a. substances produced by living organisms, such as molds and fungi; used to fight disease

b. a disease-producing organism so small it can pass through the finest filter

c. substances in the tissues or fluids of the body which help fight germs and the poisons produced by the germs

d. a state of the body in which antibodies help it resist the development of a given disease

e. capable of being communicated or passed from person to person

f. affected by or causing some form of rheumatism

Health facts. Read the sentences below. Then write on your paper *T* after the number of each sentence that is true and *F* after the number of each sentence that is not true.

1. Malaria is the greatest health problem of the world.

2. It is very hard to spread influenza from one person to another.

3. A streptococcus infection can usually be cured by antibiotics.

4. A positive tuberculin skin test proves that you have tuberculosis.

5. A person with active tuberculosis will probably have to stay in bed a long time.

6. Poliomyelitis is caused by a virus that invades the nervous system of the body.

7. Malaria is spread by a certain kind of female mosquito.

8. There is no need to have a chest X ray taken for tuberculosis if the tuberculin skin test is negative.

9. Unless a strep sore throat is cured, it may be followed by rheumatic fever.

10. Examination of the sputum under a microscope is one way of determining whether a person has active tuberculosis.

11. You can help control the spread of communicable diseases by practicing good health habits — by eating the right foods in the right amounts and by getting enough rest and sleep.

LOOKING AHEAD TO CHAPTER NINE

Do You Know?

1. Is there a perfect food that contains all the food elements in the proportions you need?

2. What is the Daily Food Guide?

3. Name some of the many factors that affect the amount of food your body needs daily.

4. Is the nutritional value of foods affected by the kinds of soil and the places where the foods are raised?

5. What fraction of your daily requirements in calories and proteins should be supplied by your breakfast?

6. What safeguard does the body have to insure that you will get enough water daily to offset the water lost through body wastes?

7. What is the main food contribution of fruits to the body?

8. Does the food value of milk change when it is kept in cold storage for some time?

9. Are you likely to need a smaller amount of energy-giving foods as you grow older? Why?

10. Do those who don't eat enough protein for breakfast usually make it up at the next meal?

11. What is the relationship between proteins and blood pressure?

12. Why are eggs a popular food?

13. What is the main value of vegetables in the diet?

14. Are your personal tastes in food influenced by your emotions?

9. Foods and Health

How Foods Are Related to Health

Why you eat as you do. Did you ever stop to think about your eating habits, and did you ever wonder why you eat the kinds of foods you do? When you have an opportunity to choose your own food, do you eat only what you like? Do you eat the same foods over and over again?

To some extent, your eating habits depend upon the place where you live. If you live along a seacoast, you may eat much fish and other sea food. If you live in the southwestern part of our country, perhaps you like many highly seasoned foods. Wherever you live, your food should supply the basic food essentials, such as proteins, carbohydrates, fats, vitamins, minerals, and water.

There are also other factors that influence your food preferences. You will learn more about some of these later in the chapter. It is important, however, to know that the food you eat has a definite relationship to the way you feel and to your health.

In the following pages you will find out what foods you should be eating each day in order to attain and keep the greatest possible degree of health and well-being.

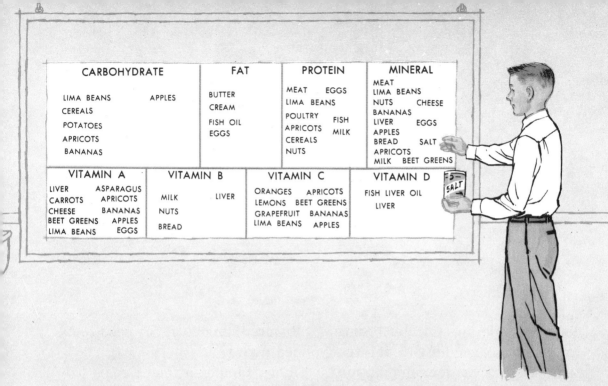

CARBOHYDRATE		FAT	PROTEIN	MINERAL
LIMA BEANS	APPLES	BUTTER	MEAT EGGS	MEAT
CEREALS		CREAM	LIMA BEANS	LIMA BEANS
POTATOES		FISH OIL	POULTRY FISH	NUTS CHEESE
APRICOTS		EGGS	APRICOTS MILK	BANANAS
BANANAS			CEREALS	LIVER EGGS
			NUTS	APPLES
				BREAD SALT
				APRICOTS
				MILK BEET GREENS

VITAMIN A		VITAMIN B		VITAMIN C		VITAMIN D
LIVER	ASPARAGUS	MILK	LIVER	ORANGES APRICOTS		FISH LIVER OIL
CARROTS	APRICOTS	NUTS		LEMONS BEET GREENS		LIVER
CHEESE	BANANAS	BREAD		GRAPEFRUIT BANANAS		
BEET GREENS	APPLES			LIMA BEANS APPLES		
LIMA BEANS	EGGS					

Your class may wish to make a survey of the breakfast habits of the class. Each person could write down what he had for breakfast on the morning chosen. Names need not be signed on the papers. A committee could summarize the results and list the foods on the board. The class could then make a menu or menus for what they thought would be a nourishing breakfast, using foods from those listed, if possible. After reading this chapter, the class members could check the menu or menus to see whether they contained the essential nutrients for a nourishing breakfast.

▼

Make a Survey

▲

The nutrients your body needs. You need foods containing substances that your body can use: (1) to make heat and energy; (2) to build and repair cells; and (3) to regulate body processes and protect you against disease. These substances are proteins, fats, carbohydrates, vitamins, minerals, and water.

It is a known fact that about 70 per cent of the total weight of an

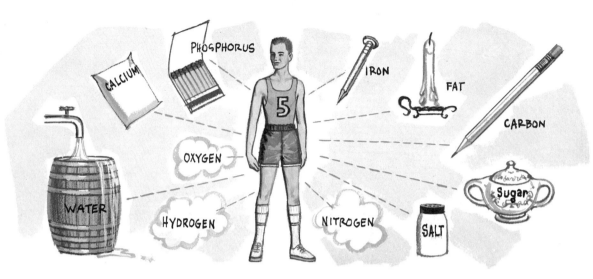

adult is made up of water. Since water is lost each day through respiration, perspiration, elimination, and sometimes in other ways, too, it must be replaced. A loss of even 10 per cent of the body water may make a person sick; but since people who go without water develop a strong thirst, they can usually get water before their health is seriously damaged. There is another safeguard, too. Water is furnished in most foods. Green vegetables, for example, are usually about 90 per cent water.

No "perfect" food. There is no food that contains everything in the proportions you need. There is no food that is "perfect" from this point of view. Most foods, however, have more than one *nutrient* (nū′ trĭ · ĕnt) and can be used to fill more than one of the needs outlined above.

For example, a food that is primarily an energy-giving food might also contain some *protein* (prō′ tĕ · ĭn), which is needed for the growth and repair of cells. But it might not have very much protein, and it might not have any vitamins and minerals that are needed for the regulation of body processes. So it would not be a "perfect" food.

To get enough of the right nutrients each day, you need a variety of foods; and to be certain that you get the right amounts of the right foods each day, you need to follow a daily plan, or guide.

The Essential Four. A guide that is easy to use is one that was prepared by the *research* (rĕ · sûrch′)

service of the Department of Agriculture of the federal government. This guide includes four groups of foods that are essential to your health. You should eat some food from each of these groups each day. For this reason, the food guide is sometimes referred to as the Essential Four.

There are enough different kinds of foods in each group so that it ought not to be very hard to find foods that you like in each group. Or at least you should be able to learn to like some of these foods.

These four essential food groups are not strangers to you. In earlier books in this series you learned something about them. Our purpose now in calling them to your attention is to refresh your memory and also to give you some additional information about the kinds of foods in each of these food groups.

Variation in needs. The Daily Food Guide is just a foundation for an adequate diet. You will need to add other foods, such as fats and sugars, in order to get enough food for your needs.

You will notice that the number of servings you should have from each group each day is indicated on the chart. These are the *minimum* (mĭn′ ĭ · mŭm) amounts. Various things affect the amount of food you need. Physical activity, age, sex, and body build are some of the factors affecting your food requirements, or the number of *calories* (kăl′ ȯ · rĭz) you need. A calorie, you may remember, is a unit which measures the heat- or energy-giving value of foods.

For example, a boy who engages in a strenuous physical activity such as football requires more calories than a boy of the same age who is not active physically. A boy with a larger frame and a heavier, muscular build requires more calories than one with a smaller frame. Girls, in general, require fewer calories than boys for this reason.

Those who are growing rapidly also require more calories than those who are not growing so rapidly. Most young people of your age are beginning a period of rapid growth, if they have not already done so. Your food requirements for the next few years will be greater than they will be in the years immediately following this period of growth.

After you have become an adult,

DAILY FOOD GUIDE

MILK Group
3 to 4 cups daily

MEAT Group
2 or more servings
per day

BREAD-CEREAL
4 or more servings
per day

VEGETABLE-FRUIT
4 or more servings
per day

your needs for food will not always be the same. The amount of energy-giving foods you need will vary as your activities vary. Older people, such as those in their sixties and seventies, usually require less food that is rich in calories than they did in their middle years, and much less than they did during their teens. Some older people, however, are still very active. Their food requirements will differ from those in their age group who are less active.

About 280 calories per hour

About 56 calories per hour

Try This

Write down all the foods that you ate at your last meal, excluding breakfast. Were there some foods from each of the food groups in your list?

Variation in quality of foods. Foods that are grown in certain soils and in certain parts of the country may be more *nutritious* (nŭ · trĭsh′ ŭs) than the same kinds of food grown in another soil and under other conditions. For example, strawberries grown in rich soil under good conditions are more nutritious than strawberries grown in poor soil and under poor conditions, provided they have

been stored and shipped properly and reach you fresh and in good condition. Similarly, meats and poultry vary in nutritional qualities. Meat from chickens raised on a superior type of feed would likely be more nutritious than that from chickens raised on inferior feed, if the food value were not lost in some way. Even the most nutritious food loses some of its

About 562 calories per hour

About 112 calories per hour

food value if it is improperly cooked.

Storage of food is important, too, in preserving food values. Fruits and vegetables should be kept cool and out of the sun after they have been picked. The freshness of foods affects their nutritional qualities, as you can understand.

The Bread — Cereal Group

The value of breads and cereals. You will notice on the chart of the Daily Food Guide that you should have four servings from this group each day. The foods in this group are important for their energy value; but they also supply other food essentials such as vitamins, minerals, and proteins.

The amount of energy provided by a slice of bread is approximately the same, whether it is white bread, whole-wheat, or rye. In other words, there are the same number of calories in each slice of bread. The amount of wheat protein in white or whole-wheat bread is about the same for each, too.

There is, however, a difference in the amount of B vitamins in the different kinds of bread. Whole-wheat bread contains more of these vitamins than white bread, unless the white bread has been enriched. If the white bread has been enriched, it may have almost as much Vitamin B as whole-wheat bread.

In addition to supplying protein and calories, breads and cereals supply small amounts of calcium and phosphorus, as well as varying amounts of the B vitamins. Enriched breads and cereals also contain a certain amount of iron. Cereals usually supply you with protein and other nutrients the same as bread.

Breakfast cereals. There have been many studies made on breakfasts and their importance to health. As a result of such studies, it was found that a "good" breakfast should supply about one-fourth of your daily food requirements in calories and in proteins. One such breakfast might contain: fruit, cereal and milk, buttered toast, and cocoa or other beverage. Another nutritious breakfast could contain: fruit, egg and buttered toast, and milk. To these could be added sausage, bacon, or other meats.

It has been found that people

who eat these kinds of breakfasts feel less tired during the morning than those who do not eat a nutritious breakfast. They feel less fatigue during the whole day, in fact, and their physical and mental reactions are more accurate. This means that when you eat a good breakfast, you can do better schoolwork. You also have more strength and can play better in team sports. You look better, too.

In a study of the eating habits of teen-agers it was found that those who don't eat enough protein for breakfast usually don't make it up at their next meal, which is lunch. Instead, since they are extremely hungry, they tend to eat quick-energy foods such as candy and snacks that do not supply what they need for good nutrition. They often do not wait until lunch before they eat these energy foods,

thus taking care of their hunger but taking away their appetite for lunch and the protein and other nutrients they should be eating at that time, too.

You can see that it is important to start out right with the right kind of breakfast. Studies show that it doesn't matter whether the protein and calories are supplied by cereal and milk or by bacon, eggs, and milk. The important thing is that the breakfast contain enough protein and enough calories.

Other meals, too, are important to your health. The reason that so much attention is paid to breakfast is because it is a meal that is often hurried, and sometimes omitted altogether. The other meals are not so likely to be skipped over; but it should be remembered that lunch and dinner are also necessary for good nutrition.

The Meat Group

The value of meats. Meats are especially valuable because of the proteins they furnish. They also contain other substances, such as vitamins and minerals; but it is because of their protein that they are so valuable in the diet.

As you recall, protein is needed for the proper growth and development of the body. This food substance is needed in great amounts while you are growing; but it is also needed by people of all ages. Older people, for example, need

185

protein for the repair of worn-out tissue, for resistance to infections, and for other reasons.

Proteins are needed to maintain a proper blood pressure. When there are not enough proteins in the blood stream, there is liable to be a shift of the fluid in the blood vessels out into the body tissues. The body then swells. Perhaps you have seen in magazines or other places pictures of very under-nourished children. Their mis-shapen bodies showed the results of poor nutrition. A diet rich in meats and meat products protects

the body against this kind of disorder.

To be in good health, you must have enough red blood cells of good quality to carry oxygen from the lungs to all the different cells of the body. If a person eats a diet that is very low in protein, he may suffer from anemia. You may recall that this is a condition in which there aren't enough red blood cells, or the cells themselves do not contain enough hemoglobin. The hemoglobin in the red blood cell is made up mostly of protein. As you can see, a diet rich in meats helps to keep your health at a high level, partly because you are less likely to develop anemia.

Foods that are rich in protein also help in the absorption of *calcium* (kăl' sǐ · ŭm). About one-half of the calcium in the blood exists in combination with proteins.

Proteins are needed by the body so that it can fight disease germs and the infections produced by them. As you may remember, anti-bodies are made by the body to fight germs that cause disease. Since antibodies are made partly from proteins, it is important that you eat enough foods containing proteins. If one's body is low in proteins and his antibody-producing ability is not normal, he can restore the normal ability by eating enough high-quality proteins, such as those found in meats.

Some meats are especially rich in food values. One of these is liver. This meat not only is a source of protein and calories, but it is especially rich in *phosphorus* (fŏs′ fȯ · rŭs), iron, Vitamin A, and *niacin* (nī′ a · sĭn), which is one of the B vitamins. Liver also contains some Vitamin C, as well as some calcium. The main value of liver, however, lies in its content of protein, iron, and Vitamin A.

Other sources of protein. Perhaps you have wondered why eggs seem to be such a popular food, especially for breakfast. This is partly because eggs are rich in protein and other essential food elements. As you recall, you should have approximately one-fourth of your daily requirements of protein at breakfast. Eggs are good sources of protein, especially the white portion. Eggs are less expensive than most meats, and they are easily and quickly prepared. In addition to protein, eggs contain fat, calcium, phosphorus, Vitamin A, and some iron.

Milk, cheese, poultry, fish, and beans are very high in their protein content. Though foods in the meat group are excellent sources of protein, some grains and vegetables also contain protein.

Amino acids. Protein contains substances called *amino* (a · mē′ nō) *acids*. There are over twenty different kinds of these acids. Not all of them are found in all proteins, however. The proteins found in the various foods differ in the kinds and numbers of the amino acids they contain.

The foods listed in the meat group are especially rich in proteins, as you remember. The foods listed in this group also have the greatest numbers of the amino acids that you need.

The Vegetable-Fruit Group

Food values of vegetables. Vegetables are valuable mostly because of their vitamin and mineral content. Vitamins and minerals, you may recall, are needed for the regulation of body processes, such as digestion of foods. Vegetables also contribute roughage and bulk to the diet.

Ordinarily, vegetables do not contain much fat or many proteins, although they may have both. Vegetables differ quite a bit in the vitamins, minerals, and other nutrients they contain, as you will see in the chart on page 179.

Freshly-cooked lima beans, for example, contain vegetable protein, *carbohydrates* (kär′ bȯ · hī′ drāts), calcium, phosphorus, iron, Vitamin A, and Vitamin C as their principal food values. Lima beans also contain small amounts of other vitamins and some fat.

The main value of asparagus lies in its Vitamin A content. It also has some Vitamin C and small amounts of other food substances.

Cooked beet greens have a relatively high content of Vitamin A and some Vitamin C and phosphorus, as well as iron and small amounts of other vitamins and minerals. In comparison with beet greens, the beet roots themselves contain hardly any Vitamin A, but they do contain calcium. Except for the calcium they lack, beet greens are superior to beets as a source of vitamins and minerals.

As you can see, many different vegetables contain the same kinds of vitamins and minerals, though they may have different amounts of these nutrients. If you do not like one vegetable, you can get the needed vitamins and minerals by eating another kind. There are enough different kinds of vegetables so that you should be able to learn to eat a number of them.

Food values of fruits. Fruits are valuable mostly because of the vitamins and carbohydrates they contain. Many fruits, however, are also a good source of minerals and even provide a few vegetable proteins. Fruits, like vegetables, differ greatly in the vitamins and minerals they furnish.

For example, apples and bananas are a good source of carbohydrates, phosphorus, and vitamins A and C. Though they both contain these nutrients, the amounts they contain differ greatly. Bananas have almost three times as much phosphorus as apples, about four times as much Vitamin A, and about twice as much Vitamin C. These fruits contain little fat.

Apricots are especially rich in Vitamin A, though they also contain Vitamin C as well as carbohydrates, calcium, phosphorus, and small amounts of vegetable proteins and iron. The citrus fruits, including oranges, grapefruit, and lemons, are rich in Vitamin C.

Since Vitamin C is stored in the body in only small amounts, it is important that people eat some type of citrus fruit or a fruit or vegetable rich in Vitamin C daily in order to meet the body's daily needs for this vitamin.

The Milk Group

The value of milk. Milk is one of the best foods that we can consume. It is one of the better sources of protein, and is a good source of fat. Milk is one of the very best sources of calcium and phosphorus, as well as Vitamin A. In addition, milk contains certain other vitamins and minerals, including a trace of iron. Fresh, whole milk is also a good source of calories.

Although milk is not a rich source of *thiamine* (thī′ à · mēn), which is a part of Vitamin B, or *ascorbic* (à · skôr′ bĭk) *acid*, (Vitamin C), it does have some of these vitamins. However, as you recall, there is no "perfect" food. Milk is not a perfect food. If a person had to live on milk alone, he would need other foods, especially in order to get the Vitamin C and thiamine he needs.

The food value of milk does not change when it is kept in frozen storage for many months. Nor are the food values of milk destroyed to any extent by evaporating, or by concentrating milk into milk powder.

Pasteurization does not damage the protein, the fat, the carbohydrates, the minerals, or most of the vitamins in milk. The only vitamin that is destroyed to any extent by pasteurization is Vitamin C. Since milk is not a rich source of this vitamin anyhow, it does not matter that pasteurization causes any loss of Vitamin C.

In the United States the average person drinks about 250 quarts of milk a year. This may seem like a large amount; but our country does not lead the world in the drinking of milk. The people in certain Scandinavian countries, Switzerland, and the Netherlands drink more milk than we do.

Milk is a good food to take between meals. It is a real addition to the diet. Furthermore, it does not seem to destroy appetites at regular mealtimes.

Cheese, butter, and buttermilk. Cheese is a milk product that has rich food values. Like milk, all the cheeses have good quantities of calcium, phosphorus, and Vitamin A. They also have a reasonable number of calories and proteins. Cottage cheese is especially rich in protein, but not in fat. The cheeses have smaller amounts of other vitamins and minerals, just as milk does.

Butter, another important milk product, contains mostly fat and Vitamin A. Butter has only a trace of most other vitamins or minerals.

Buttermilk is a good source of calcium, phosphorus, protein, and riboflavin. Many people think that buttermilk is rich in butterfat; but it has very little fat because most of the butter has been removed from the milk.

The Digestion of Food

Eating habits. Your eating habits are affected by many things. The place where you live, your family customs, the food preferences of your friends—all of these have an effect on the kinds of food you eat. The season of the year influences you, too. Pumpkin pie, for example, is eaten more often in the fall and winter months than in the warm months. The amount of food you eat is affected by your physical activity. Your personal taste for various foods also influences your choice of foods. Some of these personal tastes are connected with your emotions.

Think for Yourself

Do you feel like eating when you are upset or troubled about something? Why?

Emotional factors. Eating is in part, at least, an emotional experience. Much of the pleasure of eating comes from the association with family or friends at mealtimes. One digests his food better when he enjoys not only the food he eats but also the company of the people with whom he eats his food.

It is interesting to note that many times friendship is expressed through the gift of foods. This is especially true among primitive tribes, though a gift of food is still considered a very welcome one in our highly civilized society.

It is true that our eating habits are greatly affected by those of our friends; and our eating habits are most likely to be changed for the better when our friends make improvements in their eating habits. On the other hand, we are likely to distrust, or at least avoid, new foods, especially if these foods have been prepared by strangers, or if the foods represent countries with which we are not familiar. The food of foreign peoples is, of course, just as wholesome as our foods if the soil in which it is grown is similar in quality. But just the fact that it is different or perhaps prepared in a different manner doesn't make it less wholesome.

Food likes and dislikes. It is normal and natural for a person to have food preferences and some foods he doesn't like very well. One who is growing up in a wholesome way, however, is usually learning to like an increasing number of foods. As you may have observed, a child will reject a food sometimes as a means of getting additional attention. In somewhat the same way, one who dislikes a very large number of foods may be immature or may have a tendency toward emotional problems.

Many foods have associations with age and maturity, too. For example, most children do not like olives, but they do like peanut butter. Adults, on the other hand, prefer olives to peanut butter. When you can look back a few years to a time when you didn't like a certain food, but which you now eat and enjoy, you are showing signs of maturity.

Sometimes it is the preparation of a food, rather than the food itself, that is disliked. For example, you may not like boiled spinach. But if it is put into a cream sauce with perhaps some cheese on top and then baked for a few minutes, you might find spinach very tasty.

Often eating just a small amount of a new food, at first, will help one acquire a taste for it. There will probably still be some foods that you never will like particularly well. This is natural and normal; but if you are becoming more mature, you should be learning to eat more and more different kinds of foods.

Activity for Health

Badminton. If you like tennis, you will probably like badminton, which is also in the tennis family of sports. It is a faster game than tennis, and it calls for greater endurance. By playing badminton you can not only build up your endurance but also train your muscles to work together smoothly.

Boys and girls can play badminton together indoors, or outdoors when there is little or no wind. The playing court is 20 feet wide by 44 feet long, and is divided into two equal parts by a net made of light cord. The net is 2 feet 6 inches wide and should be 5 feet from the ground at the center when stretched between two posts.

The badminton racket is 26 inches long and weighs about 5 ounces. Instead of a ball, a shuttlecock is used. It also is called a "bird" because good shuttlecocks are made of feathers. Plastic shuttlecocks can also be used.

As in tennis, there may be singles games with two players, one on each side of the net, or doubles games with four players, two on each side of the net. The same court can be used for both singles and doubles games. In singles, the alleys are not used, thus narrowing the court. In doubles play, the serve is made from the long service line, whereas in singles play the serve is made from the back boundary line.

The object of the game is to hit the "bird" back and forth across the net without allowing it to fall to the ground or the floor or go out-of-bounds. To start the game, the "bird" is served with an underhand stroke; but after it is served, the "bird" may be hit underhand, overhead, or from the side.

To serve the "bird," hold it in your left hand by a feather tip in front of, and a little to the right of, your body at your waist. As you drop the bird, swing your racket up under it in an underhand stroke. Hold the racket with your fingers closed lightly and comfortably around the handle with the thumb on the left. The end of the handle should not extend beyond the heel of the hand.

Service is begun from the right-hand court, and only one serve is allowed. The "bird" must be sent into the court that is diagonally opposite the server and beyond the short service line. The "bird" may be hit any place within the boundary lines after a serve.

The serving alternates to the left and right courts as long as the serving side continues to score. In a doubles game, partners receive the serve alternately. Points are made only when a side is serving. Fifteen or 21 points may constitute a game. The side that wins two out of three games or the best of three games wins the set. Points in badminton are called "aces."

In boys' singles, or in doubles games, when both sides have 13 points in a 15-point game, the first team to reach 13 may choose whether to play 5 or more points. When the score is 14 on both sides, or 14-all, the first team to reach 14 may set the game at 17.

In girls' singles, game is set at 11. If both sides reach 9, the first to reach 9 can decide whether to play 3 more points; at 10-all, the first to reach 10 can decide whether to play 2 more points.

After the "bird" is served, it is

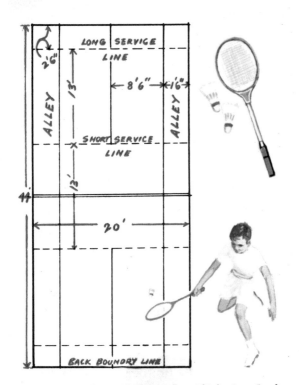

Figure labels: ALLEY, LONG SERVICE LINE, 8'6", 16", ALLEY, SHORT SERVICE LINE, 2'6", 13', 12', 20', BACK BOUNDARY LINE

hit back and forth until it lands in the court, goes out-of-bounds, or strikes into the net. As you recall, the serve alternates to the left and right courts as long as the serving side continues to score. At the end of the first game, the players change courts. If there is a third game, the players change courts again after the second game.

Service is lost if the "bird" does not reach the proper service court, if it goes into the net, or if it goes out-of-bounds. The served "bird" may touch a boundary line of the receiver's court, however. If the "bird" touches the top of the net

but would have reached the proper court, it is called a *let service*. The serve is then repeated. (A returned "bird" may touch the top of the net and still be in play.)

Service is lost also if, at the moment the "bird" is hit, it is higher than any part of the hand holding it, or if the racket is higher than the hand holding the "bird." The server also may not touch a boundary line with his feet, or lift a foot from the floor while serving.

A point is made by the serving team if the receivers send the "bird" out-of-bounds, into the net, or to the ground or floor. Touching the net or posts with racket, clothing, or with any part of the body also costs the receiving team a point. The "bird" also must not be struck before it crosses the net.

If you are in good physical and mental condition, you will play a better game. You can play better, too, if you are dressed properly. You should wear comfortable clothing that will allow you to move fast and to use your arms and legs without being hampered. And, of course, tennis shoes should be worn for safety in playing this fast, exciting game.

194

HELPS TO UNDERSTANDING

Points to Remember

1. Your body needs food substances (a) to make heat and energy; (b) to build and repair cells; (c) to regulate body processes and protect you against disease. These substances are proteins, carbohydrates, fats, vitamins, minerals, and water.

2. People who have many food dislikes are often immature persons.

3. You can show that you are growing up and maturing by learning to eat a wide variety of foods.

4. You should eat some foods daily from each of the four essential food groups: the bread-cereal group, the meat, the vegetable-fruit, and the milk groups.

5. Milk is one of our best foods. Its food value is not altered when pasteurized or when kept in cold storage for many months.

6. Vegetables are valuable in the diet for their vitamin and mineral content. Fruits are needed for their vitamins and carbohydrates.

7. Thirst is a good guide to the water needs of the body. The signs should be heeded and the thirst quenched accordingly.

Questions to Discuss

1. Are your eating habits likely to be influenced by the place where you live? For instance, if you live near the ocean, are you likely to eat much fish and other seafood?

2. Why do you need a variety of foods rather than one perfect food to get enough of the right nutrients?

3. How are your food needs affected by your age, sex, body build, physical activity, and rate of growth?

4. Why is the fact emphasized that you need a well-rounded breakfast?

5. In what way does a lack of protein cause anemia?

6. How does an adequate supply of protein aid the body in building antibodies?

7. Is milk a perfect food? Why?

8. Are our eating habits influenced by our friends' eating habits?

Some Things to Do

Make observations

1. Look at the labels on boxes of dry cereals and observe the variety of nutrients they contain.

2. Make a list of 15 vegetables.

If your mother will cook them for you, try to eat at least one teaspoonful of a different vegetable each day for the next 15 days. Observe the difference in taste, the time required for preparation and cooking, and the relative cost of each vegetable.

To Help You Learn More

1. Ask your mother if you may learn to cook one vegetable properly. If the family is agreeable, serve this vegetable to the family.

2. Ask your mother to cook and serve some kind of meat dish that you have never tasted before. See if you like it immediately or if it is one you may have to learn to like.

3. Try to eat a complete meal of some national group other than your own, such as a Mexican, Swedish, German, Chinese, or Japanese dinner. Try to eat every part of the meal.

Words to Remember

amino acids	nutritious
calcium	phosphorus
calories	protein
carbohydrates	research
nutrients	vitamins

 CHECKING YOUR UNDERSTANDING

Health facts. Number your paper from 1 to 9. Beside each number write the letter of the food in column 2 that contains the food element listed.

1. vitamin A   a. eggs

2. vitamin B   b. meat

3. vitamin C   c. milk

4. proteins   d. asparagus

5. carbohydrates   e. liver

6. calcium   f. bananas

7. phosphorus   g. oranges

8. iron   h. lima beans

9. fat   i. bread

Health words. On your paper write the word that is missing in each sentence below. Choose from these words: *amino acids, anemia, calorie, hemoglobin, nutritious, research, vitamins.*

1. If you eat a diet low in protein, you may suffer from _____, a condition in which there are not enough red blood cells, or the cells do not contain enough _____.

2. The _____ service of the U. S. Department of Agriculture prepared the Daily Food Guide.

3. A _____ is a unit with which to measure the heat or energy supplied by food.

4. Foods grown in certain soils may be more _ _ _ _ _ than the same kinds of food grown elsewhere.

5. Proteins contain substances called _ _ _ _ _ _ _ _ _ _.

6. _ _ _ _ _ are special substances in foods which are necessary to health and normal growth.

Health rules. Arrange the words in each group that follows so that they make a health rule. Write each rule on your paper.

1. enough a variety of foods in order each day Eat to get of the right nutrients.

2. each day in the Daily Food Guide You should eat from each of the four groups some food.

3. breakfast Start with a good day the right.

4. each day the bread-cereal group should have four servings from You.

5. Feed the disease germs each day so that it can fight some proteins body.

LOOKING AHEAD TO CHAPTER TEN

Do You Know?

1. In what way does one's general health affect his vision?

2. By what means does the eye normally keep itself clean?

3. What is muscle imbalance?

4. Does the act of seeing take place in the eyes or in the brain?

5. What first-aid steps should be taken at once if a chemical gets into the eye?

6. Why is it important that inflammation of the eyes receive prompt medical attention?

7. What communicable diseases are associated with the eyes?

8. In normal health, does the eye require special care daily to insure proper functioning?

You Will Need

a ruler, metal or wood

a water glass   water

10. Taking Care of Your Eyes

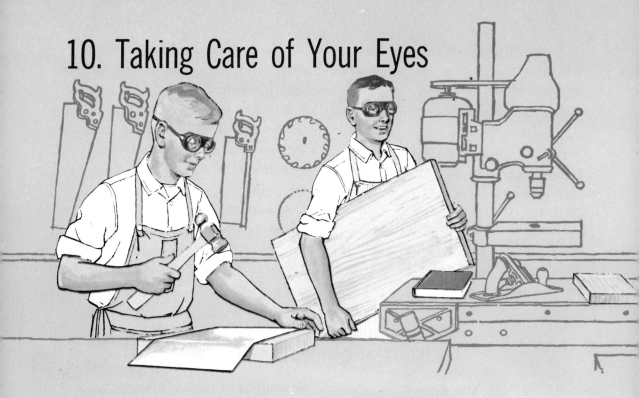

Your Eyes and Their Care

What would it be like? Perhaps you think that you have a good imagination. But can you imagine what it would be like to lose your eyesight? Can you picture what your life would be like if you couldn't see the members of your family or your friends? Can you even begin to name all the things you wouldn't be able to enjoy as much as you do now? What would life be like without color, form, or design?

There is really no point, however, in trying to speculate about things such as this, except perhaps to help yourself realize the importance of learning how to take care of your eyes properly to protect your vision.

In this chapter you will learn something about the parts of the eye and the way these parts work together so that you can see. You will find out what kinds of things affect your ability to see. You will also read about some of the things you should be doing to take care of your eyes and to protect your sight.

▼

**Make a
Demonstration**

▲

To demonstrate how light rays can be bent, place a wooden or metal ruler in a glass of water that has been filled about two-thirds full. The ruler should be taller than the glass, and part of the ruler should be above the water level. You will notice that the ruler seems to be bent at the point where it enters the water. Does this prove that light rays are bent when they pass through substances of different densities, such as water or glass?

Factors affecting your sight. There are many factors that have an influence on your vision. One of the most important of these is your health. Anything that affects your general health also has an effect on your eyes. A severe nutritional deficiency can affect the eyes. Sometimes tobacco and alcohol may cause a partial impairment of vision. Serious diseases such as diabetes may cause changes

in the eye as well as elsewhere in the body. Infections often cause a temporary or even a permanent impairment of vision. A serious case of anemia also can affect one's sight. In addition, many other diseases have an influence on the eyes.

In fact, the relationship between eye health and general physical condition is so close that the presence of illnesses in the body is sometimes discovered by the *oculist* (ŏk′ ū · lĭst), or eye specialist, when he examines the eyes. The presence of diabetes and hypertension, for example, may be discovered by the eye specialist.

In addition to your general health, your ability to see can be affected by such things as accidents to the eyes. Sight can be affected temporarily by other things, too, such as a lack of sleep. You can't see well if you don't have enough light, either; and very small type is hard to see as you may recall from a personal experience.

Some persons are born with eyes that are faulty in structure or function. For example, the eyeball may be too long or too short from front to back, or the eye muscles may not work properly.

General principles of care. As a rule, the eyes need very little special care. Eyes should be examined at regular intervals, however; and you should, of course, eat well-balanced meals and follow other good health practices that help you build a healthy body.

You should also take some precautions to protect your eyes from accidents and from such things as excessive amounts of dust, glare, and from other harmful agents. The eyelids, eyelashes, and the bony socket of the eye give some protection against accidents and dust and dirt; but goggles or other protective equipment should be worn by one who is exposed to glare, to large amounts of dust, or to flying particles of such things as sand.

To some extent, the eyes are equipped to protect themselves against too much light; but excessive brightness, such as the glare on a white, sunny beach is harmful to the eyes. So also is the glare around a blast furnace. You may have seen pictures of men who work near blast furnaces. They wear protective glasses, goggles, or a shield of some sort.

The eye is admirably prepared to keep itself clean by the secretions from the tear ducts that constantly moisten the eyeball and help to wash away dust and dirt. Under normal conditions, there is no need to use eyewashes; in fact, it is not wise to use an eyewash unless this kind of treatment has been advised by a doctor. However, you should help to keep your eyes clean by not touching or rubbing them, because of the danger of introducing germs into the eyes.

To learn more about the way the eye works and some ways it should be protected from harm, you should know something about the structure of the eye.

Parts of the Eye

The eyeball. Under normal circumstances only a small part of the eyeball can be seen when you look at a person. The eyeball is larger than you perhaps realize; and it is very complicated in structure.

A mucous membrane called the

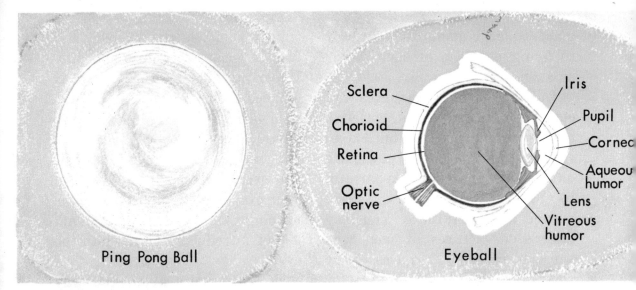

Labels in figure: Sclera, Chorioid, Retina, Optic nerve, Iris, Pupil, Cornea, Aqueous humor, Lens, Vitreous humor

Ping Pong Ball

Eyeball

conjunctiva (kŏn′ jŭngk · tī′ vȧ) covers the front part of the eyeball, except for the cornea. This membrane extends upward to line the inside of the upper eyelid and downward to line the lower lid.

The eyeball itself has three coats, or coverings. The first, or outside, coat is white and fibrous and is called the *sclera* (sklē′ rȧ). This coat covers the whole eyeball except for the part that is covered by the *cornea* (kôr′ nė · ȧ). The sclera has the job of supporting and protecting the eyeball. The cornea is the front, transparent part of the eye, through which light rays enter your eyes.

The second, or middle, coat of the eyeball is called the *chorioid* (kō′ rĭ · oid). This coat is brown,

and one of its functions is to darken the inside of the eyeball. The major work of the chorioid, however, is to bring food and oxygen to the inside parts of the eyeball and remove waste products from them through the blood vessels it contains.

The inner, or third, coat of the eyeball is known as the *retina* (rĕt′ ĭ · nȧ). This inner coat is made up mostly of nerve tissue, for it is actually an expansion of the optic nerve. Light rays are received and changed into nerve impulses by the retina.

The retina contains the rods and cones. These are the nerve cells that receive the light rays that reach the back portion of the eyeball. The rods are nerve cells that

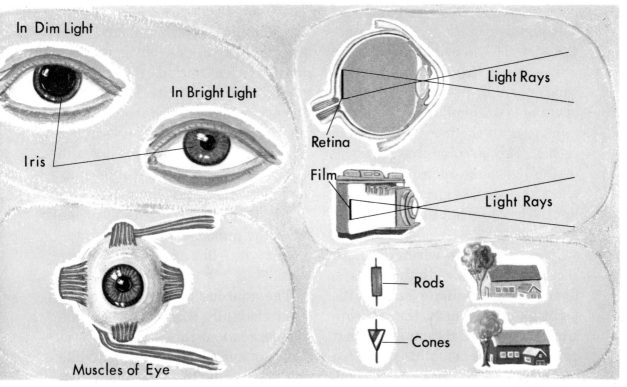

In Dim Light

In Bright Light

Iris

Light Rays

Retina

Film

Light Rays

Rods

Cones

Muscles of Eye

help a person see in dim light. The cones are the nerve cells that permit one to see in brighter light.

The muscles of the eyeball. The eyeball has six muscles whose purpose is to permit the eye to turn in various directions and to keep both eyeballs working together when you look at something. These muscles are attached to the outside of the eyeball in various places.

As you recall from your study of Chapter 2, if a muscle on one side of the eyeball is stronger than the muscle on the other side, the eye may turn inward or outward, de-

pending on which muscle is the stronger. If the eye turns inward, because of the stronger pull of a muscle, a person is said to be cross-eyed. If the eye turns outward, a person is said to be wall-eyed. These are popular terms; the doctor calls these conditions *muscle imbalance*. Fortunately, the eye surgeon can help to correct muscle imbalance of this kind.

The iris and the pupil. The *iris* (ī′ rĭs) is a round membrane just behind the cornea. It is a front part of the chorioid and is made of small muscle fibers and pigment.

The pigment in the iris determines the color of the eyes.

The iris is like a curtain with a small opening in the center. This opening is the pupil, through which light goes to the nerve cells in the retina. The circular muscle fibers of the iris make the pupil smaller when the eye is exposed to bright light. Then less light can enter the eye.

In darkness, or whenever light becomes dimmer, radiating muscle fibers in the iris dilate, or open the pupil. In other words, the iris controls the size of the pupil so that usually neither too little nor too much light will enter the eyeball.

Try This

You might ask a friend to stay in a darkened room for several minutes and then come out into the light. Examine the pupils of his eyes. Notice that the pupils are larger when he first comes out of the room and that they become smaller in the bright light.

The lens and humors. Most of you have seen a *lens* (lĕnz). A telescope, a pair of binoculars, and many other things with which you are familiar contain a lens. The eye, too, has a lens, but it is not a hard, dry lens such as the kind you already know about. The lens in the eyeball is thin and transparent, and it is held in place between the *aqueous* (ā′ kwė · ŭs) *humor* and the *vitreous* (vĭt′ rė · ŭs) *humor* by a ligament. This ligament suspends, or holds, the lens in a line with the pupil of the eye, with the humors in front and in back of the lens.

The aqueous humor is a watery fluid that fills the cavity between the cornea and the lens. The vitreous humor is a clear, jelly-like material that fills the space between the lens and the retina. Thus, the lens and the two humors are all transparent and permit the passage of light from the pupil back to the retina.

Besides permitting the passage of light, the lens has another important function. This is to bend light rays so that they are brought to a focus on the retina. Focusing is necessary in order to see clearly.

The act of seeing. You could not see without your eyes; but other parts of the body are also involved in seeing. The actual "seeing" takes place in the brain.

The lens of the eye bends light rays to form an image on the retina. The retina contains the nerves that transmit nerve impulses to the optic nerve, and thence to the nerve center in the brain.

In normal vision light rays are focused directly on the retina of the eye. If the shape of the eyeball is not normal, or if the lens does not bend the light rays properly, they may be focused in front of the retina or behind it. In each case, glasses can be used to send the light rays where they belong. The image as it appears on the retina is upside down; but it is "interpreted" by the brain in such a way that we see the object as it is, right side up.

The eyes can focus on objects near at hand or on objects at a distance. In order to focus on things close at hand, the lens thickens. It does this by a contraction of the *ciliary* (sĭl′ ĭ · ĕr′ ĭ) *muscle*. This muscle is relaxed when the eye is focusing on things at a distance.

Think for Yourself

Why does it rest your eyes when you are doing close work to stop for a moment and look at something in the distance?

Some Emergency Situations

Kinds of emergencies. An emergency, as you probably know, is a situation or a happening that calls for immediate action. There are some emergencies of the eye that require medical attention within a very short period, within minutes if possible. In others, medical care may be delayed for a few hours, or even for a day or two; but no difficulty with your eyes should be permitted to continue for weeks or months without medical attention. Usually the nature of the difficulty is such that you would not be tempted to delay getting help; but sometimes the difficulty isn't so urgent, and in some cases isn't even recognized as an emergency.

It is important that you learn how to recognize some of the various emergencies and also learn some general principles concerning what to do and what not to do until you can get medical help. To know

these things may save someone from possible blindness.

Though there are exceptions, it is usually wise never to attempt to give very much first aid to a damaged eye. However, there is one major exception to this rule. When a chemical has gotten into the eye, it should be washed out immediately with water.

The commonest kinds of emergencies include injuries or blows to the eyes, pain or inflammation, or sudden loss of vision. Cuts or tears of tissues surrounding the eyes, such as the eyelid, are also emergencies and they should have medical attention as soon as possible.

Foreign bodies in the eye. You may have had some soot blown into your eyes on a windy day. Particles of other materials such as sand, wood splinters, glass, iron, copper or other materials may get into the eye in one way or another, too. Such foreign bodies may cause serious injury. The eyeball may be cut or punctured and infection may result.

As in most emergencies, medical aid is the best kind of aid for such injuries; great damage may be done by one searching the eye carelessly or roughly. In general, it is wise not even to touch an injured eye except to wash it very gently or to lift out a foreign body that is easily seen and removed—one that has not penetrated deeply into the eyeball.

Only a specialist should attempt to remove foreign bodies deeply imbedded in the eyeball. Sometimes a doctor will use a magnet to pull metallic foreign bodies out of the eye. But only one who is medically trained should attempt this, or any other, method of extracting something from the eye. The doctor has the knowledge and the tools to do this delicate job.

Since any foreign body in the eye may cause an infection, it may be necessary for the patient to be treated with antibiotics or other medicines to prevent infection. Antibiotics should be used with great care, however, since a patient may be allergic to some kinds of antibiotics. No one but a doctor should ever give antibiotics. The doctor may also wish to test the vision in each eye after an injury caused by a foreign body.

Chemical burns. Time is of the greatest importance in this kind of emergency. First aid that is given within the first ten minutes after an eye has been burned may save the sight of an injured eye. Great amounts of water should be used immediately to wash out the eye. Fortunately, water is usually available nearby. Water dilutes, or makes weaker, any chemical substance in the eye.

The person giving first aid should not waste time trying to find a neutralizing agent. It is much more important that the eye be washed out immediately. Especially if the chemical is an alkali, it is wise to wash the eye over and over again with water. An alkali penetrates the eye and may cause damage deep within the tissues. Even while the patient is en route to the doctor's office, it would be well to have the patient washing his eye with water from a bucket, for example.

Lime is an alkaline substance that seems to penetrate the cornea, or outer surface, of the eye more easily than some chemicals. It sticks closely to eye tissues and is not easily removed. Therefore, it is important that every particle of lime be removed by a doctor as quickly as possible. Meanwhile, washing with water is helpful.

| Foreign Bodies | Chemical Burns | Allergic Reaction | Disease |

Some Causes of Eye Inflammation

Inflammation of the eyes. Inflammation of the visible parts of the eye is a common disorder, and one for which there may be several causes. It is also an emergency that might be neglected, since it may not cause much discomfort at first. Sometimes the causes may be temporary. In other cases the inflammation may be caused by a serious condition. For this reason, it is important that all inflammation of the eyes receive prompt medical attention.

Sometimes a difficulty of this kind may be a reaction to an injury from a foreign body in the eye. Chemical burns also cause inflammation. An allergic reaction such as that caused by pollen in the air may inflame the eyes. Disease elsewhere in the body can cause inflammation of the eyes, as can infections of the eye, such as *conjunctivitis* (kŏn · jŭngk′ tĭ · vī′ tĭs) or *iritis* (ī · rī′ tĭs).

Conjunctivitis is an infection of the conjunctiva. As you recall, this is the membrane that lines the inside of the eyelids and covers the front of the eyeball, except for the cornea.

Iritis is an infection of the iris. The iris, you know, is the part of the eye that surrounds the pupil. It is the part that shows the color. An infection of the iris is more serious than an infection of the conjunctiva because it is a deeper type of infection.

Glaucoma (glô · kō′ mȧ) can also cause inflammation. This is a disease in which a great deal of pressure is built up inside the eyeball because more fluid is getting into the eyeball than is getting out. When the pressure is built up to a certain point, it results in a hardness of the eyeball. The retina may be damaged, thus causing blindness. As you recall, the retina contains the nerve cells.

Glaucoma is one of the leading causes of blindness in our country.

Often the only sign of this disease is the inflammation that can be seen by one examining the eyes. Sometimes, however, glaucoma develops without any inflammation.

Think for Yourself

Why can't you see if the retina is damaged?

Virus infections. Inflammation of the eye may be caused by a virus or some other germ. A popular name for one type of infection of this kind is "pink eye." Although it is not realized by many people, fluid from the eye can spread disease just as droplets from the nose can spread infections. A number of epidemics have been shown to be caused by virus infections of the eyes. Because many people wipe their eyes with their hands from time to time and then touch someone else, there is an opportunity for disease germs to be spread in this manner.

A virus infection that is still troublesome in some parts of the world is *trachoma* (trȧ · kō′ mȧ). This infection of the eye may follow conjunctivitis, and it can cause partial loss of vision. In fact, it has this effect more often than that of

causing complete blindness. *Aureomycin* (ô′ rẻ · ȯ · mī′ sĭn) and some other drugs have been found to be very effective in the treatment of conjunctivitis and the prevention of trachoma.

Sudden loss of vision. The sudden loss of vision, especially of central vision, is always an emergency. There is a loss of central vision when a person is able to see the outside part of what he is looking at but cannot see the middle part of it.

There can be several causes of this loss of vision, but prompt medical attention is necessary no matter what the cause. If treatment is begun in time, vision can be saved.

Loss of central vision can be caused by a spasm of the central artery in the eye. The arteries carry blood, oxygen and other nutritional substances to the eye. If something stops the flow of blood and oxygen through the arteries, the tissues are damaged and sight is lost, at least temporarily.

In cases of this kind, the doctor gives the patient medicine to *dilate* (dī · lāt′), or open up, the artery and let the blood flow through to the eye tissues again. As you can see, it is important to get the blood and oxygen to the eye as quickly as possible.

Another possible cause of sudden loss of vision is a blood clot in a blood vessel. The clot stops the flow of blood to the eye, and vision is cut off. The treatment consists of medication that will dissolve the blood clot and allow the blood to be circulated to the eye again.

Sometimes a part of the retina may come loose from its normal position. This is known as a *detached retina*. It may be necessary to have surgery on the eye within twenty-four to forty-eight hours after a part of the retina has become detached.

No one but an eye specialist can tell which of these things is caus-

ing the loss of vision. No matter what the cause, however, prompt medical attention is necessary because any loss of vision is a serious emergency.

Blows to the eye. Various amounts of damage may be done when one is struck in the eye. In almost all cases, however, prompt washing of the eye with water is good first aid. This helps to remove dirt, debris, and perhaps blood or chemicals that may have gotten into the eye.

A person who has been struck in the eye may suffer some shock. One who has had a serious eye injury should lie down until medical care can be secured. A stretcher and an ambulance may also be needed to get the patient to a doctor.

Prompt treatment of this kind of injury is important, since tissues in or around the eyes may have been torn or cut. Sometimes the aqueous humor or the vitreous humor that is inside the eyeball may escape. If eyelids that have been torn or split are cleaned out and repaired within twenty-four to thirty-six hours, there is a greater probability that the eyelids will close normally and not be kept open by scar tissue or by loss of some of the eye tissues.

The treatment the doctor gives will depend, of course, upon the kind of damage that was done. He may have to take care of infection, cuts, hemorrhage, or chemical burns. In case of infection, the doctor may use antibiotics or some other medicine. He frequently uses medicines to prevent eye infection that may develop after severe injury to the eye.

In injuries of this kind, the use of water to clean the eye is probably all that should be done before the doctor comes. Sometimes cool compresses can be applied to the damaged eye. Bandages may also be applied.

Ulcers of the cornea. An ulcer of the cornea may be caused by an accidental injury, by chemical burns, by infections, or by other things. An ulcer of the cornea is a loss of surface tissue of the cornea, which is the front or outside part of the eyeball through which light rays enter your eyes.

If the ulcer is caused by an injury, it is important that infection be prevented by the use of antibiotics or other medicines. When the cause of the ulcer is found, it

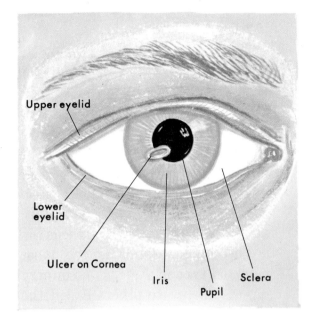

is possible for the proper remedy to be given and then the ulcer will usually heal rapidly. Such a condition should never be neglected because if the cornea is destroyed, blindness will result. This type of eye condition is, therefore, considered to be an emergency, one that should receive prompt attention.

As you have seen, proper eye care includes examination of the eyes at regular intervals and attention to health practices that affect the general health. Such measures help prevent the development of eye difficulties. In addition, a knowledge of what to do in emergency situations in order to protect your vision is an equally important part of eye care.

Activity for Health

Square dancing. Many of you have probably seen a square dance, and some of you may also have taken part in one. Such types of dances are called square dances because the four couples that make up a *set* are in the form of a square at the beginning of the dance.

The square dance is the most common type of American country dance. There are others called the round, the quadrille, the line, and the circle. All such dances are accompanied by music and usually by a *caller*. A caller is a person who knows the positions and steps of the dance and calls out directions for the dancers to follow.

The music for square dances can be provided by a fiddle, accordion, or other musical instrument or by a recording. There are advantages to the use of a recording, especially for those who don't know the various positions taken by the dancers and the steps they must follow. Recordings frequently are arranged with calls such as, "All join hands and circle left." All the couples in the set then join hands and form a circle. They move to the left with a rhythmic walking

step. Their feet are kept close to the floor and they shuffle along, keeping time to the music. This light, rhythmic walk is common to most square dances.

If you will look at the diagram on page 213, you will see how a set is formed. The square made by the dancers is about ten feet across. In the diagram each boy is represented by an x and each girl by a 0. The girl always stands at the right of the boy. Couples are numbered counterclockwise, and they stand facing toward the center of the square.

Couple number one, or the *head couple*, stands near the accompaniment or the caller, with their backs to the music or the caller. The *end couple*, or couple number three, are opposite the head couple. The other couples are called *side couples*. They stand to the right and left of the head couple.

Each square dance is built on a plan. The introductions come first, followed by the figures of the dance, and finally by the ending. The caller might begin with the call, "Bow to Your Partner," meaning that each boy should bow

to his lady and she curtsies in return. Then he might call, "All join
hands and circle left," and so on,
with similar calls.

You will want to become familiar with the meaning of some of
the calls and figures. The following
are among the more common calls:

Corner lady: The girl at the
boy's left.

Do-si-do: Back to back.

Forward and back: Walk four
steps toward the center and four
steps backward into place.

Honors right and left: Bow to
the person on your right and to
the person on your left. To bow, a
boy places his feet together and
bends forward from the waist, letting his arms hang naturally at his
sides and keeping his eyes on his
partner's face. A girl bows as the
boy does, but she extends one foot
a little forward and may curtsy.

There are also some common
dance figures that you should be
familiar with if you are going to
take part in a square dance. Some
of the more common figures are:

Allemande left: Boys and their
corners (left-hand ladies) face
each other. They walk forward,
join left hands, turn around each
other in a counterclockwise direc-

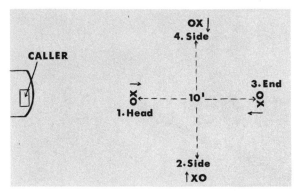

tion, and walk back to their
original places to meet their
partners.

Grand right and left: This figure is done in circle formation.
Girls move clockwise and boys
move counterclockwise, weaving in
and out. To start, partners face
each other, join right hands and
move forward, passing right shoulders. Each joins left hands with
the next person and passes left
shoulders. Each then joins right
hands with the next person and
passes right shoulders, continuing
alternately joining right and left
hands and passing right and left
shoulders.

Ladies chain: This figure is performed by two couples. The girls
walk toward the center, join right
hands and walk past each other,
passing right shoulders. They continue walking forward toward the
boys opposite them, with whom
they join left hands. They turn

counterclockwise around the boys, as the boys pivot in place, and finish at the boys' right, all facing the center. The girls again walk to the center, join right hands and walk past each other, passing right shoulders. They meet their own partners, join left hands, and turn counterclockwise into their original places, all facing the center.

Promenade: This figure is performed by one or more couples in a set. Usually all couples move at the same time. Partners stand side by side, facing counterclockwise. They join hands, right hands joined above left hands, and walk counterclockwise around the set.

Swing: Two people stand in social dance position, but with

right shoulder to right shoulder. In this position they turn each other clockwise two complete turns.

You will enjoy square dancing more when you are in good health. This kind of dance requires the co-ordinated use of your whole body as well as mental alertness. Taking part in square dances, in turn, helps your physical growth and development. Such dances also help you keep mentally alert, too, as you take your part and watch the dance patterns unfold.

Since square dances are enjoyed by young and old alike, you and your friends can learn them and have fun dancing together. Your parents may appreciate being asked to join you, too. You will have fun, find such dancing good exercise, and have the satisfaction of learning dances that are truly American.

HELPS TO UNDERSTANDING

Points to Remember

1. Many things may cause "pink eye," and some of these things may also cause loss of eyesight.

2. When a person gets something in his eye, great care should be taken not to injure the eye further.

3. Do not try to take anything from the eye that cannot be removed by washing the eye with water or by gently lifting out the foreign body.

4. It is important to wash the eye over and over with water if a chemical has splashed into the eye.

5. Glaucoma is an eye disorder in which the pressure inside the eyeball becomes so great that it damages the nerve cells of the eye.

6. If there is a sudden loss of sight, the person should be rushed to a doctor as quickly as possible.

7. A torn eyelid should be treated as a medical emergency.

Questions to Discuss

1. Does it help you to appreciate your vision when you realize that without sight human life would have no color, form, or design?

2. Can anemia affect one's sight?

3. What is muscle imbalance?

4. What determines the color of a person's eyes?

5. Why should you not attempt to remove foreign bodies embedded in the eyeball?

6. Can virus diseases of the eyes be spread to other persons?

7. Can you improve your sight by using an eyewash daily?

8. How does the eye normally keep itself clean?

Some Things to Do

Make investigations

1. Write to the National Society for the Prevention of Blindness, 1790 Broadway, New York 19, N. Y. Ask for free educational materials on vision and blindness.

2. Find out if there is a voluntary group in your community that works for the welfare of the blind. If one exists, perhaps someone from the group will visit your class and tell of the work of the organization.

3. Discover what provision your local and state libraries have made for the blind. How does a blind citizen obtain reading materials in braille and recordings?

To Help You Learn More

1. Try to make a model of an eye. Bring it to class and explain the parts to your classmates.

2. Perhaps you can get the name and address of a blind person in your community through a voluntary group such as was mentioned in *Some Things to Do*. You do not want to intrude, but perhaps you can do something for this person's welfare, such as making a personal visit, reading to him, or rendering some other kindness.

Words to Remember

aqueous humor	iris
cornea	pupil
emergency	retina
imbalance	vision
inflammation	vitreous humor

CHECKING YOUR UNDERSTANDING

Health words. On your paper write the word that is missing in each sentence below. Choose from the *Words to Remember* above.

1. Anything that affects your general health may affect your _ _ _ _ _.

2. The _ _ _ _ _ is the part of the eye through which light enters.

3. The third, or inner, coat of the eyeball is known as the _ _ _ _ _. It contains the rods and cones.

4. A doctor calls the lack of muscular balance in the eye _ _ _ _ _ _.

5. The pigment in the _ _ _ _ _ determines the color of the eye.

6. An _ _ _ _ _ is a situation that calls for immediate action.

7. All _ _ _ _ _ of the eyes should receive prompt medical attention.

8. The lens in the eyeball is held in place between the _ _ _ _ _ _ _ _ _ and the _ _ _ _ _ _ _ _ _ by a ligament.

Health facts. On your paper write the word that completes the meaning of each sentence in the paragraphs that follow.

An injury to the eye should be taken care of within (1) _ _ _ _ _ or (2) _ _ _ _ _ _. When chemicals have been spilled into the eyes, they should be washed with (3) _ _ _ _ _. A person, who suffers sudden loss of (4) _ _ _ _ _ should be taken to an eye specialist at once.

"Pink eye" is an (5) _____ of the eye caused by a virus or some other germ. Infections of the outer lining of the eye and eyelid are known as (6) _____. When an infection spreads into the deeper tissues of the eye around the pupil it is (7) _____.

Trachoma is a (8) _____ disease of the eyes. Increased pressure within the eyeball is known as (9) _____. This is a leading cause of (10) _____ in the United States.

Health rules. Arrange the words in each group below so that they make a health rule. Write each rule.

1. Protect dust and glare from your excessive eyes.

2. by touching or rubbing your eyes Help not to keep them clean.

4. wash the eye with a chemical eye immediately If water gets into the.

4. Keep in top shape by avoiding accidents, rest and sleep, and eating well-balanced meals, getting plenty of your vision.

5. if anyone suffers medical care Try to get eye an injury at once.

LOOKING AHEAD TO CHAPTER ELEVEN

Do You Know?

1. What usually happens to a person's physical and mental reactions when he drinks excessive amounts of alcohol?

2. What is alcoholism?

3. Is one type of personality more likely to become an alcoholic than other types?

4. How are the safety and well-being of others endangered by every person who drinks to excess?

5. How do members of Alcoholics Anonymous assist in rehabilitating alcoholics?

6. What is drug addiction?

7. What is drug habituation?

8. Do normal persons become drug addicts, or is a certain type of personality more likely to become addicted?

9. Can a drug addict be cured?

10. What measurable effects are produced on the body by smoking?

11. Health, Addiction, and Habit-Forming Substances

Addiction and Your Health

What you should know. How much do you know about the use of alcohol, narcotics, and other habit-forming substances? You probably have read in newspapers or magazines about some of the effects of the use of alcohol. You may know, for example, of the relationship between alcohol and traffic accidents. Do you know that the repeated use of excessive amounts of this and other habit-forming substances has a measurable and noticeable effect on the health of the user, and sometimes on the safety and well-being of others as well?

In this chapter you will read about some of these effects. You will also learn of some of the things that are being done to help prevent addiction to the use of habit-forming substances and to aid those who are already addicted to their use.

You may wish to have a class discussion on the ways in which the sale and distribution of drugs are controlled. To obtain information on which to base your discussion, a committee of pupils or your teacher might interview a druggist. They could find out what kinds of records the law requires the druggist to keep in order to show what is done with codeine, morphine, and other such drugs that he uses in making up prescriptions for medicine.

▼

Have a
Discussion

▲

Some effects of alcohol. The temporary effects of alcohol, both on the mind and on the mental processes, have been carefully studied. It has been found that alcohol acts like *anesthesia* (ăn′ ĕs · thē′ zhĭ · à) because it depresses, or lessens the activity of, the brain and the central nervous system. For this reason, worries, anxieties, and nervous tensions are reduced for the time being. One who is very shy and insecure, or one who is tense or anxious a great deal, or one who feels guilty about things should be especially careful to avoid the use of alcohol, for it may come to dominate him.

When a person drinks excessive amounts of alcohol, his physical

219

Drinking of alcohol affects the split-second timing necessary to be a good batter.

as well as his mental reactions are slowed down, though he feels as if he were more capable and efficient than he usually is. After a while, his speech becomes unintelligible and his muscular co-ordination poor. If he drinks large enough amounts, he may go into a *coma* (kō′ mȧ), or a sleep-like state. And too much alcohol kills a person.

The amount of alcohol that would be *fatal* (fā′ tăl) varies somewhat. The amount which would cause death is in proportion to the drinker's size and weight. A fatal blood-alcohol level may be caused by 6 cubic centimeters of pure alcohol to each kilogram of body weight. One quart of 100-proof whiskey (50 per cent alcohol) contains about this amount for a person of average weight. In other words, if a person of average weight drank a quart of 100-proof whisky within a short period of time, it could be fatal. At least his life would be in danger.

Think for Yourself

Could a quart of alcohol, taken in a short period of time, be fatal to a person of less than average weight?

Effects of repeated doses. The long-term, or lasting, effects of repeated doses of alcohol on the body are not so well known. Our knowledge of the permanent effects of repeated small doses is still incomplete, though we know something about the effects of repeated large doses of alcohol.

The general health of one who drinks large amounts of alcohol at frequent intervals seems to be affected adversely. His resistance to infections, such as pneumonia, is lessened. His mental judgments are weakened, and there is a general mental and moral breakdown. Evidence seems to indicate that the life span of such persons is shortened, also.

What is alcoholism? *Alcoholism* (ăl′ kỏ · hŏl · ĭz′m) is a disease that has become so widespread that in one way or another it affects a large part of our population. It is estimated that there are about five million alcoholics in our country; and, counting the families and others who are closely connected with each alcoholic, there are at least twenty million people who are affected to some degree by this disease. For this reason, much time and money have been spent in trying to find out more about alcoholism.

Alcoholism is the result of the use of excessive amounts of alcohol; and an *alcoholic* (ăl′ kỏ · hŏl′- ĭk) is one who has this disease. Not everyone who takes alcoholic drinks, of course, becomes an alcoholic; only about one in ten drinkers ever becomes an alcoholic. There is often some question in people's minds, therefore, as to

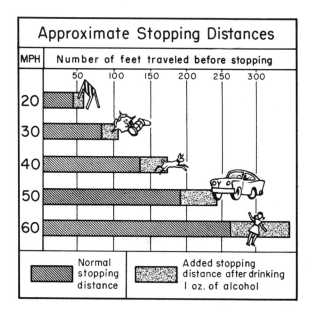

Approximate Stopping Distances

MPH	Number of feet traveled before stopping
	50 100 150 200 250 300
20	
30	
40	
50	
60	

Normal stopping distance

Added stopping distance after drinking 1 oz. of alcohol

221

who could be considered to be an alcoholic.

An alcoholic may be defined as someone who is unable to control the amount of alcohol he drinks. Alcohol "takes over." The alcoholic loses control of his life. His normal or usual activities are interfered with because of his excessive drinking. The alcoholic also uses alcohol to build up his courage or to help himself face unpleasant or unhappy situations. This is not a normal, healthy situation. An alcoholic, then, is one who uses alcohol in an abnormal way, a way which is harmful to himself and which may be harmful to others as well.

Factors in alcoholism. Why are some people more affected by alcohol than others? Why do some continue to drink even though they know of its effects on them? Are there some people who, because of their personality, are more likely than others to become alcoholics?

One of the subjects of much research has been the personality of one who drinks too much alcohol.

These are some of the excuses for heavy drinking given by alcoholics....

POOR ENVIRONMENT

JOB PROBLEMS

As a result of these studies it was found that a badly-adjusted person, or one who is unhappy most of the time and unable to adjust to the circumstances of his life, is more likely to develop alcoholism than others in his social group. In general, a well-adjusted, healthy personality isn't likely to go to excess in the use of habit-forming substances such as alcohol. There are exceptions, of course; but usually the person who begins to drink large amounts of alcohol is already badly adjusted. And his problems become worse as he continues his drinking.

Environment also seems to make a difference in the drinking habits of people. Sometimes the personality traits of a *potential* (pȯ · tĕn′ shăl) alcoholic would not be enough to cause him to become an alcoholic. However, he might become an alcoholic if he lived among people who, because of unreasonable ideas, made community adjustment impossible.

Costs of alcoholism. As you have seen, the costs of alcoholism to the individual are very great. The whole way of life of the alcoholic is threatened by this disease. In addition to the costs to the individual, there is also the cost to society. The safety and well-being of others is endangered by every person who drinks to excess.

ho end here . . . .

FAMILY TROUBLE

ALCOHOLIC WARD

The mental reactions and muscular co-ordination of one who drinks large amounts of alcohol are slowed down, as you have seen. His judgment is greatly impaired, too. For this reason, one who has drunk too much alcohol is apt to be involved in traffic accidents, thus harming others as well as himself. Even a small amount of alcohol can have an effect on driving ability, too.

One who has lost part of his mental facilities because of the drinking of alcohol is apt to do things he wouldn't otherwise do, too. As a result, he might break a law or harm someone.

Mental health of the alcoholic. As you have read, the alcoholic usually begins to drink because he is unhappy. The more he drinks, however, the more unhappy he becomes and the fewer friends he has. People begin to criticize him because of his drinking, and this often makes him drink even more. He is likely to get into quarrels with his family, and he may lose his job, too, thus creating further troubles. He loses much of his self-respect as a result of all of these failures. As you can see, his mental health is greatly affect-ed by his excessive use of alcoholic beverages.

Helping the alcoholic. In the past, alcoholism was treated in various ways. At one time alcoholics were put in jail, with very little attention paid to their welfare and with little effort made to help them overcome their problem. Recently, however, alcoholism is being thought of as a disease, and its physical and mental aspects are being carefully studied.

One thing has become clear as a result of these studies. The alcoholic must stop drinking alcoholic drinks completely if he is to be cured. No alcoholic can drink moderately.

As you have seen, many alcoholics have personality traits that contribute to their illness. Some have nervous and emotional disorders that can be treated by physicians and *psychiatrists* (sī · kī′ a · trĭsts), thus aiding them to recover from their illness. A psychiatrist is a doctor who is specially trained to help those with mental disorders.

A psychiatrist tries to help the alcoholic see his problems as they really are. He also tries to help him "face up" to his problems and set up new and attainable goals for himself.

Frequently, too, alcoholics are able to stop their excessive drinking as a result of spiritual or religious help. When the alcoholic finds spiritual help, he may be able to re-establish his confidence and self-reliance and develop strong resistance to alcohol.

Sometimes by making adjustments in his environment the alcoholic can help himself. Other members of his family may help the alcoholic build up his self-respect and strengthen his ability to meet his problems.

An organization called *Alcoholics Anonymous* has frequently been found to be effective in aiding the alcoholic who really wants to be helped. This organization is made up of people who have once been alcoholics, but who have made a successful recovery. There are no dues and no requirements for membership, except a desire to stop drinking. The names of the members are not told. Members remain anonymous, except to other members.

One of the problems in bringing the alcoholic back to a normal way of life is to destroy, or lighten at least, his sense of guilt and to increase his self-respect and his hope. When the alcoholic sees other respected members of society who were once alcoholics, it helps him to gain some hope. The people in Alcoholics Anonymous are living evidence that the disease can be cured. The members of this organization, of which there are more than 200,000, help each other overcome their problem. They give encouragement and guidance to the alcoholic, and help him in his effort to abstain from alcoholic drinks completely, since an alcoholic is unable to drink moderately. The alcoholic gains strength from being in a group of people who are all trying to do the same thing. In many cases this organization has been successful in rehabilitating the alcoholic, or restoring the alcoholic to a normal way of life.

The Problem of Drug Addiction

An important distinction. The terms *drug addiction* (ă·dĭk′shŭn) and *drug habituation* (hȧ·bĭt′ ŭ· ā′ shŭn) are frequently confused. It is important that the difference between these terms be understood.

225

There are certain drugs such as *heroin* (hĕr′ ȯ·ĭn) and *morphine* (môr′ fēn) to which a person may become greatly addicted. There are other drugs, less powerful, that are used to relieve nervous tensions such as tranquilizing drugs, sedatives, and sleeping pills. A person may develop the habit of taking such drugs, but the risk of becoming addicted to them is probably less. The danger from sleeping pills should be pointed out. The drugs contained in sleeping pills are powerful and should be taken only under a doctor's guidance and direction.

In order to help clear up the understanding of the terms addiction and habituation, the World Health Organization recently approved two definitions. Drug addiction was defined as a state of intoxication produced by the repeated use of a drug. Such a drug creates an overpowering desire or need for the addict to continue its use. The addict has a tendency to increase the dosage of the drug. He also will obtain it by any means, even though he must resort to violence to get it. There is both a mental and a physical dependence on it and its effects. Such effects are harmful, both to the addict and to society.

A habit-forming drug, on the other hand, is a drug that causes the user to develop a habit from the repeated use of the drug. Though there is a desire on the user's part to continue taking the drug, there is little or no tendency to increase the dosage. The user does not develop physical dependence on the drug; and harmful effects, if any, are confined mostly to the person himself. In other words, the user of a habit-forming drug does not become antisocial, nor does he turn to crime in order to get money to buy his drug.

Mental health and personality of

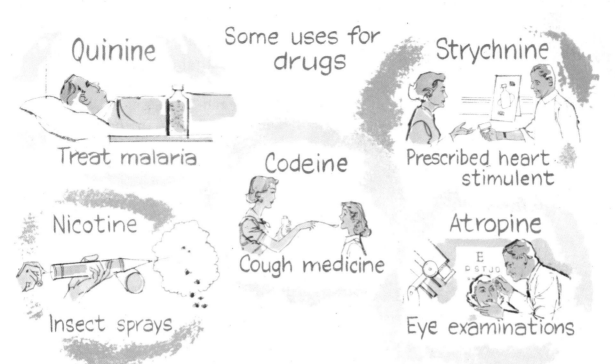

Some uses for drugs

Quinine — Treat malaria

Strychnine — Prescribed heart stimulent

Codeine — Cough medicine

Nicotine — Insect sprays

Atropine — Eye examinations

addicts. With the use of *narcotic* (när·kŏt′ĭk) drugs, the personality of the addict is greatly affected. Since the changes that occur affect not only the addict himself but the health and safety of others as well, many studies have been made on this topic. What personality traits are developed or emphasized with the use of narcotics? Is a certain type of personality more likely than others to become addicted? Is drug addiction caused by the drug itself or by the personality of the user, or by both?

As a result of the research that has been carried on in this field it was found that, as in the case of alcoholics, few addicts had normal, well-adjusted personalities before addiction. Although most addicts do not have a past history of mental disease, most of them have had personality defects before they began to use the drug. Some normal persons became addicted to the use of drugs when they were prescribed to kill pain; but such persons are in the minority and usually are the easiest to cure.

With the use of the drug, the mental health and personality of the addict becomes much worse. He is unable to think clearly or concentrate. This inability to use his mind, of course, has an effect on

A police laboratory chemist prepares to analyze pills in a check for narcotics.

Since it is illegal to buy drugs, he must get them from people who are criminals and lawbreakers. Thus he degrades himself further.

Some other effects of addiction. One who becomes addicted to drugs develops physical disorders, too. The drug decreases his appetite for food, and he becomes thin and poorly nourished. His resistance to infection is probably lessened, also.

It is very difficult for the addict always to know just how much of the drug he is taking. As you know, he gets his drug where he can. Sometimes it is "pure," and sometimes it is mixed with other substances. Since he can't be sure of what he is taking, he may take too much. And a dose that is too large could be fatal.

Those who are addicted to drugs sometimes become so depressed that they commit suicide. Frequently they are involved in accidents, since they aren't as alert to the dangers around them as a normal person would be.

If an addict wishes to stop taking the drug, he suffers from what is called withdrawal illness. Not all drugs are followed by such illness. *Marijuana* (măr′ ĭ · wä′ ná) and the *cocaine* (kō · kān′) drugs

all his activities. If he is still in school he doesn't do well in his studies. If he is working, he frequently loses his job. He meets with an increasing number of failures, thus adding to loss of self-respect.

The main interest of the *addict* (ăd′ ĭkt) is in his own reactions to the drug that he is using. Increasingly, he is occupied almost solely with his own thoughts and feelings, with little or no interest in others.

The doses he takes are increased, as you have learned, and he needs more money to get his drug. He will do anything to get it, too, though he usually does not resort to violence except for this purpose.

are not followed by withdrawal sickness. However, users of marijuana or cocaine often begin to take heroin or similar drugs that do have withdrawal illnesses connected with them. In effect, then, anyone who begins to take drugs will be faced with this illness, in addition to the other problems he will surely create for himself, such as loss of friends, job, health, and most of the things that make life worthwhile and happy.

Think for Yourself

Should a person ever take drugs of any kind without the advice of a physician?

Treatment of the addict. Those who wish to be helped can find help, though they may not be permanently cured. Some think that they are cured, only to become addicts again. As in the case of the alcoholic, psychiatric care is often very helpful and is, indeed, the most important part of the rehabilitation of addicts who have been physically cured. Attitude is of very great importance. The addict must be led to gain an insight into why he takes the drug—an understanding of his inner thoughts and feelings. He also must be guided in setting up new patterns of thinking.

Institutions that are run by the federal health authorities in Lexington, Kentucky and Ft. Worth, Texas are especially equipped to help addicts. Treatment, to be effective, must be in some kind of institution where the addict has no access to drugs of any kind, and is given every possible help in overcoming his addiction.

The Use of Tobacco

What happens when you smoke. The effects of tobacco on the body have been carefully studied. Both a moderate and an excessive use of tobacco have been the subject of much research. Although there is some disagreement among the conclusions that can be drawn from these studies, certain facts have been proved.

For example, it has been found that the pulse rate and blood pressure are raised by the smoking of just one cigarette. This fact has been proved by many experiments. Although most persons would not

Some Effects of Smoking

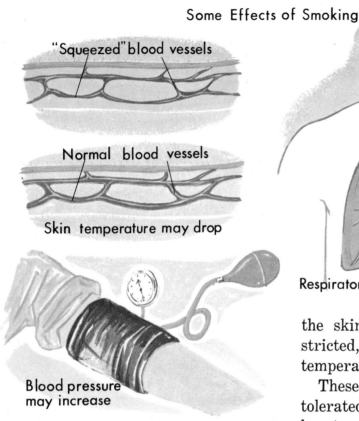

"Squeezed" blood vessels

Normal blood vessels

Skin temperature may drop

Blood pressure may increase

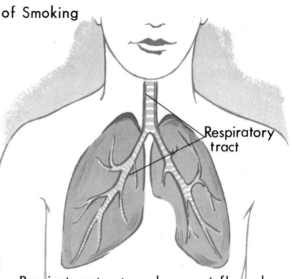

Respiratory tract

Respiratory tract can become inflamed

have such a reaction, in one study the pulse was increased by 36 beats per minute and the blood pressure by 19 points. These rates continued for a period of 15 minutes after the cigarette was finished. The effects from one cigarette would usually be milder but along the same lines. Also, the temperature of the skin is lowered as a result of smoking. Because of the stimulation of the sympathetic nervous system, the tiny blood vessels near the skin are "squeezed" or constricted, thus lowering the skin temperature.

These effects are probably easily tolerated by one with a healthy heart and circulatory system. On the other hand, the effects on a person with poor blood circulation or a faulty heart would be harmful, as you can understand.

There are other measurable effects that are produced by smoking. It is known that the throat and the upper respiratory tract are irritated, to a greater or lesser degree, by smoking. The heavy smoker frequently has a chronic inflammation of his respiratory tract. He often has a chronic cough.

For several years there has been much interest in the research that is concerned with the relationship between smoking and lung cancer. During the past twenty-five or more years, the death rate from lung cancer among the male population has gone up by more than 700 per cent. Though there are other factors to be considered, such as the pollution of the air, and others, research is being conducted to establish the relationship between excessive smoking and the incidence of lung cancer.

Evidence seems to show that the harmful effects of tobacco in this regard can be lessened by the addition of filters to cigarettes, and in other ways. There is much research still being carried on in an effort to find ways of lessening the harmful effects of heavy, or excessive, smoking. Meanwhile, it should be pointed out that excessive smoking is a health hazard and should be avoided.

Emotions and smoking. The fact that many people enjoy smoking seems to indicate that there must be some *psychological* (sī′ kŏ · lŏj′ ĭ · kăl) or emotional factors involved. Some people think that tension and stress cause people to become excessively heavy smokers. Others feel that excessive smoking is a cause of stress or emotional tension. As you recall, the blood pressure is raised during smoking. This fact would seem to show that the use of tobacco actually makes a person more tense without his being aware of it. The effect of tobacco on the individual may vary greatly, however.

Some doctors feel that the smoking of tobacco is related in some way to ulcers and to the tensions that may be the cause of the ulcers. It is probable that ulcers of the stomach or duodenum may be caused, in part, by worries, tensions, and anxieties. Such tensions and worries increase the produc-

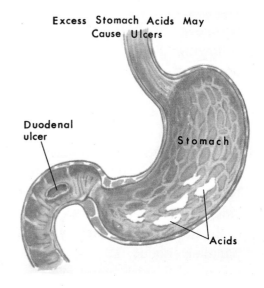

Excess Stomach Acids May Cause Ulcers

Duodenal ulcer

Stomach

Acids

tion of acid in the stomach; and it is the acid that causes the ulcer. Though it has not been definitely proved, doctors believe that smoking increases the flow of acid, and therefore either helps to cause stomach ulcers or makes them worse after they already exist. This effect, too, depends to a great extent on the individual; but many doctors advise ulcer patients not to smoke anyhow, because it may aggravate the ulcer by adding to the tensions of the smoker.

As you have seen, the use of tobacco, especially excessive use, carries with it certain risks. The degree of these risks varies to some extent with the individual; but it is safe to say that the wise course, from a health point of view, is not to smoke at all or at least to avoid heavy smoking. All of the effects of alcohol in the body are not entirely known, as you have learned, but the use of excessive amounts has been found to be harmful. And the taking of drugs in any amount, unless under the specific directions of a physician, can have a harmful and permanent effect on health.

Activity for Health

Baseball skills. To play baseball well, there are certain skills that you should master. Learning to bat is one such skill. Practicing the following points will help you to become a skillful batter:

1. Take a comfortable position about 6 inches to a foot away from home plate, depending upon your height. Stand close enough to the plate so that you can reach the balls that are pitched over the outside and inside corners.

2. Stand tall, with your feet parallel, about 12 to 18 inches apart, and with your weight almost evenly distributed over the balls of your feet. There should be slightly more weight on the foot nearest the catcher.

3. Your shoulders and hips should be level, with the shoulder nearest the pitcher pointing almost directly at him. Elbows should be kept away from the body. The back elbow (the one nearest the catcher) should be slightly lower than the front elbow.

4. Hold the bat slightly above shoulder level and back of the shoulder, but not on it. Grip the bat about two inches from the end,

with the hands together and the knuckles pointing away from the body. Hold the bat lightly. Relaxed muscles help the wrists to swing the bat. The forward hand should be almost in line with the back shoulder.

5. Keep your eyes on the ball and be ready for it.

Another important skill is *base running*. These points will help you:

1. Start for first base as soon as you hit the ball. Run at top speed. Watch first base, not the ball, as you run. In this way you are more likely to touch the base and not miss it or stumble over it.

2. Remember that each base must be touched or tagged as you run around the bases.

3. Try for second base if you think you have a chance to make it. Remember that you may be put out on your way to second base. As you near first base, run outside the base line, lean to the left, and touch first base on the inside corner with either foot. Learn to run at top speed without making a big curve while rounding first base.

4. Watch the pitcher very closely and be alert to opportunities to steal bases. Stand with one foot against the edge of the base and the other toward the next base. Most of your weight should be on the ball of the foot that is not on the base. Your knees should be bent and the upper part of your body should lean slightly toward the next base.

5. When you are on third base, stand outside the base line. When you advance toward home with the pitch, stay in foul territory, outside the base line, to avoid being hit by a ball.

6. Do not pass a runner who is ahead of you or run out of line to avoid being tagged by the ball. Also, be careful to touch every base.

Another baseball skill that you can practice is *catching*. To become a skillful catcher, one who is very helpful to a pitcher, remember these hints:

1. Squat with the feet together, knees apart, and the upper part of the body in a slightly forward position. Your gloved hand should rest on your knee, leaving your right hand free to give the signals to the pitcher. Your glove is the target for the pitcher's aim.

2. When pitched balls are thrown above the batter's waist, catch the

of the right foot on wide pitches to the right. Shift to the left with a sideward step of the left foot on wide pitches to the left.

6. If you throw with your right hand, shift your weight to the right foot and get into a throwing position as you catch the ball.

Pitching is another important skill that should be mastered. Hold the ball on the seams, using your thumb and your first and second fingers. To be able to send the ball just where you want to is important. So also is the ability to throw a fast or a slow ball. Practice pitching balls to various locations to see if you can control the ball.

In addition to your skills, your ability to play will depend, to a great extent, on your general health. One who doesn't feel physically strong and mentally alert wouldn't make a good team member, as you can easily understand. Your diet each day is important. So also is the proper amount of exercise and rest and sleep. Following the good health habits you have learned about will help you build a strong, healthy body, thus making it possible for you to be a good team member and one whom others will want on their team.

ball with the fingers pointing up. On low pitched balls, catch the ball with your fingers pointing down.

3. Keep the fingers of your bare hand in a cupped position. You are less likely to injure them than if they are pointed toward the pitch.

4. Let your hands give slightly as the ball is caught.

5. Never cross your feet. Shift to the right with a sideward step

HELPS TO UNDERSTANDING

Points to Remember

1. A person with a stable personality is less apt to become a heavy drinker or to use narcotics than an immature person.

2. The blood pressure of most people who smoke goes up. This suggests that smoking does not relax a person.

3. The heavy drinking of alcohol creates more problems than it solves.

4. The narcotic addict may be as intelligent as a normal person, but his personality is immature — he has never grown up emotionally.

5. A drug addict feels inadequate and insecure. A normal person may think he is inadequate and inferior also, but as he gets older he usually develops confidence in himself.

Questions to Discuss

1. In what ways are habit-forming substances such as tobacco, alcohol, and narcotics related to mental health?

2. List several differences between drug addiction and drug habituation.

3. What is an alcoholic?

4. How does alcohol affect the mental health of a person who drinks?

5. What steps must be taken if an alcoholic is to be cured?

6. Is drug addiction caused by the drug, the user's personality, or both?

7. Does drug addiction make a person more self-centered or more interested in the welfare of others?

8. Why has the increase of deaths from lung cancer increased the use of filter-tip cigarettes?

Some Things to Do

Keep records

1. Study your daily newspaper for two weeks and keep a record of the kinds of trouble people get into while intoxicated. See if you can learn about their mental health from the newspaper stories.

2. If your parents will permit you to cut out the articles on drugs in your daily newspaper, keep a scrapbook for a full school year in which you paste all the articles on drug addiction. Save the scrapbook for a future report on addiction in some high school class.

To Help You Learn More

1. Ask your father to take you to a local court where people are tried for drunken driving. Try to get per-

235

mission from the court to listen in during out-of-school hours. Note the kinds of trouble caused by heavy drinking. What must be its effect on the drivers' mental health?

2. If there is a mental hospital in your town or nearby, ask your teacher or father if you can visit it. If it can be arranged, ask questions about the mental health of the people who were sent to the hospital for alcoholism or drug addiction.

Words to Remember

addiction	narcotics
anxieties	personality
emotions	psychiatrist
immature	spiritual
inhibitions	tension

CHECKING YOUR UNDERSTANDING

Health words. On your paper write the word in parenthesis that belongs in each sentence below.

1. When an alcoholic finds (financial, spiritual) help, he may be able to re-establish his self-reliance.

2. A person who is (mature, immature) has never grown up emotionally.

3. Drug (addiction, habituation) is defined as a state of intoxication produced by repeated use of a drug.

4. Few drug addicts had a well-adjusted (personality, mentality) before addiction.

5. Some alcoholics have emotional disorders that can be treated by a (psychiatrist, orthodontist).

Health facts. On your paper write *T* for each sentence below that is true and *F* for each sentence that is false.

1. Tobacco smoking usually causes a fall in blood pressure.

2. The more alcohol a person drinks, the more friends he has.

3. Some doctors believe that heavy smoking helps to cause stomach ulcers.

4. Many doctors advise patients to smoke heavily so they will relax.

5. A heavy drinker of alcohol is less

236

apt to get married and more apt to become divorced than a non-drinker.

6. Most drug addicts have immature personalities; they are not normal, well-adjusted people.

7. Drug habituation is a less serious problem than drug addiction.

8. In drug addiction, the addict increases the amount of drug he uses as time goes on.

LOOKING AHEAD TO CHAPTER TWELVE

Do You Know?

1. Why must a person be punished for wrong conduct?

2. Name some of the factors that contribute to the development of desirable personality traits.

3. What factors determine whether punishment is effective as a means of directing or guiding conduct?

4. Why doesn't every person grow up into normal, mature behavior, with a sense of responsibility for his actions and the desire to do what is right for its own sake?

5. Why might rewards for good conduct be a surer way of making you a responsible individual than physical punishment for wrongdoing?

6. What should you learn from being punished?

7. Would a truly mature person, concerned with being fair to all people, be likely to break laws and need to be punished?

8. Should the aim of all punishment be to correct the individual's conduct, or to build strength of character and respect for the rights of others?

12. Understanding Punishment

Behavior and Punishment

Values of punishment. Have you ever visited a courtroom and watched the *proceedings* when someone was being tried for an offense? Perhaps the one being tried, or the *defendant* (dĕ·fĕn′dănt), had been accused of breaking a traffic law; and if he was found guilty, perhaps he was fined. There are other kinds of punishment he might have been given.

In general, it is thought that if people are punished in some way they may not commit the same offense as readily a second or even a third time. Sometimes punishment does have this effect, though not always. If, as a result of his punishment, the lawbreaker described above did not repeat his offense and did not break other traffic rules, the correction he received had an additional value. It had the effect of protecting others from his careless and unsafe driving, as well as making a desirable change in his behavior.

It is easy to understand the need for laws to protect the rights of the individual, as well as for courts to interpret the laws and punish those who break the laws. Courts are also needed to protect people against false *accusations* (ăk′ ŭ·

zā′ shŭnz) and to provide a fair hearing for those who are accused of breaking the law.

You can probably see that the kinds of punishment mentioned above are necessary. However, you may not understand so well the kind of punishment that is used to help build strength of character and prevent wrongdoing. In this chapter you will learn something about punishment and how it can be used to help develop personality in wholesome and healthful ways.

Have a Discussion

▼

▲

You may wish to have a class discussion about what should be done to punish *offenders* (ŏ · fĕnd′ ẽrz) in the following situation: A class had decided to take an examination under the honor system. That is, each student was "on his honor" not to give or receive help during the examination. Two students did not keep their word, and the teacher discovered this as she entered the room after the examination.

If you were the teacher, how would you handle this situation? You may wish to discuss whether or not it is important that such offenses be punished. What would be a just punishment? Is it fair to the rest of the class if the offenders are not punished, or if their punishment is very slight?

The need for laws and standards of conduct. You can easily imagine the confusion that would result if there were no laws to *regulate* (rĕg′ ŭ · lāt) traffic. Most people can see the need for controls of this kind, not only to prevent confusion and keep traffic moving, but to protect their own safety as well as that of others. Traffic signals and other ways of controlling traffic can be effective, however, only when people realize the importance of living up to their responsibilities in obeying the laws. Only as the individual citizens develop inner controls, will these regulations become effective.

Every individual has certain rights; and along with these rights,

he also has certain responsibilities. He has the responsibility of being sure that when he exercises his own freedom, he does not harm others or interfere with their rights and their freedom in any way.

For example, when you are old enough you will have the freedom or the right to own and drive a car; but you also have the responsibility of driving in such a way that you do not endanger the lives of others or interfere in any way with their right to drive also or to cross a street on foot in safety.

Have you ever heard someone say, "This is a free country. I'll do as I please." Such a person is aware of the fact that he has certain freedoms. He doesn't seem to be aware of the fact that others have freedoms, too; and that a person is free to do as he wishes only when his actions do not interfere with someone else's rights and freedoms.

In all areas of life people must follow certain standards of conduct. If this were not so, your rights as well as those of your neighbor would not be protected. Fire regulations should be followed in putting out a campfire, for example, so that you protect others from a possible fire. In a similar situation of course, others also

have the same responsibility for your safety. Everyone has a right to own personal property, too. You do not expect others to take your property from you, and you also have a responsibility not to take what belongs to someone else.

As you have no doubt observed, there are some people who have not formed the habit of following rules and regulations or of obeying laws. There are some who have not learned to respect the rights of others. When their behavior affects others in undesirable ways, and when their behavior interferes seriously with the safety and well-being of others, they must be corrected.

Think for Yourself

Can you see the need for the regulation of conduct according to certain standards? What are some agencies or departments of government that are concerned with protecting the rights and safety of the people?

The development of character. Did you ever wonder why some people become lawbreakers, whereas others usually follow rules and regulations? Did you ever wonder why some people never develop the strength of character and the self-discipline, or the inner controls, that would keep them from breaking laws and getting into trouble?

There are many factors that contribute to the development of desirable personality traits. As was pointed out in an earlier chapter, both heredity and environment have an effect on personality development. Equally important are habits and attitudes. It is essential that healthful habits and attitudes be developed early in life. Much of a person's happiness as an adult depends upon how well he has learned to distinguish right from wrong, and upon the kinds of attitudes he developed at an early age. His attitude toward others is especially important.

For example, at a very early age

242

one should be taught the value of honesty. He must also learn not to take things that belong to others. He must learn to be considerate of others. No one is born with this knowledge or these habits of thought and action. He must be guided by his parents or others until he has developed a strong character and high ideals. He needs guidance until he is able to make wise decisions and distinguish right from wrong. He must practice these healthful habits until they are a part of him. Then, when he meets a situation that tests his strength of character, the right course of conduct will come to mind quickly. For example, one who is in the habit of being honest will be likely to return money if he is given too much change at a store.

Ways of Influencing Behavior

The role of punishment. The effectiveness of punishment as a means of directing or guiding behavior depends to a certain extent on the person being corrected or guided. It also depends on how the punishment is given, whether it is a fair punishment for the offense, and on other factors, too.

To be effective, punishment also depends upon the ability of the person being corrected to understand the need for the correction and his willingness to accept it.

Rewards and punishments. Often a *psychological* (sī′ kȯ · lŏj′ ĭ · kăl) form of punishment is more effective than a physical form. If a person is denied a privilege, such as attending a party or a motion picture, he is likely to be influenced to a greater degree than he would be by the use of a physical type of punishment.

Rewards vary, too, in their effectiveness and in the form they may take. A reward may be an expression of praise, a gift, or the granting of a special privilege.

Some children respond very well to praise and to some type of reward for good behavior. The kinds of punishment usually vary also according to the age of the person being corrected. For example, in training a three-year-old not to write on the wall with crayons, several methods could be used. He could be given a physical form of punishment, with little or no explanation as to why he was being punished. He could be reminded that he knew better than to do this and that he would be punished by not being allowed to do something he very much wanted to do. Or, he could be praised or rewarded for good behavior over a stated period.

Maybe the first method of correcting a three-year-old would not accomplish very much for most children, or if it did, the child might also develop a feeling of resentment toward the one giving the punishment. A combination of the last two methods might be a very effective way of handling this situation. Of course, the punishment must vary according to the child and his ability to understand an explanation.

Try This

What methods of punishment are most effective in improving your behavior? Do rewards influence you more than punishment, or is a combination of reward and punishment most effective?

Adjusting to Punishment

Accepting punishment. Did you ever receive punishment that you thought was unfair? If you did, you probably found it hard to accept the correction.

To be effective, punishment

should be accepted as well as understood. The one punished should realize that he deserved a correction. He should know exactly why he is being punished. The kind of explanation given must vary with the age of the person being punished, as you have learned. A very young child could not understand, and does not need, a detailed explanation. An older child or a young person needs a full explanation of the ways in which he failed to live up to certain standards of behavior.

The punishment should be in proportion to the offense, too, with a more severe punishment given for a greater offense. Nor should anyone in a family be punished for doing something he did not know was wrong. Instead, he should be given an explanation and be punished for a repetition of the offense.

It is easier to accept punishment, too, if one realizes not only that he deserves the punishment he has received but that his parents are trying to help him by correcting him. Good parents do not punish children because they dislike them. Rather, they discipline their children because they are so concerned that they develop desirable habits of thought and action. Such helpful habits and attitudes will help them to be happy and well-adjusted to life. It is important to remember that your parents still love you even though they disapprove of some of your behavior and must

PARENTS' ATTITUDES TOWARD POOR BEHAVIOR BY A CHILD...

...WILL INFLUENCE HIS BEHAVIOR AS AN ADULT

try in some way to influence your behavior.

Your mental health as an adult will depend to a large extent on the habits that are formed in your early years. A child or young person who is not corrected for bad conduct is really being trained to "get away" with bad behavior. And it should be pointed out that the punishment for bad behavior as an adult is more severe than that received in childhood.

If you really accept the punishment you are given, you shouldn't complain about it to others. Accepting punishment also includes trying to learn from it and improve your behavior as a result of it.

Try This

See if you can explain to a friend why you deserved some punishment you have received, without complaining about it.

Learning from punishment. Finally, if punishment is effective, the one being punished learns something from it. Punishment can help you distinguish more clearly between right and wrong. When you are punished, think about the reasons for it. Try to see exactly why your conduct was bad. In what way did your behavior affect other people? Did it interfere with someone else's rights? Did your behavior endanger someone's safety? Was someone actually hurt by something you did? It often takes courage and determination to give up something you want to do because you know that your behavior will hurt someone.

THOUGHTLESS BEHAVIOR CAN CAUSE SERIOUS INJURY

Perhaps you were punished for failing to do something. Did your failure to do this affect someone else or did it simply contribute to your own bad habit of putting things off? Are you forming the habit of "getting by" and not doing your share of household duties, for example? All such behavior, of course, should be corrected.

Now that you are older, you can probably look back to your earlier years and remember specific times when you were punished for various misdeeds. Do you have a better understanding, now, of the reasons why you were punished?

If you are really learning from the correction you receive, and if you are not repeating the same misbehavior, you are beginning to develop self-discipline, or inner controls. There is no longer the need for as much correction. Eventually, these inner controls will be developed to such a point that punishment will be unnecessary.

Responsible, or Grown-up, Behavior

Adults and punishment. You have probably noticed that all through this chapter there has been much discussion of the punishment of children or young people. This is because children and young peo-

Getting along well with others helps young people grow into well-adjusted adults.

cepted standards of conduct as the average adult does.

Developing mature behavior. Over a period of years, the normal person develops what is known as mature behavior. As you have seen, there are some adults who still have not developed mature, or responsible, behavior. Normally, however, a person develops a sense of responsibility for his actions as he grows older, especially in respect to those actions that have an effect on others. The ability to get along well with others and to treat them fairly is a good sign of maturity.

This ability to get along with others, and the attitudes and habits of thought that foster this ability are developed, usually rather slowly, over a period of years. A very young baby does not appear to be interested in those about him. Soon, however, a baby becomes aware of others around him, and feels the need of their company. In fact, if deprived of the company of those he is accustomed to, he may even become ill. Increasingly, as he grows from infant to child, he becomes interested in others around him. He learns of his relationship to them and begins to show affection and concern for others in

ple usually have more to learn about behavior than a grown person. An adult who has developed in a wholesome way has very little need of punishment. He is, in fact, hardly aware of the rules and regulations he follows. His attitudes toward others are such that he isn't likely to infringe on others' rights or break the law. Of course, as you have learned, there are some adults who break laws. They have never really grown up and developed inner controls to the point where they are able to conform to achis family and in his immediate circle.

As a child grows older, he comes into contact with more people. There are more and more *conflicts* (kŏn′ flĭkts) of needs and wants. One of the first conflicts a child encounters may involve just one other person, perhaps a brother or sister. They may both want the same toy at the same time. In one way or another, the child adjusts to this situation and others like it. Gradually, he learns what is considered acceptable behavior in such situations. Later he learns to adjust to more complex situations involving more people and more difficult adjustments.

He learns how to fulfill his needs and wants in socially acceptable ways. For example, when a person works and saves his money until he has enough to buy something he wants instead of expecting someone else to provide it for him, he is acting in a mature and socially acceptable way.

Especially when a child enters school he becomes increasingly aware of his relationship to others and his responsibilities to them. He learns to be considerate of others. He learns that their rights are as important to them as his rights are to him. If he does not learn this easily, he is helped to do so by the opinions of his classmates and by punishment of one kind or another from those in authority.

One who is growing into maturity learns, finally, to do what is right for its own sake. He does what is right not because someone is watching him or because he knows he will be punished for fail-

Earning one's own spending money is a sign of mature thinking and behavior.

THIS and **THIS**

knows and likes, but also those whom he doesn't know well. He is as concerned with protecting the rights of others as he is with protecting his own freedom and rights. One who is really mature, then, would have no need of punishment.

ing to do what is right. One who is truly developing into maturity is concerned with being fair to all people—not only those whom he

Activity for Health

Baseball. In the last chapter you learned about some skills that you should acquire in order to play baseball well. You learned some pointers to help you bat, run the bases, catch, pitch, and field. It is important to practice these skills until you have learned them thoroughly.

Your physical condition is important, too, in helping you to play a good game. You must be in good physical condition to be a fast runner. You need strong leg muscles and good, strong lungs, too. Skillful batting requires good coordination. In fact, all of the skills used in baseball require a body in top physical and mental condition for the best performance. Eating a diet that contains all the necessary nutrients, as well as getting the proper amount of exercise and sleep, will help you attain and keep good physical and mental health.

You probably know many of the details of the game already. Most of you have watched baseball being played or have played it yourself. You probably know that baseball is played on a diamond-shaped field that has bases at its corners. The bases are 90 feet apart. The pitcher's box is called the *mound*. It is 60 feet, 6 inches from *home plate*. The bases are also marked in some way, usually by means of bags that are stuffed with material so that they are hard and firm.

The object of the game is to score runs. A run is scored when a batter moves all the way around the bases. The team making the greater number of runs wins the game. The teams take turns at bat, the visiting team batting first. When three players on the team at bat are put out, or *retired*, it takes the field and the other team has its turn at bat.

When each team has had a turn at bat, the play is called an *inning*. There are usually nine innings in a game. If there is a tie score at the end of the ninth inning, more innings are played until one team is ahead at the end of a complete inning. A game may be called, or ended, because of darkness or rain. The last half of the ninth inning, or of any extra inning, will not be played if the home team is ahead at the middle of that inning.

Teams are made up of nine players each. The players are called catcher, pitcher, first baseman, second baseman, third baseman, shortstop, left fielder, center fielder, and right fielder. The positions of the players are shown on the diagram on page 252. Players bat in turn according to a batting order that is decided upon before the game.

You will notice the foul lines on the diagram. If a ground ball stays within the foul lines until it goes past first or third base, it is called a *fair ball*. A fly ball that first strikes the ground outside the foul line is a *foul ball*. A

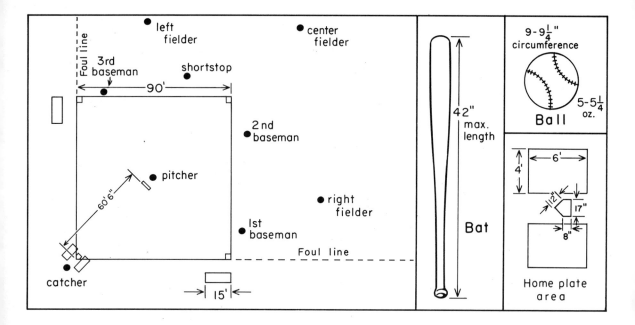

left fielder

center fielder

Foul line

3rd baseman

shortstop

90'

2nd baseman

pitcher

60'6"

right fielder

1st baseman

Foul line

catcher

15'

42" max. length

Bat

9-9¼" circumference

Ball

5-5¼ oz.

6'

4'

2'

17"

8"

Home plate area

batter cannot advance to first base when he has batted a foul ball. An *umpire* is an official who decides whether a ball is fair or foul. He also calls balls and strikes and rules on all other plays during the game.

A batter can decide whether or not to try to hit a pitched ball. A pitched ball which crosses the plate above the batter's knees and below his shoulders, is a *strike*, whether the batter tries to hit it or not. A ball batted into foul territory is a strike, except when there are already two strikes against a batter. A batter may have three strikes before he is *out*. Then the next batter comes to bat.

A pitched ball that does not cross home plate, or one that goes below the batter's knees or above his shoulders, is called a *ball*. A batter *walks* to first base when four balls are called. He also goes to first base if he is hit by a pitched ball.

A batter is out, too, if the ball he bats, either fair or foul, is caught in the air by a fielder.

If the ball is batted far enough, and is a fair ball, the batter, who now becomes a base runner, may be able to run around all four bases, making a *home run*. If he reaches only first base, the hit is called a *single*. If he reaches second base, it is called a *double*. If he reaches third base, the hit is called a *triple*.

BATTING

Batting Stance

Bunting Stance

FIELDING

Ground Ball

Fly Ball

There are many opportunities to use strategy and skill in playing baseball. A pitcher who watches the batting order of the opposing team may deliberately "walk" a batter who is more skillful than the next due to bat. A pitcher also studies each batter and tries to pitch balls that will be hard for him to hit.

A pitcher must be able to pitch a ball in a variety of ways. He

UMPIRE'S SIGNALS

Safe

Out

Batter

Catcher

Path of Curve Ball

CURVE BALL

253

must not pitch all balls the same way, or the opposing batters would find it easy to hit his pitches. A good pitcher can throw fast, slow, and "curve" balls. Many batters find it difficult to hit a curve.

Teamwork plays a great part in the success of any baseball team. As you play, you will find the ways in which you can be of the greatest value to your team. You will also learn how important it is to have teammates each of whom will also do his part. Once you and your teammates have learned to play together well, each doing his best for the team, you will find more fun and greater satisfaction in playing the game of baseball than ever before.

HELPS TO UNDERSTANDING

Points to Remember

1. The best training in good conduct for the young child is a combination of reward for good behavior and of punishment for bad behavior.

2. A child who is not punished for misconduct is really being trained to "get away" with bad behavior.

3. When you do things that are wrong, you should expect punishment.

4. Always try to understand clearly why you are being punished. This will help you to accept your punishment.

5. It is important for every child to know that when he is punished his parents still love him. Good parents punish their children because they want to make them into good citizens.

6. If you are learning from the correction you receive and are not repeating your misbehavior, you are developing inner controls or self-discipline. Eventually these inner controls will develop to the point where punishment is unnecessary.

Questions to Discuss

1. Why must a person be punished for wrong conduct?

2. Can traffic laws, signals, and policemen fully serve their purpose if individual citizens do not realize their responsibility for obeying the laws and traffic regulations?

3. Every individual has certain rights, but does he have the responsibility of being sure when he exercises his rights that he does not harm others or interfere with their rights and freedom in any way?

4. Why must people follow certain standards of conduct in all the areas of life?

5. Does much of a person's happiness as an adult depend upon his distinguishing between right and wrong and upon his attitude towards others?

6. Is a person acting in a mature way when he works and saves his money to buy something he wants instead of expecting someone to provide it for him?

Some Things to Do

Talk it over

1. Ask your parents if either can remember a time when he or she was punished unjustly. Did this parent learn a lesson from this experience? See

if you can discover how this parent now determines what is right and fair punishment.

2. The next time you should be punished for wrongdoing, see what a good job you can do of suggesting punishment that is just and fair. Try to take the responsibility off your parents and see if they will accept your self-punishment. Don't make it too severe nor too easy.

To Help You Learn More

1. Discuss with your teacher and the class whether or not the imprison- ment of adults is effective punishment and whether or not it teaches an adult how to do right.

2. Try to find out what rehabilitation steps are taken in your city or county jail and in your state reform schools and penitentiaries to return prisoners to society with a better understanding of how to live with other people.

Words to Remember

character	punishment
conduct	self-discipline
misbehavior	wrongdoing

CHECKING YOUR UNDERSTANDING

Health words. On your paper write the word that is missing in each sentence below. Choose from the *Words to Remember* above.

1. You must be guided by your parents until you have developed a strong _ _ _ _ _.

2. You must learn to accept _ _ _ _ _ for wrongdoing.

3. In all areas of life, people must follow certain standards of _ _ _ _ _.

4. Inner controls, or _ _ _ _ _, will keep you from breaking laws and getting into trouble.

Health rules. Arrange the words in each group below so that they make a health rule. Write each rule.

1. when exercising others rights and freedom harm You must not your.

2. if your behavior must be corrected You interferes with the safety of others.

3. early in life healthful habits and attitudes must develop You.

4. in proportion for wrongdoing should be the offense to Punishment.

5. and accepted Punishment should be understood.

Health facts. In the paragraphs that follow are several situations. On a sheet of paper write the problem number and the letter of the solution you believe would bring the best results in mental health.

Problem 1. A two-year-old child is visiting someone with his mother. He takes a vase off a low table and breaks it. What would you do?

a. I would punish the child for breaking the vase.

b. I would pay for the vase. At home I would practice with the child until I felt sure he would leave a vase alone when we again went visiting.

c. I would tell my friend that she should have kept the vase out of reach, but I would do nothing to my child.

Problem 2. Your three-year-old son takes a crayon and marks up the living room wall quite badly.

a. I would spank him and put him to bed without supper.

b. I would point out the damage and remind him that he knew better than to do this. I would punish him by taking away some privilege.

c. I would hide the crayon so he could not get it again.

Problem 3. Your ten-year-old daughter has been very lazy around home and has refused to help you clean up the kitchen.

a. I would tell myself that I am the grown-up one and that I should clean the kitchen myself.

b. I would explain to my daughter why she should help in the house and would give her another chance before I did anything about punishing her.

c. I would whip my daughter, put her to bed, and tell her that she must help me or I will not let her go to any party for six weeks.

HANDBOOK

The important health facts in this book have been gathered together for you here. You may use this Handbook for review or for quick reference. It is divided into sections such as "Body Structure and Function" and "Community Health." The section titles are arranged alphabetically. The numbers in parentheses show the pages in the book where a particular subject is discussed.

Body Structure and Function

A. The Work of the Glands

1. **Two kinds of glands:**

   a. Glands manufacture chemical substances from materials they take from the blood. Some secrete these substances into small ducts. (6, 9)

   b. Glands lacking ducts are called ductless or *endocrine glands*. Their secretions, called *hormones*, enter the blood stream and travel to body parts. (9-10)

2. **The endocrine glands secrete powerful chemicals:**

   a. Secretions from the thyroid gland (*thyroxin*) regulate your basal metabolism—the rate at which your body makes energy and heat. A lack or excess of thyroxin may affect your physical development and your personality. (10, 11-13)

   b. An excess of the parathyroid glands' hormone may cause a decrease in the calcium deposits in the bones. Muscle weakness may result and a person may be fatigued. Lack of parathyroid may cause muscle spasms. (13)

   c. The pancreas gland produces *insulin*, a hormone which controls the rate at which the body uses blood sugar. An excess or lack of insulin may have negative effects. (14-15)

   d. The adrenal glands produce a number of hormones, an excess or lack of which causes problems. (15-16)

   e. Little is known about the function of the pineal gland in the head or the thymus gland in the chest. (17)

   f. The pituitary gland is the master gland of the endocrine system. Its secretions affect those of other glands, such as influencing growth through the thyroid gland. (16-17)

3. **Maintaining glandular balance:**

   a. The glands usually function properly and secrete the right amount of hormones. (19)

   b. If your body is damaged, nature may make an adjustment to sustain the production of body chemicals. (19-20)

B. The Parts of the Eye

1. **The eyeball:**
    a. The eyeball has three coverings of membrane. One of these, the *retina*, receives light rays and changes them to nerve impulses. (202)

    b. The retina contains *rods* and *cones*, nerve cells that help one see in dim or in bright light. (202-203)

    c. Six muscles permit the eyeball to turn in various directions. If one muscle is stronger than another, you may have *muscle imbalance.* (203)

    d. The *iris* controls the amount of light entering the eyeball through a little opening in its center called the *pupil.* (203-204)

    e. A *lens* is held in line with the pupil by a ligament. The lens permits light to pass from the pupil to the retina and bends light rays so they come to a focus on the retina. (204)

2. **The act of seeing:**
    a. In seeing, the lens focuses an image on the retina. There nerves transmit nerve impulses to the *optic nerve* and thence to the brain. The actual "seeing" takes place in the brain. (204-205)

    b. In normal vision the image is focused directly on the retina, but if the focus is imperfect, glasses can be used to send the light rays where they belong. (205)

    c. The image on the retina is upside down, but the brain interprets it so that we see the object as it is, right side up. (205)

C. The Brain and Nervous System

1. **Intelligence is shown through various characteristics:**
    a. An intelligent person has the ability to think quickly, to solve problems, to adjust to new situations, to see relationships between objects, to say exactly what he means. (135-136)

    b. Individuals differ in intelligence much as they differ in athletic or artistic ability. (136-137)

    c. Native intelligence can be developed to different levels through desire and effort. Abilities, to a great extent, seem to be inherited. (137)

2. **The nervous system is made up of two chief parts:**
    a. The brain, spinal cord, and the nerves associated with them compose the *central nervous system.* It is concerned with voluntary actions and with thoughts. (137)

    b. The *autonomic nervous system* is concerned with involuntary actions or bodily functions such as digestion and breathing. (138)

    c. The two systems are interdependent. Without the messages carried to it over the sensory nerves, the brain would lack the information it needs when making interpretations and decisions. (138)

3. **The central nervous system:**
    a. The brain is a spongy mass of tissue protected by the skull. (138)

    b. The spinal cord is made up of 31 pairs of nerves and the cord itself, which is protected by the spine. (138)

c. Nerves connect the brain and spinal cord with all parts of the body. (138)

d. Twelve cranial nerves emerge from the brain. Some are motor, some sensory, some sensory-motor. (139-140)

e. The neuron, or nerve cell, is the basic unit of both nervous systems. Neurons receive and pass along nerve impulses, or messages. (140)

f. All sensory nerve impulses originate as messages from one or more sense organs. Motor nerve impulses originate in the brain. (140-141)

4. **The autonomic nervous system:**

a. This system is composed of the sympathetic and parasympathetic divisions. Both divisions regulate vital body processes, thus freeing the thinking part of the brain to express intelligence. (141-142)

b. The sympathetic and parasympathetic systems tend to counterbalance each other. (142)

5. **Intelligence should be protected:**

a. The ability to think well seems to be tied up with proper diet and rest. Prolonged nutritional deficiencies can damage the brain. (142-144)

b. Avoid infections, accidents, and drugs, all of which can have harmful effects on the brain. (144)

c. Alcohol has an effect on the way you think. Brain damage may result from its continued use. (144-145)

d. You can develop study and work habits that will help you to make the most of your intelligence. (145-148)

D. Work of the Respiratory System

1. **Your breathing apparatus is equipped to supply the body with oxygen:**

a. Oxygen is needed for oxidizing food materials supplied to the body cells by the blood. (115-116)

b. The respiratory system carries away carbon dioxide from the cells. It helps to regulate body temperature by releasing heat and moisture from the lungs in exhalation. (116)

2. **Anatomy of the breathing apparatus:**

a. The principal parts include the nose, pharynx, trachea, bronchial tubes, lungs, chest and ribs, diaphragm, and capillaries. (116-117)

b. On its way to the lungs, air is filtered and warmed in the nostrils by the cilia. (117)

c. The windpipe divides into tubes that go to each lung. Inside the lungs these re-divide until each tiny part ends at an air cell. (118)

d. The two lungs fill most of the space inside the chest. A thin membrane, the pleura, covers them. (119)

3. **The process of breathing:**

a. Breathing includes the lungs' inhalation and exhalation of air and the exchange of oxygen and carbon dioxide in the lungs and body cells. (119-120)

b. The rate of breathing is controlled by a nerve in the brain. (120)

c. The efficiency of the respiratory system is partly dependent upon the red blood cells. There must be enough of them and they must contain a proper amount of hemoglobin. (121)

E. The Effect of Exercise

1. **What physical activity does for you:**

    a. Exercise helps to develop co-ordination or the efficient functioning together of all the parts of your body. (72)

    b. Exercise helps develop the ability to work or play for long periods without getting too tired. (72)

2. **Exercise improves the skeletal system:**

    a. The skeleton, movable joints, and their connection by muscles and tendons make it possible for you to move as you do. (74-75)

    b. The bones are nearly hollow and filled with marrow. (75)

    c. The joints partly determine the kinds of movement you can make. (76)

    d. Joints are protected and supported by tough bands of tissue called *ligaments*. (76-77)

3. **Muscles need exercise:**

    a. Muscles are bands of long, thin cells, usually ending in a cord that forms the tendon. Tendons connect muscles to the bones and other body parts and transmit the mechanical force of the muscle to the bone, causing it to move. (77)

    b. You can move the parts of your body because muscles can contract and relax. (78)

    c. The heat produced when muscles contract helps to maintain normal body temperature of 98.6 Fahrenheit. (79)

4. **Exercise improves circulation:**

    a. The heart is a hollow organ that acts as a pump to operate the circulatory system. Arteries carry the blood away from the heart; veins return it to the heart. (80-81)

    b. Tiny blood vessels (*capillaries*) lie close to the tissue cells. Food materials and oxygen pass through the capillary walls into the blood. (81)

    c. When you exercise, the contraction of the muscles keeps pushing the blood back toward the heart through one-way valves. This helps the heart to do its work. (81)

    d. The heart's contractions are mirrored in your pulse. A slow pulse (50 or 60 or less) may indicate that a heart is superior in mechanical efficiency and the owner has good endurance. (82)

    e. The blood, made up of plasma and blood cells, carries food materials, oxygen, endocrine gland secretions, and other substances to and from the body cells. (82-83)

    f. Blood plasma helps to regulate body temperature. (83)

    g. Physical activity increases the blood pressure temporarily, but it is only when blood pressure remains high much of the time that it becomes a health problem. (83-84)

5. **The lungs and exercise:**

    a. During physical exercise the lungs may take in as much as seven times the air normally inhaled. The rate of breathing also increases, and more oxygen is needed. (84)

b. The respiratory and circulatory systems co-operate to supply needed oxygen and to remove carbon dioxide from body cells. (84-85)

Community Health

A. Taking Safety Measures

1. **Local authorities should be ready for emergencies:**
   a. The weather bureau can inform radio and TV stations when to warn the public of approaching floods, tornadoes, and hurricanes. (48)
   b. Health, police, and Civil Defense authorities should broadcast instructions on what to do in emergencies. (48-49, 54, 56, 57-58, 60-63)
   c. The U.S. Weather Bureau maintains stations that tell where hurricanes are forming and the direction they are moving. (56)
   d. The Civil Defense authorities should inform the public of the plans for meeting a nuclear explosion and be sure people know what they must do. (59-63)
2. **Citizens should take precautions during emergencies:**
   a. Drinking water should be boiled to guard against contamination. (50)
   b. People should have on hand a supply of canned food for emergency use during floods. (51)
   c. To be prepared for a tornado, people in many communities arrange to be informed when weather conditions are favorable to tornado formation or when one is sighted. (54)

B. Avoiding Dangerous Conditions

1. **Community problems after a disaster:**
   a. Clean up after a flood. Remove all debris. Repair or tear down damaged buildings. (51)
   b. After a tornado, enter carefully any house that was struck. Do not touch loose wires. Report injuries. (53-54)
   c. After a hurricane, tune in the radio to learn what you can do in the clean-up. (57-58)
   d. After an earthquake, shut off the gas, be sure drinking water is safe. Avoid dangling wires. (59)
   e. Protect yourself against radioactive fall-out by following instructions of authorities. (62)
2. **The problem of air pollution:**
   a. In recent years many large cities have suffered from smog—a condition in which the air is polluted with fumes. (127)
   b. Some cities have tried to cut smog. They analyze the air and ask the public to co-operate in measures designed to reduce the pollution. (128)

Diseases

A. Communicable Diseases

1. **Major diseases in childhood:**
    a. Communicable diseases are caused by germs and may be passed from person to person. They can be spread by water, food, air, animals, and insects. (156)
    b. In the United States, the most serious communicable diseases among teen-agers are influenza, pneumonia, streptococcus sore throat, rheumatic fever, tuberculosis, and poliomyelitis. Others include measles, diphtheria, whooping cough, typhoid fever, and dysentery. (156)
2. **Prevention and control of illness:**
    a. Germs can be spread in many ways, but your body has defenses against those bearing disease. (157-158)
    b. In major infections, the body can produce antibodies which build immunity against recurrence of a particular disease. Artificial immunity can also be built with use of vaccines. (158-159)
    c. You can do much to avoid illness by practicing good health habits, such as eating the right amounts of the right foods and having enough rest and sleep. Have regular health examinations. (159-160)
    d. If you become ill, you can help control the spread of germs to others by observing precautions. (160)

B. Respiratory Diseases

1. **Five diseases common at your age level:**
    a. Influenza, caused by viruses, usually begins with a fever and may leave you feeling weak and tired, or may be followed by pneumonia. (161-162)
    b. The lungs become inflamed in pneumonia. The disease may be controlled by antibiotics. (162-163)
    c. Streptococcus infections of the throat can be treated with sulfa drugs and antibiotics if treatment is undertaken before rheumatic fever develops. (163-164)
    d. By taking care of a cold, you may prevent other diseases. (164)
2. **Tuberculosis, poliomyelitis, malaria:**
    a. Tuberculosis is not hereditary, but it is easily spread by the sneezing or coughing of the infected person, or by eating from contaminated utensils. (164-165)
    b. It is difficult to detect tuberculosis, but doctors use several tests for that purpose. (165-166)
    c. A tuberculosis patient needs rest and a diet rich in food essentials. (166)
    d. Poliomyelitis causes inflammation of the nervous system. (167-168)
    e. When the spinal cord is damaged by polio, the affected person often becomes paralyzed. (167)

f. The best protection now is to take three shots of Salk vaccine and repeat them every year or two. (168)

g. A disease of chills and fevers, malaria is a serious problem in many countries. It can be prevented by destroying its carrier, the Anopheles mosquito. (169-170)

C. Controlling Communicable Diseases

1. **Public health authorities do their part in controlling disease:**

    a. They safeguard the community water supply. Water is sometimes filtered; sometimes chloride compounds are added. Water is tested for purity. (160)

    b. They safeguard the milk supply by inspecting dairies and requiring the milk to be pasteurized. (160-161)

    c. They have restaurants inspected and require food handlers to take physical examinations. (161)

    d. They are responsible for disposing of sewage and garbage in sanitary ways and for the eradication of rodents and insects. (161)

    e. Our public health program on malaria includes drainage of swamps and other places where mosquitoes breed, spraying individual homes with DDT, and dusting areas where mosquitoes are thickest. (170-171)

2. **National organizations lend a hand:**

    a. The National Tuberculosis Association aids in controlling tuberculosis. (166-167)

    b. The National Foundation helps to fight polio. (168-169)

Food and Nutrition

A. Foods and Health

1. **How foods are related to health:**

    a. You need foods your body can use (1) to make heat and energy; (2) to build and repair cells; (3) to regulate body processes and protect you against disease. (179)

    b. The substances in foods needed to do the above three things are proteins, fats, carbohydrates, vitamins, minerals, and water. (179)

    c. About 70 per cent of an adult's weight is water, but some of this is lost daily through respiration, perspiration, and elimination. Some of the lost water is replaced by the water in foods. (179-180)

    d. No food contains every nutrient in the proportions you need. To get enough nutrients each day, you need a variety of foods and a daily plan or guide to follow. (180)

    e. The *Daily Food Guide* is easy to use. It includes four groups of foods essential to health. You need to eat foods from each group daily. (180-181) *f.* The number of calories of food each person needs varies, affected by physical activity, age, sex, body health, and other factors. (181-183)

2. **The digestion of food:**

a. Your eating habits are affected by your environment, family customs, the food preferences of your friends, your physical activity, and your personal tastes. (190)

b. If you are growing up in a wholesome way, you are learning to like many foods. (191-192)

B. Food Groups

1. **The bread-cereal group of foods:**

a. These foods are important for their energy value. (184)

b. Studies on breakfasts indicate that a good breakfast should supply one fourth of your daily calorie and nutrient needs. If you eat a nutritious breakfast, you feel less tired during the morning. (184-185)

c. Studies of teen-age eating habits show that if you don't have enough protein for breakfast, you tend to eat quick-energy foods, such as candy, and lose your appetite for lunch. (185)

2. **The meat group of foods:**

a. Meats are particularly valuable for the protein they provide. Proteins have many values. They help maintain proper blood pressure and enough red blood cells. They help fight disease germs and make antibodies. (185-187)

b. Other good sources of protein include eggs, milk, cheese, poultry, fish, and beans. (187)

3. **The vegetable-fruit group:**

a. Vegetables are valuable for their vitamin and mineral content—substances needed for regulating body processes. Vegetables also give you roughage and bulk. (188)

b. Fruits provide vitamins, carbohydrates, and minerals. (188-189)

c. People should eat citrus fruit daily or a fruit or vegetable rich in Vitamin C to meet the body's requirements for Vitamin C. (189)

4. **The milk group of foods:**

a. Milk gives you protein, calcium, fat, phosphorus, Vitamin A, other vitamins, and minerals. (189)

b. The food value of milk does not change when in frozen storage nor when it is pasteurized. (189-190)

Growth and Health

A. Dental Health

1. **Safeguarding your teeth helps safeguard your general health:**

a. You need your teeth to prepare food for digestion. (96)

b. Most people have 52 teeth in a lifetime. The first 20 are later replaced by permanent teeth. (97-98)

2. **Take care of your teeth:**

a. The enamel of the teeth is subject to decay. (96-97, 99) *b.* Bacteria in the mouth make acids of food particles, especially sugar, remaining in the teeth. Such acids break down the enamel. (100)

c. To avoid decay, brush the teeth after eating before bacteria can act. If you can't brush, rinse the teeth with water. (101-102)

d. Some communities add fluorides to the water to reduce tooth decay. (102-103)

e. A diet that makes for good general health is adequate for dental health. Eat very few sweets and drink plenty of milk. (104)

f. Visit the dentist every six months. (104-105, 107-108)

g. Malocclusion should be prevented. If it occurs, let an orthodontist correct it. (37-38, 105-107)

B. Care of the Eyes

1. **Various factors affect vision:**

    a. Your vision is affected by your general health. It may be impaired by such things as a severe nutritional deficiency or by disease. (199-200)

    b. Your ability to see can be affected by accidents, lack of sleep, poor light, or by faulty eye structure and function. (200)

2. **To protect your vision, take care of your eyes:**

    a. Have them examined at intervals. Eat well-balanced meals. (200)

    b. Wear goggles or glasses to protect your eyes from accidents, excessive glare and dust, and from flying objects such as sand. (200-201)

    c. Do not use eyewashes. (201)

▶▶*See also* **Body Structure and Function** *and* **Safety and First Aid** in this Handbook.

C. Air and Its Pollution

1. **The condition of the air affects body comfort:**

    a. The body is affected by temperature, air pressure, and the presence or absence of air currents. (122)

    b. The discomfort felt in a crowded, poorly ventilated room is due to the moisture in the air and to the lack of air movement. (123-124)

    c. It is difficult to breathe in enough air at high altitudes because there are fewer molecules in the air and they are farther apart. (124)

2. **Dust and pollen affect our health:**

    a. Most dust in the air is harmless unless there is a large amount. (124)

    b. Radioactive dust from nuclear explosions can be harmful. (125)

    c. Pollens known as allergens may cause people sensitive to pollen to have hay fever or asthma. Air-conditioning devices that wash and filter air may be helpful to such victims. (125-126)

    d. Germs in the air may cause respiratory infections. (126)

    e. People can suffer discomfort and illness from breathing smog— air polluted with chemicals from auto exhausts and smoke from factories, incinerators, and burning garbage. (127-128)

D. Habit-forming Substances

1. Some effects of alcohol on health:

a. Alcohol acts like an anesthesia, depressing or lessening the action of the brain and the central nervous system. A person's reason, anxieties, and tensions are temporarily reduced after he drinks alcohol. (219)

b. When one drinks large amounts of alcohol at frequent intervals, his resistence to infections is lessened, his mental abilities weakened, and there is a general mental and moral breakdown. (219-221)

c. Alcoholism is a disease which affects a large part of our population. (221)

d. Studies of their personality indicate that alcoholics were usually badly adjusted before they became alcoholics. (222-223)

e. An alcoholic's mental health suffers. People criticize him, he loses his friends, he may quarrel with his family, and lose his job as well as his self-respect. (223-224)

2. Alcoholics can be helped:

a. Alcoholics were once jailed, but we now consider them the victims of disease. (224)

b. An alcoholic must stop drinking if he is to be cured. (224)

c. The nervous and emotional disorders of alcoholism can be treated by physicians and psychiatrists. (224)

d. Alcoholics are often enabled to stop drinking through spiritual or religious help. (225)

e. Alcoholics Anonymous has helped many. The members of this organization help others to stop drinking and to build worthwhile lives. (225)

3. The problems of drug addiction must be faced:

a. A person may become *addicted* to drugs such as heroin and morphine. A person may form the habit of taking other drugs such as sedatives and sleeping pills, but he is less likely to become addicted to them. (225-226)

b. Studies show that badly adjusted personalities are the more likely to become drug addicts. While under a drug, an addict is unable to concentrate. His activities are affected; he meets with increasing failure even to losing his job. (227-228)

c. The addict is mainly interested in his reactions to the drug he is using. He increases his doses and needs more money to buy his drug. Since it is illegal to buy drugs, he must get them from lawbreakers, thus adding to his disgrace. (228)

d. Drug addiction decreases the user's appetite for food. He becomes poorly nourished; his resistance to infection is lessened. He becomes depressed and frequently is involved in an accident because he isn't alert to danger. (228)

e. Those who want help can get it. Psychiatric help has been the most important part of rehabilitating addicts in the past. The addict is helped to understand why he took the drug; is guided in setting up new patterns of thought. (229)

4. **The problem of smoking faces you:**

    a. Some studies show that the pulse rate was raised 36 beats per minute and the blood pressure was raised 19 points by smoking just one cigarette. The higher rate continues for 15 minutes after the cigarette is finished. (229-230)

    b. Smoking irritates the throat and upper respiratory tract. Chronic inflammation of the tract or a chronic cough may develop. (230)

    c. There is evidence of the relationship between smoking and the incidence of lung cancer. (231)

    d. Some doctors feel that smoking is related to ulcers and the tensions that produce ulcers of the stomach and duodenum. (231-232)

E. Exercise and Health

1. **Young people need exercise to promote their growth and to develop their muscles and nerves:**

    a. You exercise in order to develop the co-ordination of all parts of your body. After co-ordination is developed, exercise helps you to keep fit. (72)

    b. Regular physical activity can improve endurance, which you need all your life. (72)

    c. Skill in standing, sitting, and walking properly gives others the impression that you are poised and self-confident. (73)

    d. Participation in sports can influence your mental health and the development of your personality by helping you relax mental tensions. Your dexterity and ability to take your place in a group increase your confidence. (73)

    e. To be a good team member, you must control your actions, respect the rights of others, and work together smoothly. (73-74)

2. **Exercise affects various groups of body parts:**

    a. Plenty of activity in the air and sunshine, enough rest, and a well-balanced diet help to build good bones. (76)

    b. Much remains to be learned about the adjustments that take place in the body during exercise, but we know that when you exercise you help the body circulate oxygen and food material to the cells more rapidly. (79)

    c. Exercise improves nerve and muscle co-ordination. The voluntary muscles are the principal ones used in physical activity and they are directed by the brain. (79-80)

    d. As a result of exercise, more oxygen is carried to the cells, and waste products are removed from the cells more rapidly. (80)

    e. Strenuous physical activity over a period of years helps to develop the respiratory system. A bigger chest results, with more lung space and breathing power. (85)

Mental Health

A. Glands Affect Your Health

1. **The nature of good mental health:**
   a. A mentally healthy person usually gets along well with others. (8)
   b. He controls his emotions. (8)
   c. He works toward a goal. (8)
   d. He thinks clearly and realistically. (8)
   e. He faces difficulties and problems. (8)
   f. He has the ability to solve problems. (8)
2. **Factors affecting mental health:**
   a. You inherited certain characteristics from your parents. (9)
   b. Your environment has a part in building your mental health and personality. (9)
   c. Chemicals secreted by your glands affect the way you think, feel, and act. (6)
   d. The amount of chemicals produced varies, making you feel different on different days. You have to adjust to the normal bodily changes caused by these glands if you are to have well-balanced mental health. (11)

B. Appearance and Mental Health

1. **The importance of a good appearance:**
   a. The way you look influences others to want or not to want you in their group. (26)
   b. Knowing that others like you helps you to have self-confidence in your relations with others and aids you in acquiring poise. (28-29)
2. **You can improve your appearance:**
   a. Developing good health habits helps to give you a "glad-to-be-alive" look. (30-31)
   b. Practice good grooming until it is a natural part of everyday living. (31)
   c. Select your clothing with care and take care of it. (31)
   d. Control your weight by developing correct eating habits. (31-32)
   e. Develop good posture. (32-34)
   f. Keep your hair, teeth, nails, and skin clean. (34-35)
3. **Overcome your handicaps:**
   a. Such defects as muscle imbalance, a harelip, or a cleft palate can often be corrected by surgery. (36-40)
   b. Teeth can be straightened. (37-38)
   c. Unless corrected, body defects reduce our acceptance by others and may harm one's personality. (39-40)

C. Behavior and Punishment

1. **We need laws and standards of conduct to protect human rights:**
   a. Every individual has certain rights, but he has the responsibility of being sure that when he exercises

his freedom he does not interfere with the rights and freedom of others in any way. (240-241)

b. To protect everyone's rights and freedom, people must follow certain standards of conduct. (241)

c. To insure that these standards are maintained, rules, regulations, and laws are set up. (241)

2. **Behavior must be directed and guided:**

a. Much of an adult's happiness depends upon his skill at distinguishing right from wrong. (242)

b. No one is born with a standard of right and wrong. He must be guided by his parents or others until he has developed a strong character. (243)

c. The individual must practice healthful habits until they are part of him and he does the right thing without thinking. (243)

3. **Behavior can be influenced by punishment:**

a. The effectiveness of punishment in guiding behavior depends on the person being guided and on how the punishment is given. (243)

b. Effective punishment also depends upon the ability of the corrected person to understand the need for the correction and his willingness to accept it. (244-245)

c. Desirable behavior might be maintained by rewarding good behavior. (244)

d. Punishment to achieve good behavior may be physical or psychological. (244)

e. If punishment is effective, it can help the person distinguish more clearly between right and wrong. It can help a person develop self-discipline or inner controls. Eventually these inner controls will make punishment unnecessary. (245-248)

4. **Over the years you are developing adult or mature behavior:**

a. A person develops a sense of responsibility for actions that affect others to the extent that he isn't likely to infringe on others' rights or break the law. (248-249)

b. A person who develops in a normal way has little need of punishment. He becomes hardly aware of the rules he is following. (250)

Safety and First Aid

A. Meeting Emergencies

1. **Health and safety during a flood:**

a. Follow the instructions given by the authorities when warning you of an approaching flood. (48-49)

b. Safeguard your water supply. Boil drinking water and avoid the danger of typhoid fever. (50-51)

c. Avoid contaminated food. (52)

2. **When tornadoes strike:**

a. The community can prepare itself to meet a tornado by taking certain precautionary steps. (54)

b. If you see a funnel-shaped tornado cloud, take shelter—preferably underground. If you are outside, get to a ditch, cave, or ravine that is low and out of the wind. (52-53)

3. **Safety during hurricanes:**

   a. A hurricane wind moves in a circular pattern. (55)

   b. When warned that a hurricane is approaching, people should get ready for it. Medical and sanitary crews can be organized. Water can be stored. People can board up windows, brace doors, and bring in items that would blow away. (56-57)

4. **Protection during earthquakes:**

   a. It is difficult to predict when an earthquake will occur, so buildings should be well constructed in earthquake regions. (58-59)

   b. To avoid the common danger of falling objects, stay inside and take shelter under furniture or in a doorway. (58)

5. **Meeting a nuclear explosion:**

   a. The community's Civil Defense authorities can hold practice drills to familiarize citizens with warning signals. (60)

   b. When you hear an alert signal, tune your radio to 640 or 1240 kilocycles, the Conelrad frequencies, and stay tuned in for instructions on what to do. (60)

   c. Follow all broadcast instructions, especially to take cover. Get to a shelter or lie face down in or behind some kind of cover. Be sure to close your eyes to protect them from nuclear flashes. (61-62)

   d. You can take certain safety steps now. Someone in the house should be trained in first aid. Decide the safest place in the house to take shelter. Store a survival kit there. Clear the house of fire hazards. Know what to do after an alert sounds, such as disconnect gas and electricity, close all windows and doors. (62-63)

   e. Get information by tuning your battery-operated radio to a Conelrad frequency. Leave the telephone lines free for emergency calls. (63-64)

B. Emergencies and the Eye

1. **No difficulty with the eye should be allowed to go uncared for:**

   a. Some emergencies of the eye require attention within minutes. (205)

   b. In general, give little first aid; call a doctor. (207)

   c. Give prompt attention to any sudden loss of vision. (209-210)

2. **Some immediate first aid for the eye is necessary:**

   a. If a chemical gets into the eye, don't waste time looking for a neutralizing agent, but wash it at once, with water. (207)

   b. When someone is struck in the eye, wash the eye promptly with water. If the victim suffers from shock, have him lie down until the doctor comes. An ambulance may be needed to move him. (210)

GLOSSARY

This section of your book has been made so that you will have short explanations of some health words when you want them in a hurry. Most of these words are also explained in the text.

The more difficult words in the Glossary are marked so that you will know how to pronounce them. Use the key below when you are not quite sure how to pronounce some marked letter or combination of letters.

Key to Sounds

ā, āte	ȧ, ȧmong	ĕ, momĕnt	ks, for x,	ŏ, cŏnduct	û, ûnite
å, våcation	ē, bē	ī, mīce	text	oi, noisy	û, bûrn
â, bâre	ė, dėmand	ĭ, fĭll	ō, gō	ōō, fōōd	ŭ, cŭp
ä, ärt	ẹ, hẹro	ĭ, famĭly	ô, ôbey	ŏ, sŏft	ŭ, circŭs
ă, hăt	ẽ, aftẽr	k, for ch	ô, ôrder	ŏŏ, gŏŏd	
ȧ, ȧccount	ĕ, sĕnd	chorus	ŏ, nŏt	u, ūse	

Abscess (ăb′sĕs), a pocket of infection or pus, such as sometimes forms in the gum at the root of a tooth.

Accusations (ăk′ŭ·zā′shŭnz), charges that a person has committed a fault or an offense.

Addict (ăd′ĭkt), one who has a habit which he cannot break, such as the use of drugs.

Adjustment, becoming used to a new situation; learning to live with a difficult condition, such as blindness.

Adrenal (ăd·rē′năl) **glands,** a pair of endocrine glands, located at the upper end of each kidney, which secretes hormones necessary to good mental and physical health.

Alcoholic (ăl′kŏ·hŏl′ĭk), one who is

addicted to the excessive drinking of alcoholic beverages.

Alcoholics Anonymous, an organization composed of former alcoholics for the purpose of helping others successfully overcome their alcoholism.

Alcoholism (ăl′kŏ·hŏl·ĭz′m), a diseased condition resulting from excessive drinking of alcoholic liquors over a period of time.

Allergens (ăl′ẽr·jĕnz), substances which can cause allergy; for example, pollens.

Allergy (ăl′ẽr·jĭ), extreme sensitivity to a certain substance, such as pollen or dust, which may cause such reactions as a rash, coughing, or sneezing.

Amino (ȧ·mē′nō) **acids,** substances

necessary to body growth and development; a group of acids found in proteins.

Anemic (*à·*nē′mĭk), having too few red blood cells or too little hemoglobin in them.

Anesthetic (ăn′ĕs·thĕt′ĭk), an agent capable of producing complete or partial loss of feeling; for example, alcohol.

Anopheles (*à·*nŏf′ĕ·lēz), a type of mosquito. The bite of the female spreads malaria.

Antibiotic (ăn′tĭ·bī·ŏt′ĭk) **drugs,** medicines that contain antibacterial substances which are very helpful in fighting disease and infection.

Antibodies (ăn′tĭ·bŏd′ĭz), substances produced by the body to help fight disease germs.

Apprehensive, fearful; afraid; expecting something unfavorable.

Aptitude (ăp′tĭ·tūd) **tests,** examinations for measuring special ability or the capacity to learn certain kinds of things, such as painting pictures or playing a musical instrument.

Aqueous (ā′kwė·ŭs) **humor,** a watery fluid that fills the cavity between the cornea and the lens of the eye.

Arteries (är′tĕr·ĭz), the large blood vessels that carry blood away from the heart.

Ascorbic (*à·*skôr′bĭk) **acid,** Vitamin C, especially found in fresh fruits, tomatoes, and vegetables.

Association neurons, nerve cells and fibers that transfer messages from one part of the brain and spinal cord to another.

Athletic heart, a term for what was at one time thought to be a kind of heart disease resulting from too much exercise.

Auditory (ô′dĭ·tō′rĭ) **nerves,** the nerves that enable one to hear.

Aureomycin (ô′rĕ·ô·mī′sĭn), an antibiotic drug which is used for the treatment of certain diseases and infections, such as conjunctivitis.

Auricles (ô′rĭ·k'lz), the upper chambers of the heart.

Autonomic (ô′tô·nŏm′ĭk) **nervous system,** the part of the nervous system concerned with involuntary actions, such as breathing and the digestion of food.

Basal metabolism (bās′ăl mĕ·tăb′ô·lĭz′m), the rate at which the body makes heat and energy from the oxygen and food substances in the blood.

Bronchial (brŏng′kĭ·ăl) **tubes,** the tubes from the windpipe which are located inside the lungs.

Calcium (kăl′sĭ·ŭm), a chemical element necessary to the growth of bones and teeth; found in such foods as milk, cheese, and cauliflower.

Calories (kăl′ô·rĭz), units of measurement used to express the heat-producing or energy-producing value of food.

Capillaries (kăp′ĭ·lĕr′ĭz), tiny, thin-walled blood vessels through which food materials and oxygen are exchanged between the cells and the blood.

Carbohydrates (kär′bŏ·hī′drāts), food nutrients, such as starch and sugar; good sources of heat and energy.

Caries (kâr′ĭ·ēz), tooth decay; cavities in the teeth.

Cavity (kăv′ĭ·tĭ), a hole in a tooth caused by decay.

Cementum (sĕ·mĕn′tŭm), a bone-like material which encloses the roots of teeth.

Central nervous system, the brain, spinal cord, and the nerves associated with them; the part of the nervous system concerned with voluntary thoughts and actions.

Chlorine (klō′rēn), a chemical frequently used to purify water.

Chorioid (kō′rĭ·oid), the second covering of the eyeball. It brings food and oxygen to the inner parts and removes wastes from them.

Cilia (sĭl′ĭ·à), hairlike projections of membrane, as found in the nostrils.

Ciliary (sĭl′ĭ·ĕr′ĭ) **muscle,** the muscle used in focusing the eye.

Cleft palate, a crack in the roof of the mouth; an improper development of the roof of the mouth in the period before birth.

Cocaine (kō·kān′), a narcotic drug obtained from coca leaves.

Coma (kō′mà), a sleep-like state of unconsciousness produced by disease, injury, or poison.

Communicable (kŏ·mū′nĭ·kà·b′l) **diseases,** diseases that can be spread from person to person or from one place to another by such things as water, insects, animals, or food.

Conelrad (kŏn′ĕl·răd) **frequencies,** the name given to the radio frequencies of 640 and 1240 kilocycles. They would be used to broadcast information in case of a nuclear attack.

Confident (kŏn′fĭ·dĕnt), poised; sure of one's self.

Conflicts (kŏn′flĭkts), clashes; differences of opinion or goals, as a struggle between one's wishes and one's conscience.

Conjunctiva (kŏn′jŭngk·tī′và), the mucous membrane that lines the eyelids and covers the front part of the eyeball, except for the cornea.

Conjunctivitis (kŏn·jŭngk′tĭ·vī′tĭs), an infection of the conjunctiva of the eye.

Contaminated (kŏn·tăm′ĭ·nāt′ĕd), made impure or unfit; for example, water made unsafe for use by the entry of bacteria or sewage.

Contracting, drawing together; shortening and thickening, as of a muscle.

Co-ordination (kŏ·ôr′dĭ·nā′shŭn), the smooth, efficient working together of different parts, such as the members of the body.

Cornea (kôr′nĕ·à), the front, transparent part of the eye through which light rays enter.

Cortex (kôr′tĕks), the outer part of the adrenal glands.

Cranial (krā′nĭ·ăl) **nerves,** the twelve nerves of the central nervous system that emerge directly from the brain or brain stem, such as the nerves of sight, smell, and hearing.

Debris (dĕ·brē′), rubbish; trash, such as broken glass or fallen branches.

Deciduous (dĕ·sĭd′ū·ŭs) **teeth,** baby teeth; primary teeth; the first teeth that fall out and are replaced by permanent teeth.

Defect, a blemish; a flaw; a handicap, such as poor eyesight or a cleft palate.

Defendant (dĕ·fĕn'dănt), the one who is accused or required to defend himself; a person on trial in court.

Dentifrice (dĕn'tĭ·frĭs), toothpaste, tooth powder, or other substance used to clean the teeth.

Dentine (dĕn'tēn), the ivory-like material that makes up the body of the tooth.

Detached retina, a condition in which the retina of the eye has come loose from its normal position.

Detected (dĕ·tĕkt'ĕd), discovered; revealed, as to have found the existence of an approaching storm.

Devastation (dĕv'ăs·tā'shŭn), destruction; ruin; severe damage.

Dexterity (dĕks·tĕr'ĭ·tĭ), quickness; skill and ease of movements.

Diabetes mellitus (dī'à·bē'tĕz mĕ·lī'tŭs), a disease that may develop if too little insulin is secreted by the pancreas.

Diaphragm (dī'à·frăm), the partition separating the chest and lungs from the abdominal cavity; a part of the breathing apparatus.

Diastolic (dī'ăs·tŏl'ĭk) **pressure,** the blood pressure when the heart is resting.

Dilate (dī·lāt'), enlarge; expand; open up, as to dilate an artery.

Drug addiction (ă·dĭk'shŭn), physical and mental dependence on the use of narcotic drugs; a state of intoxication produced by the repeated use of drugs.

Drug habituation (hà·bĭt'ū·ā'shŭn), the state of being accustomed to the use of certain drugs; repeated usage of drugs through habit, not through physical dependence upon them.

Ducts, small tubes into which the glands secrete chemical substances.

Dysentery (dĭs'ĕn·tĕr'ĭ), a disease involving inflammation of the large intestine.

Emergencies (ê·mûr'jĕn·sĭz), unexpected situations that call for immediate action.

Enamel (ĕn·ăm'ĕl), the hard, white outer covering of the teeth.

Endocrine (ĕn'dô·krīn) **glands,** ductless glands that discharge their secretions, called hormones, directly into the blood stream instead of into ducts as do the other glands.

Endurance (ĕn·dūr'ăns), the ability to work or play effectively for long periods without getting too tired.

Environment (ĕn·vī'rŭn·mĕnt), the total surroundings of a person, including home, family, school, neighborhood, and country.

Enzymes (ĕn'zīmz), juices secreted by the pancreas which aid digestion.

Epiglottis (ĕp'ĭ·glŏt'ĭs), the flap of cartilage at the top of the voice box. It closes as one swallows to keep food from entering the windpipe.

Epinephrine (ĕp'ĭ·nei'rĭn), a hormone produced by the adrenal glands. Secreted in larger amounts when one is nervous or excited, it causes certain bodily changes, as a faster pulse.

Erupted (ê·rŭpt'ĕd), to have come through, as a tooth that has cut through the gum.

Esophagus (ē·sŏf′a·gŭs), the food tube leading from the pharynx to the stomach.

Evacuate (ē·văk′ū·āt), to leave one's home or dwelling at a time of danger.

Fatal (fā′tǎl), causing death.

Fluoride (flōō′ō·rīd), a chemical that helps prevent tooth decay when added to drinking water or applied directly to the teeth.

Glaucoma (glô·kō′ma), a disease in which the eyeball becomes hardened. Poor vision or blindness may result if the condition is not corrected.

Grooming, all that contributes to a good appearance, including care of hair, teeth, skin, and clothing.

Harelip, a defect of the mouth, present at birth; a condition in which the two sides of the lip (usually only the upper one) have not joined properly.

Hazards (hăz′ērdz), risks or dangers.

Hemispheres (hĕm′ĭ·sfērz), the two parts of a certain object, such as the brain.

Hemoglobin (hē′mō·glō′bĭn), the substance which carries oxygen in the red blood cells and gives them their red color.

Heroin (hĕr′ō·ĭn), a powerful narcotic drug; a product of morphine; extremely habit-forming, it is judged to be undesirable even for medical use.

Hormones (hôr′mōnz), the powerful chemicals that are secreted into the blood stream by the endocrine glands.

Immunity (ĭ·mū′nĭ·tĭ), the natural or acquired ability to resist disease or infection.

Impacted (ĭm·păk′tĕd), wedged, such as a tooth that is lodged against another tooth in the jawbone.

Inheritance (ĭn·hĕr′ĭ·tăns), qualities and characteristics received from one's ancestors, such as a strong body or brown eyes.

Insulin (ĭn′sŭ·lĭn), the hormone produced by the pancreas; important in controlling the amount of sugar in the blood.

Iris (ī′rĭs), the membrane just behind the cornea; the colored portion of the eye.

Iritis (ī·rī′tĭs), inflammation of the iris of the eye.

Larynx (lăr′ĭngks), the voice box; the upper part of the windpipe which contains the vocal cords.

Lens (lĕnz), a thin, transparent membrane of the eye which focuses rays of light so as to form clear images.

Ligaments (lĭg′a·mĕnts), tough, flexible bands of tissue that help to hold bones in position.

Malocclusion (măl′ō·klōō′zhŭn), a condition in which the upper and lower teeth do not meet properly.

Marijuana (măr′ĭ·wä′na), a harmful narcotic drug which is sometimes made illegally into cigarettes.

Marrow (măr′ō), the soft, lightweight tissue that fills the centers of most bones.

Mature, adult; grown-up.

Medulla (mē·dŭl′a), the name of the inner part of the adrenal glands.

Micron (mī′krŏn), a unit of measure; about 1/25,000 of an inch.

Minimum (mĭn′ĭ·mŭm), the smallest

or least amount that is attainable, or possible, or advisable, etc.

Morphine (môr′fēn), a narcotic drug, produced from opium, which relieves pain.

Muscle imbalance, the result of one eye muscle being weaker than the matching muscle on the other side of the eyeball.

Narcotic (när·kŏt′ĭk) **drugs,** drugs such as heroin and marijuana, which in small doses relieve pain and dull the nerves. In larger amounts they can produce a coma, convulsions, and even death.

Neurons (nū′rŏnz), nerve cells with all their processes.

Niacin (nī′à·sĭn), one of the B vitamins.

Nostrils (nŏs′trĭlz), the outer openings of the nose.

Nutrient (nū′trĭ·ĕnt), a food substance which the body can use to produce heat and energy, to build, repair, reproduce, and maintain body tissues.

Nutritious (nŭ·trĭsh′ŭs), nourishing; supplying the body with needed food substances.

Oculist (ŏk′ŭ·lĭst), an eye specialist.

Offenders, persons who break laws or rules of behavior.

Olfactory (ŏl·făk′tô·rĭ) **nerves,** the nerves that enable one to smell.

Optic (ŏp′tĭk) **nerves,** the nerves of sight.

Orthodontist (ôr′thô·dŏn′tĭst), a dentist who specializes in the correction of crooked or poorly fitting teeth.

Oxidation (ŏk′sĭ·dā′shŭn), the burning of food materials in the body to produce heat and energy.

Parasympathetic (păr′à·sĭm′pà·thĕt′-ĭk), **division,** one of the two main divisions of the autonomic nervous system.

Parathyroid (păr′à·thī′roid) **glands,** small glands located on the thyroid gland in the neck. A lack of the hormone they secrete can cause a calcium deficiency.

Pellagra (pĕ·lā′grà), a nutritional disease resulting from a lack of B vitamins in the diet.

Periosteum (pĕr′ĭ·ŏs′tà·ŭm), the membrane of connective tissue covering the bones, except at the joints. The tendons and ligaments are connected to the periosteum.

Pharynx (făr′ĭngks), a tube leading downward from the back of the mouth and the back of the nasal cavity. Food passes through the pharynx to the esophagus, and air passes through to the windpipe.

Phosphorus (fŏs′fô·rŭs), a mineral needed by the body for growth and repair; found in foods such as meat and milk.

Pineal (pĭn′ē·ăl) **gland,** a gland located deep inside the head. Very little is known about its functions.

Pituitary (pĭ·tū′ĭ·tĕr′ĭ) **gland,** a very important ductless gland that partly controls the activities of many other glands in the body.

Plasma (plăz′mà), the thick, yellowish liquid of the blood.

Platelets (plāt′lĕts), blood cells that aid in clotting.

Pleura (ploͦor′a͏̇), a thin membrane that covers the lungs and lines the chest cavity.

Pneumoccal (nū′mo͏̇·kŏk′ăl) **pneumonia,** a serious kind of pneumonia involving pneumococcus bacteria.

Pneumonia (nu͏̇·mō′nĭ·a͏̇), a serious disease in which the lungs become inflamed.

Poise (poiz), the ability to feel confident and at ease in social situations.

Poliomyelitis (pō′lĭ·o͏̇·mī′ĕ·lī′tĭs), a disease of the spinal cord which especially strikes children.

Potential (po͏̇·tĕn′shăl), possible; capable of becoming actual, as a potential alcoholic.

Proceedings, a series of steps or actions which are taken with a definite purpose in mind and which move toward a goal, such as the legal events of a courtroom trial.

Protein (prō′tē·ĭn), a nutrient that is necessary to body growth and repair of cells.

Psychiatrists (sī·kī′a͏̇·trĭsts), doctors who specialize in mental and emotional disorders.

Psychological (sī′ko͏̇·lŏj′ĭ·kăl), mental; having to do with the mind as separate from the body.

Pulse, a regular throbbing in the arteries caused by the contractions of the heart.

Radiation, the harmful rays of radient energy that are given off in nuclear explosions.

Regulate (rĕg′u͏̇·lāt), to control; to make orderly by the creation of rules.

Rehabilitation (rē′ha͏̇·bĭl′ĭ·tā′shŭn), the process of restoring to former ability; making one fit to earn his living again, as after a disease.

Relaxing, loosening; lengthening, thinning, and softening, as of a muscle.

Research (rė·sûrch′), study, investigation, or experimentation in the search for new information, as scientific research.

Respiration (rĕs′pĭ·rā′shŭn), breathing; the process of furnishing oxygen to the cells and carrying carbon dioxide away from them.

Respiratory (rė·spīr′a͏̇·tō′rĭ) **tract,** the air passages involved in breathing.

Retina (rĕt′ĭ·na͏̇), the inner, or third, coat of the eyeball where light rays are received and changed into nerve impulses.

Rheumatic (roō·măt′ĭk) **fever,** an acute disease which especially attacks young people and may develop from "strep" throat.

Sciatic (sī·ăt′ĭk) **nerve,** a large nerve located in the back of the thigh.

Sclera (sklē′ra͏̇), the outside covering of the eyeball, except for the cornea. It supports and protects.

Secreted (sė·krēt′ĕd), given off; discharged, as the body glands secrete certain chemicals.

Sensory (sĕn′so͏̇·rĭ) **nerves,** the nerves that carry messages from the sense organs to the brain.

Skeleton, the framework of the body which is composed of about 200 bones.

Sputum (spū′tŭm), saliva; spittle.

Stimulus (stĭm′u͏̇·lŭs), an agent that

starts an impulse in a nerve; that which begins activity.

Streptococcus (strĕp′tŏ·kŏk′ŭs) **sore throat,** an infection involving streptoccus bacteria which may lead to serious illness.

Sympathetic division, one of the two main divisions of the autonomic nervous system.

Systolic (sĭs·tŏl′ĭk) **pressure,** the blood pressure when the heart is contracting.

Thiamine (thī′à·mēn), a part of Vitamin B; found especially in cereals, nuts, and yeast.

Thorax (thō′răks), the chest.

Thymus (thī′mŭs) **gland,** a gland of uncertain function located in the front portion of the chest. It disappears or becomes small in the adult.

Thyroid (thī′roid), a large endocrine gland, located in the neck, which regulates basal metabolism and influences body growth and mental development.

Thyroxin (thī·rŏk′sēn), the hormone secreted by the thyroid gland.

Toxins (tŏk′sĭns), poisons produced by bacteria.

Trachea (trā′kĕ·à), the windpipe.

Trachoma (trà·kō′mà), a serious and contagious eye infection which may follow conjunctivitis. It can cause partial loss of vision.

Tuberculin (tŭ·bûr′kŭ·lĭn), a test material used to help detect the presence of tuberculosis in the body.

Tuberculosis (tŭ·bûr′kŭ·lō′sĭs), an infectious disease usually striking the lungs.

Vaccine (văk′sēn), a substance which is injected into the body for protection against a particular disease.

Veins (vānz), the large blood vessels that carry blood back to the heart.

Velocity (vĕ·lŏs′ĭ·tĭ), rate of motion; speed, such as wind velocity.

Ventricles (vĕn′trĭ·k′lz), the lower chambers of the heart.

Vertebrae (vûr′tĕ·brē), a series of ring-like bones which compose the backbone.

Vitreous (vĭt′rĕ·ŭs) **humor,** the transparent jelly-like material that fills the space between the lens and the retina.

Voluntary (vŏl′ŭn·tĕr′ĭ), controlled by the will, such as the act of walking.

INDEX

Attitudes and opinions: in developing mental power, 145-148; development of, 242; effects on mental health, 9; of others, 26; toward alcoholism, 224, 225; toward drug addiction, 229; toward food, 178, 190-192; toward others, 29, 242, 248; toward punishment, 244-247

B

Bacteria: and tooth decay, 100, 104; and water supply, 50-53

Blood: anemia, 121, 144, 186, 200; arteries, 80, 81, 209; and body temperature, 83; capillaries, 81, 84, 116; carbon dioxide in, 81; cells, 121, 144, 158, 159, 186; clotting of, 82, 210; hemoglobin in, 121, 144, 186; and hormones, 9, 142; oxygen in, 81, 84, 85, 116, 120, 209, 210; plasma, 82, 83; platelets, 82; pressure, 16, 83, 84, 186, 229-231; pulse, 81, 82, 229, 230; red corpuscles, 82, 84; sugar, 14, 15; veins, 81; vessels, 75, 79, 83, 116, 186, 230; white corpuscles, 82; work of, 80-84

Body, parts of: bones, 72, 74-77; brain, 12, 79, 120, 137-142, 144, 145, 205, 219; cells, 80, 116, 119-121, 186; cilia, 158; circulatory system, 72, 79-84, 119-121, 229, 230; and co-ordination, 70, 72, 220; and diet, 32, 76; and disease and infection, 13, 14, 16, 18, 19, 39, 107, 126, 143, 144, 156, 161-167, 199, 200, 205-209, 211, 231, 232; effects of alcohol on, 221; effects of tobacco on, 229-232; and exercise, 70-87; glands, 6, 9-20; heart, 80-82, 87; injuries to, 77, 85-87; joints, 16, 74, 76, 77; ligaments, 75, 76; lungs, 71, 84, 85, 161-163; mucous membrane, 117, 158; muscles, 34, 70, 72, 74, 77-80, 116, 119, 203, 205, 220, 224; nervous system, 70, 72, 79, 80, 120, 121, 134-148, 167, 168, 219, 230; respiratory system, 71, 72, 84, 85, 114-128, 158, 161-164, 230, 231; skeletal system, 72, 74-77; skin, 35, 83, 162; spinal cord, 137, 167; tendons, 74, 75, 77, 78, 88; vertebrae, 138

Body chemistry, 6, 9-20. *See also* Glands.

Body temperature: and breathing, 116; effects of smoking on, 230; and exercise, 83; and shivering, 79; and sweat glands, 9

Bones: breaking of, 76; cartilage of, 75; composition of, 75; cortex of, 75; growth of, 75, 76; of the head, 76; and joints, 74, 76, 77; marrow of, 75; minerals in, 75; periosteum, 75; and proper diet, 76; vertebrae, 76; work of the, 74-77

Brain: and allergies, 144; damage, 144, 145; effects of alcohol on, 144, 145, 219; effects of narcotics on, 144, 145, 227, 228; and infection, 144; inflammation of, 144; need for oxygen, 144; and nervous system, 138-142; and seeing, 205; and spinal cord, 138-141

Breathing: and air, 114, 115, 122-128; and asthma, 126; and body temperature, 116; and exercise, 84, 85; muscles involved in, 119; overbreathing, 121; and oxygen, 115, 116; process of, 119, 120; rate of, 84, 120-122; and the respiratory system, 114-122

Brucellosis, 171

C

Calcium: absorption of, 186; in bones, 75, 76; in food, 188-190; lack of, 13; salts in teeth, 99

Calories: definition of, 181; need for, 181, 183-185; and rate of growth, 181, 183

Cancer, lung, 231

Carbohydrates: in food, 188, 189; and health, 178, 179; and tooth decay, 104

Carbon dioxide: in the air, 122-124; and the blood, 81, 84, 85; in body cells, 116, 119; and regulation of breathing, 116, 120, 121; and the respiratory system, 116

tion to, 225, 226; narcotic, 219, 225-229; tranquilizers, 18, 19, 226

Ducts: *See* Glands.

Dusts: in the air, 114, 122, 124, 125, 157; inorganic, 124, 125; kinds of, 124, 125; organic, 124; radioactive, 125; silica, 124, 125

Dysentery, 156, 171

E

Earthquakes: causes of, 58; hazards of, 59; prediction of, 58; protection during, 58, 59; San Francisco, 59

Emergencies: being prepared for, 52, 53, 55-57, 60, 61, 63, 64; definition of, 205; earthquakes, 58, 59; eye, 205-211; floods, 48-52, 160; hurricanes, 55-58; kinds of, 47, 48; nuclear explosions, 48, 59-64, 125; safety during, 46-64; tornadoes, 52-54

Emotions: and alcoholism, 223, 224; control of, 8, 240, 241, 248; development of, 28, 29; and drug addiction, 226-229; and eating, 190-192; effects of glands on, 11, 13, 15, 16, 20; and smoking, 231, 232

Endocrine glands, 9-20, 120, 142. *See also* Glands.

Endurance: development of, 72; and exercise, 72, 85; and heart rate, 82; importance of, 72

Environment: and alcoholism, 223, 225; definition of, 9; and eating habits, 178; and mental health, 9; and personality, 9, 242; and physical health, 126

Enzymes, 14

Exercise: and body temperature, 79, 83; and breathing, 120; and carbon dioxide, 85; and circulation, 81; and endurance, 72, 85; and everyday activities, 72, 73; and food needs, 181, 183, 190; and growth, 70, 72, 77; and the heart, 87; and joints, 77; and the lungs, 84, 85; and mental health, 70, 73; and muscles, 77-80; need for, 70,

72, 74; and nerves, 70, 79, 80; and personality, 70, 73; and physical health, 70-87; and posture, 34; and sports, 73, 74; and supply of oxygen, 84

Experiments: Check Your Appearance, 27; Demonstrating Lung Capacity, 71; Have a Discussion, 7, 47, 219, 239; Have an Exhibit, 135; Make a Demonstration, 199; Make an Observation, 115; Make a Survey, 95, 179; Make Your Own Record, 155

Eyes: blindness, 208, 209-211; care of, 198, 200, 201, 211; chemical burns, 206, 207, 211; chorioid, 202; conjunctiva, 201, 202; cornea, 202, 211; crossed, 37, 38; detached retina, 210; emergencies of the, 205-211; examinations of, 211; eyeball, 201-205; humors, 204; and hypertension, 200; inflammation of, 206-209; injuries to, 206, 207; iris, 203, 204; lens, 204; muscles, 38, 39, 203, 205; parts of, 201-205; pupil, 203, 204; retina, 202-204; sclera, 202; and vision, 199, 200, 204, 205

F

Fat, 75, 179, 187, 188-190

Feelings: *See* Emotions.

First aid: and eye emergencies, 205-208, 210, 211; and nuclear explosions, 64

Floods: causes of, 48; cleaning up after, 51, 52; and evacuation, 49; prevention of, 48; warnings, 48, 49; and water supply, 50, 52, 160

Fluoride, 102, 103, 105

Food: allergies, 144; and appetite, 185, 190, 228; bread-cereal group, 184, 185; contamination of, 51, 52, 54, 64; deficiencies, 144, 145, 228; digestion of, 96, 116, 142, 188, 190, 191; eating habits, 31, 32, 178, 179, 185, 190-192; and emotions, 190-192; and environment, 178; essential nutrients, 178-181, 184-190; and exercise, 190; and eyesight, 199, 200; for growth, 17, 76, 181, 185, 186; guides, 180, 181; handling of, 160, 161; and health, 34, 159, 178-192; likes and dislikes, 178, 181, 190-192; meat group, 185-188; milk group, 189, 190; needs, 32, 178-183; oxidation of, 79, 116; pasteurization of milk, 160, 161, 189, 191; quality of, 183, 184; refrigeration of, 51, 52, 54; value of, 183-190; vegetable-fruit group, 188, 189; and water content, 180

G

Germs: in air, 114, 126, 157; and antibodies, 186, 187; and body defenses, 14, 158, 159; and food handling, 160, 161; and mucous membrane, 117; spread of, 157-161, 164; and tooth decay, 100, 104; tuberculosis, 166; and water supply, 50-53, 160

Getting along with others: and alcoholism, 223, 224; and appearance, 26, 28, 37, 39, 40; and drug addiction, 228, 229; and maturity, 243, 248; and mental health, 8; in sports, 73, 74

Glands: adrenal, 15, 16, 142; ducts, 9; effects on body chemistry, 11; effects on body parts, 6, 13, 15, 16; effects on growth, 10, 12, 16-18, 20; effects on mental health, 6, 9, 11-16, 19, 20; effects on personality, 6, 9, 12, 14-16, 19; endocrine, 9-20, 142; and glandular balance, 19, 20; kinds of, 9; pancreas, 14, 15; pineal, 17; pituitary, 16; thymus, 17, 18; work of the, 9-11

Glaucoma, 208, 209

Grooming, 27, 28, 30, 31, 34-36

Growth: and diet, 17, 76, 181, 185, 186; effects of glands on, 10, 12, 16-18, 20; and exercise, 70, 72, 77; and protein, 185, 186; rate of, 17, 28, 76

Gums, 107

H

Habits: and developing intelligence, 146,

147; eating, 31, 32, 178, 179, 185, 190-192; effects on mental health, 9, 31-33; eye care, 200, 201; following rules, 241; of good conduct, 29, 243, 245; grooming, 31, 34-36, 101; health, 31-33, 101, 159, 160, 171; importance of, 30, 31; posture, 32-34; and punishment, 245-247

Handicaps: adjusting to, 36-40; birth defects, 36, 39, 169; blindness, 208, 209; cleft palate, 39, 40; correction of, 36-40, 203, 205; eye defects, 205; harelip, 39, 40; Helen Keller, 37; and mental health, 37, 39, 40; muscle imbalance, 38, 39, 203; and rehabilitation, 167

Hair, 27, 30, 31, 34, 35

Health: and addiction, 218-232; and air, 114, 122-128; and appearance, 31; and communicable diseases, 154-171; co-operation for, 159, 160; effects of alcohol on, 219-225; effects of narcotics on, 225-229; effects of tobacco on, 229-232; and emergencies, 46-64; and environment, 126; examinations, 159, 200, 211; and exercise, 70-87; food for, 159, 178-192; and glands, 10-16, 19, 20; habits, 31-34, 101, 159, 160, 171; handicaps, 36-40, 167, 203, 205; and need for water, 179, 180; organizations for, 166-169, 225, 226; responsibility for, 126, 161; and rest, 159; and teeth, 94; and vision, 199, 200

Heart: athletic, 87; beat, 116, 122, 142; contractions of, 81, 82; disease, 164; effects of tobacco on, 230; examinations of, 87; and oxygen, 121; parts of the, 80; and rheumatic fever, 163, 164; the work of the, 80

Heredity: and abilities, 137; and intelligence, 137, 145; and malocclusion, 106; and mental health, 9; and personality, 242; and tuberculosis, 164

Hormones, 9-17, 120; effects on mental health, 11-16, 19, 20; effects on physical health, 10-14, 19, 20; epinephrine,

15; thyroxin, 12, 13
Hurricanes: characteristics of, 55; cleaning up after, 57, 58; detection of, 55, 56; and evacuation, 56; preparation for, 55-57; safety during, 55-58

I

Immunity, 158, 159
Immunization: for allergy, 126; and disease prevention, 159, 160, 171; records of, 155; Salk vaccine, 168, 169; against typhoid fever, 50, 51
Influenza, 161, 162
Injuries: eye, 206, 207; to joints, 77; prevention of, 86-87
Insulin, 14, 15
Intelligence: characteristics of, 134-136; developing, 145-148; and diet, 142-145; and heredity, 137, 145; individual differences in, 136, 137; measurement of, 136; and rest, 142, 143; tests for, 135, 136; use of, 142-148
Iodine, 13
Iritis, 208

J

Joints: in exercise, 77; importance of, 77; injuries to, 77; kinds of, 77; ligaments of, 75; work of the, 74, 76, 77

K

Keller, Helen, 37

L

Laws, 240, 241
Ligaments: and bones, 75; and direction of movement, 77; work of the, 76-77
Lungs, 116-120; air passages in, 84, 116, 118; cancer of, 231; diseases affecting, 167; and exercise, 84, 85; expansion of, 71, 84; inflammation of, 162, 163; the pleura, 119. *See also* Respiratory system.

M

Malaria: cause of, 157, 169, 171; control of, 169-171; treatment of, 169; and world health, 156
Measles, 156, 171
Mental health: and adjusting, 11, 19, 28, 37, 223, 245, 249; and attitudes and opinions, 9, 244-247; characteristics of, 8; and control of emotions, 8; and diet, 185; and drug addiction, 226-229; and eating habits, 191, 192; effects of alcohol on, 219-225; effects of glands on, 6, 9, 11-16, 19, 20; effects of tobacco on, 231, 232; and exercise, 70, 73; factors affecting, 9; and getting along with others, 8, 26, 28, 37, 39, 40; and habits, 9; and handicaps, 36-40; and handling problems, 8, 19; and heredity, 9; mature behavior, 247-250; and personal appearance, 26-40; and physical condition, 6, 7; and posture, 32, 33; and recreational activities, 73; and tranquilizing drugs, 18, 19
Mental illness: and drug addiction, 227-229; and psychiatry, 224, 229; and tranquilizing drugs, 18, 19
Mental power: development of, 145-148; and discipline, 146; and good books, 147; and heredity, 137, 145; and intelligence, 145
Metabolism, basal, 10, 12
Minerals, 179, 184-189; in bones, 75; calcium, 75, 76, 99, 186, 188-190; iron, 187-189; in milk, 76, 189, 190; phosphorus, 75, 76, 184, 187, 190
Moisture: in the air, 122-124; exhaled in breathing, 116, 120, 123
Muscles: and body adjustments, 79; and breathing, 116, 119; co-ordination of, 79, 80, 220, 224; development of, 34, 70, 72; effects of alcohol on, 220, 224; and exercise, 70, 72, 77-80; of the eyeball, 203, 205; facial, 78; and nerves, 79, 80; and oxidation of food, 79; relaxing and contracting, 78, 79; tendons of, 75, 78; voluntary, 79, 80; the work of the, 77

Public Health Department, 103, 175

Punishment: adjusting to, 245-247; of adults, 246-248; effectiveness of, 243, 244; kinds of, 243, 244; learning from, 246, 247; and maturity, 248-250; role of, 243; understanding, 246, 247; values of, 238-243

R

Rehabilitation: of alcoholics, 225; of drug addicts, 229; of the handicapped, 167

Reproductive glands, 11

Respiratory system, 114-128; air sacs, 116, 118, 119; and body temperature, 116; and breathing, 114-122; bronchial tubes, 116, 118; and carbon dioxide, 85, 121; cilia, 117; diaphragm, 117, 119; and disease and infection, 125, 126, 161-167; effects of tobacco on, 230, 231; epiglottis, 117, 118; esophagus, 117; and exercise, 72, 84; larynx, 117, 118; lungs, 231; mucous membrane, 117; nose, 116, 117; and oxygen, 84; parts of, 116-119; pharynx, 116-117; and physical activity, 85; rate of breathing, 120, 121; respiratory tract, 230; thorax, 119; trachea, 116, 117; vocal cords, 118; windpipe, 116, 117; work of, 116. *See also* Lungs.

Responsibility: for behavior, 247-250; for conduct, 240, 241; of dentists, 94, 99, 104, 107, 108; for health, 94, 126, 161; for laws, 240, 241; to others, 249

Rheumatic fever, 156, 157, 163, 164; dangers of, 164; treatment of, 164

Rights, 29, 73, 240, 241, 248-250

Roosevelt, Franklin D., 168

S

Safety: and addiction, 218; during earthquakes, 58, 59; during emergencies, 46-64; during floods, 48-52; during hurricanes, 55-58; during nuclear explosions, 48, 60-64; during tornadoes, 52-54; need for laws, 240, 241; responsibility for, 240, 241; and use of alcohol, 223, 224

Salk vaccine, 167-169

Secretions: *See* Glands.

Self-confidence, 28, 29, 33, 73

Self-respect, 29; and alcoholism, 224, 225; and drug addiction, 228

Skeletal system, 74-77. *See also* Bones.

Smallpox, 159

Smog, 127-128

Sports: and injuries, 85, 86; and nutrition, 185; protective equipment for, 86; and value to players, 73-74

Streptococcus sore throat, 156, 163, 164; dangers of, 164; treatment of, 163, 164

T

Teeth: and acids, 100-102; and appearance, 95-97; and calcium salts, 99; care of, 35, 94, 95, 97, 101-108; caries, 100; cleaning of, 95, 96, 101, 102; decay of, 94, 96, 97, 99, 100-104; dentifrices, 95, 101; development of, 97, 98; and diet, 95; and digestion, 96; examination of, 94, 104; and fluoridation of water, 102, 103, 105; and gums, 107; and health, 94, 96; impacted, 98; kinds of, 97, 98; malocclusion, 105-107; parts of, 96-100; and personality, 96; and research, 105; responsibilities for, 94, 99, 104, 107, 108; and speech, 96; straightening of, 36-38, 106, 107; value of, 95-97

Tendons, 75, 77, 78

Tetany, 13

Thiamine, 189

Thinking: *See* Intelligence.

Thymus glands, 11

Thyroid gland, 10; effects of, 12, 13; and iodine, 13; location of, 11; structure, 11; and thyroxin, 12, 13

Tobacco: and disease and infection, 230-232; effects on body, 229-232; effects on emotions, 231, 232; effects on length of life, 231; risks of using, 230-232; and vision, 199

Tornadoes: alerts, 52; characteristics of, 52; definition of, 52; safety measures after, 53, 54; taking shelter, 52, 53

Trachoma, 209

Tranquilizing drugs, 18, 19, 226

Trichinosis, 171

Tuberculosis, 156, 164-167; and heredity, 164; and the National Tuberculosis Association, 166, 167; spread of, 164, 165; tests for, 165, 166; treatment for, 166, 167

Typhoid fever, 50, 156, 171

U

Ulcers, 231, 232

United States Weather Bureau, 48, 52, 54, 56

V

Viruses, 166, 167; in the air, 126; diseases from, 169; infections, 209

Vision: factors affecting, 199, 200; loss of, 209-211; protection of, 198, 211; and the act of seeing, 204, 205. *See also* Eyes.

Vitamins, 178, 179, 185; A, 187-190; B, 143, 144, 184, 187; C, 188-190; effects on nervous system, 143, 144

W

Water: and body needs, 179, 180; boiling of, 50, 54, 58, 59, 64, 160; chlorine in, 50, 160; contamination of, 50-53, 54, 58, 59, 64; department, 103; and dilution of chemicals, 206, 207; fluoridation of, 102, 103; purification of, 160; and spread of disease, 157, 160, 170, 171

Whooping cough, 156, 159, 171

World Health Organization, 226

X

X rays: of mouth, 107; of teeth, 94, 104; for tuberculosis, 166

23456789   9876543